Hiking
Hot Springs
in the
Pacific Northwest

Evie Litton

FALCON®

HELENA, MONTANA

Falcon® Publishing is continually expanding its list of recreation guidebooks. All books include detailed descriptions, accurate maps, and all the information necessary for enjoyable trips. You can order extra copies of this book and get information and prices for other Falcon® guidebooks by writing Falcon, P.O. Box 1718, Helena, MT 59624 or calling toll free 1-800-582-2665. Also, please ask for a free copy of our current catalog. Visit our web site at www.falcon.com or contact us by e-mail at falcon@falcon.com.

Library of Congress Cataloging-in-Publication Data

Litton, Evie.
    Hiking hot springs in the Pacific Northwest / by Evie Litton. — [2nd ed.]
        p. cm.
    ISBN 1-56044-677-3 (pbk.)
    1. Hiking—Northwest, Pacific—Guidebooks. 2. Hot springs—Northwest, Pacific—Guidebooks. 3. Northwest, Pacific—Guidebooks. I. Title.
GV199.42.N69L58 1998
917.9504'43—dc21
                                                                        98-20202
                                                                        CIP

CAUTION

Outdoor recreational activities are by their very nature potentially hazardous. All participants in such activities must assume the responsibility for their own actions and safety. The information contained in this guidebook cannot replace sound judgment and good decision-making skills, which help reduce risk exposure, nor does the scope of this book allow for disclosure of all the potential hazards and risks involved in such activities.

Learn as much as possible about the outdoor recreational activities in which you participate, prepare for the unexpected, and be cautious. The reward will be a safer and more enjoyable experience.

♻ Text pages printed on recycled paper.

*To all the volunteers who struggle patiently and often
ingeniously to create and maintain soaking pools for everyone
to enjoy; and to those who value hot springs in a natural setting
enough to pack out the trash left by others,
this book is gratefully dedicated.*

Contents

Washington

British Columbia

Acknowledgments

My heartfelt thanks to Ellen, the best friend a writer ever had, who not only allowed me (armed with piles of scribbled notes) to attack her own computer after every field trip, but who also spent endless hours trying to teach a strictly "no-tech" novice the fine art of taming technology. Without her help, this project would never have gotten off the ground.

All of the additions in the second edition would still be in handwriting without my good friends Joanne and Dennis, who gave me full access to their home computer as well as their expertise in handling it (under April's canine supervision). I'm grateful to computer-whiz Gerry for solving jams that were beyond anyone else's nightmares to fix. Thanks are also in order to Jon, for all his honest feedback while playing the part of first-time reader.

For their input into the first edition and subsequent updates, I am indebted to the many district rangers of Umpqua, Willamette, and Mt. Hood national forests in Oregon, of Olympic National Park and Mt. Baker-Snoqualmie National Forest in Washington; and of Clearwater, Boise, Payette, Sawtooth, and Salmon/Challis national forests in Idaho.

For help with all the new hot springs and hikes in the second and third editions, I'm indebted also to the district rangers of Deschutes National Forest and the Bureau of Land Management in Oregon, of Gifford Pinchot National Forest in Washington, of BC Parks and Forests in British Columbia, and of the "Canyon Cats," and the Bureau of Land Management in Idaho. All did their best to supply me with accurate and up-to-date information.

And last but not least, I want to express my gratitude to the friendly folks at Falcon Publishing for guiding this stray missile to a safe and happy landing. Without their help, it would still be orbiting somewhere over the Pacific Northwest.

Map Legend

Interstate	🛡️00	Campground	⛺
US Highway	🛡️00	Ranger Station	
State or Other Principal Road	00 000	Cabins/Buildings	▪
Four Wheel Drive	*(4WD)*	Peak	9,782 ft.
Interstate Highway	⟹	Elevation	9,782 ft. ✕
Paved Road	⟹	Lava	
Unimproved Road	══════⟹	Glacier	
Trailhead	◯	Sand/Desert	
Main Trail(s)/Route(s)	• • • • •	Crater	
Alternate/Secondary Trail(s)/Route(s)	• • • •	Viewpoint/Point of Interest	◧
Cross-Country Route	· · · · · ·	Power Line	
Tunnel		Wilderness/Forest/ Park Boundary	
River/Creek		Wild River Boundary	
Lake	⬭	State Boundary	
Hot Spring	⚲	Map Orientation	N ▲
Bridge	⊃⊂	Scale	0 0.5 1 Miles
Meadow/Swamp	⥥		
Falls/Rapids	⫽		
Pass/Saddle	⤙		

Pacific Northwest Region

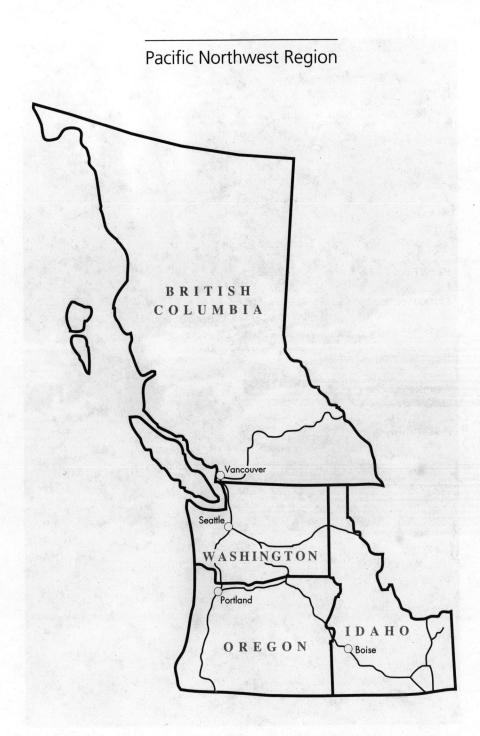

BRITISH COLUMBIA

Vancouver

Seattle

WASHINGTON

Portland

OREGON

IDAHO

Boise

Streamside pools, like this gem at Bonneville Hot Springs in Idaho, are submerged at high water and must be remodeled every summer. The temperature can be lowered by shifting rocks on the outer edge to let cold water trickle in.

Introduction

I sat on a warm rock gazing up at the Chinese Wall and eating a peanut butter and carrot sandwich when the sky suddenly started turning darker than Slate Creek below me. I gulped down the last bite as rain drops began to fall. The drizzle turned to a spitting downpour before I was halfway down the trail. I'd no sooner leaped into the car at the trailhead when the sky turned a sickly shade of yellow and let loose a wild volley of hailstones. The ground, covered with dancing snow peas, turned white in an instant. As my car tires slithered the last mile up Slate Creek Road, I had a smile on my face because the perfect antidote to foul weather was close at hand. While sleet and hail pelted the crude shelter, I was soon waiting out the storm in total comfort—immersed in a cocoon of steamy water.

Experiences like this one taught me early on that hiking and hot springing go together like cream cheese and lox on a bagel. Whether it's a hot dip sandwiched between strolls or a muscle-melting soak at the end of a rugged trek, the contrast between the hike and the soak creates a dynamite combination.

I began to comb the backwoods and wildlands of the Pacific Northwest, caught in the clutches of a powerful addiction. Between trips, I haunted the library to pour over geothermal maps for hot springs hidden in prime hiking country. As my list of hot springs lengthened, I felt a growing urge to share it with kindred souls.

The pages of this book have emerged out of my obsession. I often wrote under the most adverse conditions. I'd return to camp and just get all the paperwork spread out on a picnic table when the wind would scatter the lot or a sudden rainstorm turn it to pulp. Often I'd be scribbling away long after dark with the aid of a dim flashlight while trying to dodge the nighttime Kamikaze bugs.

With no space in my tiny car for a laptop computer on top of all the camping gear, the writing consumed an astronomical number of pencils, erasers, and notebooks in the painstaking process of stringing words together. I learned that the most grueling hike out there is nothing compared to the effort of capturing it on paper.

What it's all about

"Hot springs? What kind of hot springs?" you wonder skeptically. "Fancy resorts with wall-to-wall bodies packed into chlorinated pools, or just trickles oozing down some slimy bank into algae-coated mud puddles?" Or else, vaguely offended, you mutter, "What's this, hot springs and hikes in one book? Why on earth mix them together—what's the connection?"

The gems described in these pages aren't the commercial variety. All but a few are located on prime public land within our national forests and parks. These primitive soaking pools are improvised, strictly by volunteer labor, to collect the flow of any spring equipped with roughly the right temperature, output, and location. A hot trickle is no good to anybody without a proper pool to contain it.

Part of the adventure in seeking out these springs is that you can never be sure what you'll find. One year there might be a rock-lined pool on the bank of a sylvan stream. The next year, it may have vanished and been replaced by a different pool, a hand-crafted soaking box, or possibly even a crude bathhouse patched together to shelter users from the elements. If you're the first arrival of the season, you may have the fun of contributing to the pool design yourself.

Streamside pools are subject to washouts during the spring runoff months and by late summer may be left stranded high on the bank—too hot for comfort without cold water for a mix. For off-season use, the ideal spring would be located well above the river's grasp and have either a temperature within the comfort zone or a side stream flowing by that could be diverted to mix with the spring water.

Among the many virtues of the five-star soaks, both temperature and flow rate can be manually controlled if need be. You can often accomplish this by merely adjusting a rock or two, but sometimes you'll need more ingenious methods to channel both hot and cold water from more distant sources. A strong flow keeps the pools constantly and naturally cleaned between soaks.

The condition of each particular pool also depends on the use it gets. The soaking pools located closer to the larger population centers tend to receive more volunteer care as well as more stress, while the condition of those in more remote areas will be more primitive but more pristine as well.

What are hot springs and hikes doing together in one book, and what's the connection? You've probably gathered by now that it's entirely possible to find soaker-friendly hot pools located in precisely the kinds of places you've always enjoyed hiking, through deep river canyons or misty woods, in the mountains of some beautiful national forest or park and even in a few choice wilderness areas.

The delightful treat of a hot spring soak makes as worthy a target for a hike as a peak with a view from the top that you might just have time to catch a quick shot of—if the clouds would move over a bit. A hot spring is as good a destination as a remote lake with a finicky fish or two flipping around at the bottom and certainly no crazier.

Not all of these bubblies require a lengthy trek to locate; many lie near the road in a scenic area that offers a choice of intriguing trails nearby. The Sawtooths in Idaho are a prime example; they happen to have strategically-spaced hot dips close to almost every trailhead.

"So what?" you ask. "I came here to climb Mt. Whatzits'name, or to spend a quiet week up at Such'n'such Lake." Great! But wouldn't it feel good afterwards, back at the trailhead, to ease away all those aches and pains (not to mention the dirt) immersed in a totally natural Jacuzzi shrouded by evergreens? Or, suppose you got yourself drenched and/or frozen up there and are still faced with either a soggy roadside campsite or a miserable drive back home. You guessed it —time for a nice long soak over at Whozit's Hot Springs!

This guidebook is meant for the active outdoor hedonist who enjoys experiencing the wonders of nature on foot, but who also turns on to the contrasting idea of a blissful dip at the end of the trail in one of nature's own steamy creations.

It just so happens that the Pacific Northwest is a mecca not only for superb scenery and hiking but also for first-class primitive hot springs. A chain of these pearls runs through the Cascades of Oregon and Washington, clusters are located across southern British Columbia, and in central Idaho, you'll discover a profusion of precious gems—including no fewer than eleven buried in the River of No Return Wilderness. Idaho, astonishingly, happens to have more than twice the number of wild hot springs than the total number in Oregon, Washington, and British Columbia combined.

The best of both worlds is presented here in one package: a detailed guide to 118 of the finest natural hot soaks in Oregon, Washington, British Columbia, and Idaho, and a trail guide to 83 scenic hikes that either lead to them or begin nearby. Whether you're already a confirmed wilderness buff and hot springs fanatic or you're new to either pursuit, this guide should be a welcome companion to your travels.

How to use this guide

Hiking Hot Springs in the Pacific Northwest is a guide to both hot soaks and hikes in Oregon, Washington, British Columbia, and Idaho. The springs marked on the Locator Maps are listed numerically. Beneath them in the Contents and text, you'll find one or more hikes. For example, in Oregon we start with 1.Umpqua Hot Springs, followed by Hikes 1a,b. In Washington, 24.Olympic Hot Springs is followed by Hikes 24a-c, etc. The hikes fall into three categories: hikes that reach a hot spring, hikes that continue on from the spring, and hikes located in the same area. One or more of these catagories may be listed under each hot spring.

Headings for hot springs located less than a mile from a road

General description: Includes what you'll find, the distance from road to spring, customary swimwear or lack thereof, and elevation (a useful gauge for estimating seasonal access). Example: A quiet soaking pool cloaked in greenery at the end of a quarter-mile-long creekside path. Swimwear optional. Elevation: 2,900 feet.

General location: Approximate distance and direction of the hot spring from the nearest town. Example: 64 miles east of Roseburg.

Map: The best road map for finding your way there. In most cases this is a Forest Service recreation map.

Contact: Where to go for more information, updates on current conditions, road maps, and other pertinent sources. Agency addresses and telephone numbers are listed in Appendix B.

Finding the hot springs: The nuts and bolts of getting there. Start with the Locator Map and a highway map to get your bearings, then follow the directions with the aid of the road map listed. It's noted here whether or not the spring is marked or named on the map, or if it isn't marked on the state geothermal map (see below).

The hot springs: This short section describes the quality of the soaking pools, the temperature and any means of controlling it, the general setting and scenery, an idea of how much company you can expect, and a description of how visible the pools are. As a rule of thumb, the swimwear custom (or degree of "skinnydippability") equates with the degree of visibility or distance from the road—a useful formula.

Headings for hikes (a mile or longer)

General description: Whether it's a day hike or an overnighter, which type of hike it is and where it goes, what's there, and the customary swimwear. Example: A day hike to a bubbly soaking box in the Glacier Peak Wilderness. No need to pack a swimsuit.

Difficulty: Determined by overall steepness, with minor adjustments made for length, short steep pitches, or roughness. A hike is rated as easy if the grade is up to 5 percent, moderate between 5 and 10 percent, and strenuous if the grade is over 10 percent. You can use the following formula to calculate the grade of any hike: gain divided by 5,280 (gain in miles) divided by length of trail x 100 = percent grade.

Distance: The overall length of the hike.

General location: The approximate distance and direction of the *trailhead* (not the hot spring) from the nearest town.

Elevation gain: Given in one direction only. A round trip that gains 1,000 feet and loses 200 feet on the way in would lose 1,000 feet and gain 200 feet on the way out. This would be written: +1,000 feet, -200 feet. Another hike gains 1,600 feet, loses 400 feet, gains another 800 feet, then loses another 200 feet. The total gain and loss would be +2,400 feet, -600 feet. Only one figure is listed if the hike is all uphill or downhill. A loop hike lists just one figure because no matter how many ups and downs, the total gain is always the same as the total loss.

High point: A useful figure when trying to determine the access at different times of year.

Hiking quad(s): This heading lists one or more topographic quadrangles. In the U.S., those most commonly used are the USGS quads. Most have contour intervals of 40 feet, cover areas of about 7 by 9 miles, and are drawn on a scale of 1:24,000. In Washington and Northern Oregon, a 15-minute series by Green Trails is listed. These maps are designed for hikers. The trails are drawn in bold lines and distances are marked between points. The Forest Service offers contour maps of most wilderness areas. Although drawn with less detail than the USGS quads, they tend to be more up-to-date.

In British Columbia, the standard quads are the National Topographic Series (NTS). The newer series has a scale of 1:50,000 and contour intervals of 100 feet. Although hot springs and hiking trails often go unmarked, the more detailed scale is an improvement over the old 1:125,000 series.

A trail map is also located in the text with each hike. Intended as a general introduction, these maps should not be substituted for the hiking quads. (See Map Legend for a list of the symbols used.)

Road map: See Maps under Headings for Hot Springs.

Contact: See Headings for Hot Springs.

Finding the trailhead: See Headings for Hot Springs. It's mentioned here which map(s) the spring is marked on.

The hike: Here you'll find a description of the route, the distances between points, any nasty stream crossings or other obstacles to expect, possible extensions or side trips, campsites, and whatever outrageous viewpoints or other rewards lie in wait.

The hot springs: See Headings for Hot Springs.

A note on state geothermal maps: A map that marks hot springs along with other geothermal data is published by each state for the U.S. Department of Energy. These maps are gigantic but very useful for pinpointing possible soaks. They can be found in most university libraries.

Recreational user fees

The National Recreation Fee Demonstration Program, an experimental plan, was authorized by Congress in 1996. This three-year project, begun in 1997, tests the feasibility of user fees to help finance recreation programs on federal lands. Wherever this fee is now required, a heading has been added throughout the text.

In Oregon and Washington, the fee is called a Trail Park Pass and is required at (or within 0.25 mile of) specified trailheads and parking areas within Willamette, Mount Baker-Snoqualmie, and Gifford Pinchot national forests. The permit runs $3.00/day or $25.00/(calendar) year and is available at district offices and selected retail outlets. It covers each vehicle (all passengers) and can be transferred from one car to another. One permit is good in all forests.

The permit in Idaho is called a Recreation User Pass and is now required for parking anywhere within the Ketchum Ranger District of Sawtooth National Forest and the Sawtooth National Recreation Area. The permit, 2 dollars/day or 5 dollars/year, can be purchased from the Forest Service or selected stores. It covers each person—with a wallet card in addition to the windshield pass.

Leave no trace

Principles of Low-Impact Camping

"Some call it low-impact use or the minimum-impact method. Others refer to it as no-trace camping. Whatever you call it, the practice of outdoor ethics is essential in the backcountry. It relies on clear judgment rather than inflexible rules. And not only does common sense protect the backcountry, it can also enhance your outdoor adventures." (*Fieldbook*, Boy Scouts of America).

Three Falcon Principles of Leave No Trace
• Leave with everything you brought in.
• Leave no sign of your visit.
• Leave the landscape as you found it.

1. Concentrate use when in popular or high-use places
The key is to concentrate your use on those places that have already been damaged by previous use. Build campfires only within existing fire rings. Stay on established hiking trails. Cutting switchbacks can lead to erosion.

2. Disperse use when in pristine areas
The key is to minimize the number of times a place is stepped on and to leave nothing that will encourage others to walk or camp where you did so that the site will have time to recover. Choose a previously unused site to camp. Disperse foot traffic between camp and any water source. Minimize the use of campfires and remove all evidence of fire. Only hike off-trail if prepared to use extra care. Try to select routes on hard ground. Avoid fragile surfaces like wet places and steep slopes.

3. Other basic rules

Choose your campsite thoughtfully. Pick a spot (at least 300 feet from water or trail) where you won't have to clear any vegetation or level a tentsite. Camp on mineral soil, never in meadows.

The use of backpack stoves conserves firewood. Campfires have been prohibited in many heavily used areas. If a fire is allowed and really needed, dig out the native vegetation and topsoil and set it aside. Don't build a fire ring with rocks. When breaking camp, drown the fire thoroughly, bury the cold ashes, and replace the native soil.

Keep all wash water at least 300 feet from water sources and don't use soap or detergents near water. Even biodegradable soaps are a stress on the environment. If you must use soap, wash in a basin well away from lakes or streams.

Always answer the call of nature at least 300 feet from any campsites or open water. Dig a hole 6 to 8 inches deep, bury everything carefully when finished, then cover it with sod or topsoil.

You must carry out garbage that can't be burned. This includes tiny items like gum wrappers and cigarette butts. The foil packages commonly used by backpackers don't really burn and must be packed out as well. Never bury food scraps, because animals will dig them up.

Hot springs are as fragile as any other water source and should be treated with the same respect. Soaking pools are precisely that. They're not bathtubs where you can lather up with soap and shampoo. Whatever drains out flows directly into nearby streams, and what can't drain out is there for the next user to find. Also, the damp ground around the springs is often steep and easily eroded, and delicate plant life can be swiftly crushed.

Make it a safe trip

Backcountry safety is largely a matter of being well prepared and using common sense. This means carrying proper survival and first-aid equipment. Gather information from the ranger station nearest your destination. Rangers can tell you about any potential problems in their area as well as the current condition of roads, trails, and streams.

The basics in every hiker's gear should include sturdy but comfortable footwear, warm clothing that will keep its insulating properties when wet, plenty of water, extra food, and a dependable tent. You may enjoy beautiful dry weather, but storms can hit at any time.

Select a hike within the abilities of all in your group and stay together on the trail. If it's getting dark or a storm looks likely, make camp as soon as possible. Be aware of the dangers of hypothermia and take the proper steps to avoid it.

If you get lost, don't panic. Sit down and try to locate landmarks that will help orient you. Check out the topo map and take compass readings. Plot a rational course of action before you move on. And remember, many hikers have spent unplanned nights in the woods and survived.

Boil or treat all open water used for drinking—no matter how clean it may look. Increasing cases of backcountry dysentery, caused by a water-borne parasite called *Giardia lamblia*, show the impact that water pollution has in the wilds. Halazone and chlorine don't work against it, and iodine will kill only 90 to 95 percent of the cysts. There are also a number of filters on the market that are effective.

Don't attempt to ford major streams during the spring runoff. In early summer, creeks and rivers can have ten times their average flow. Leave your boots on for better traction. During runoff, the water will be at its lowest level during the morning hours.

Be cautious around hot springs. Some emerge from the ground at temperatures that can boil eggs and would-be bathers alike. Avoid bare feet until you're sure where any hidden hot spots are. If a soaking pool feels too hot, don't use it unless you can find a way to lower the temperature.

To prevent problems in bear country, keep all food well wrapped and hang it at night (along with garbage, lotions, and soaps) from a strong tree limb at least 12 feet above the ground and at least 5 feet from the trunk and other branches.

Driving in the backcountry often involves negotiating narrow one-lane roads—some heavily traveled by huge logging trucks and others deserted for hours just when you get stuck. Drive cautiously and exercise common sense. Carry plenty of gas, water, and spare supplies.

Oregon Locator Map

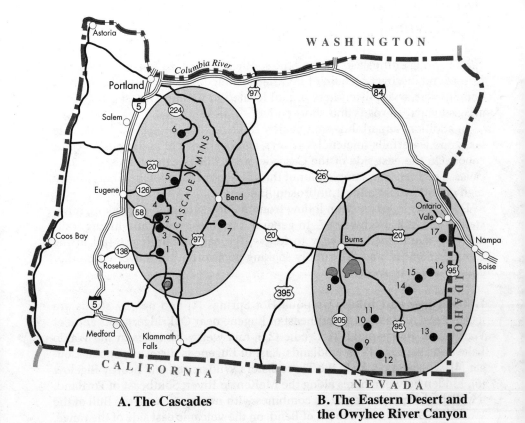

A. The Cascades

B. The Eastern Desert and the Owyhee River Canyon

Oregon

The state of Oregon is richly endowed with primitive hot springs. The ones described in this guide are located in two distinct areas. One group can be found in the Cascade Mountains to the west and another in the desert country to the east, which includes several in the Owyhee River Canyon. The reader will find a total of eighteen wild dips marked on the Oregon Locator Map—seven lined up in the Cascades and eleven spread across the eastern desert.

A. The Cascades

Hot spring enthusiasts visiting the southern Cascades can enter primeval forests and discover a chain of inviting soaking pools framed by evergreen boughs. The seven listed here are all located in national forests, with easy access via paved roads and short paths.

In addition, superb hikes on nearby trails ramble through lush woods to lakes and waterfalls, ancient lava flows, and overlooks of numerous volcanic cones. On the east side of the Cascade crest, hikers can even explore lava caves. They can also sample four of the wildlands that now link the Cascade high country in an almost unbroken line.

Directions in this section follow from major towns and cities along Interstate 5 and U.S. Highway 97. In general, the forest roads and hiking trails are well maintained and easy to follow, the campgrounds are full in the summer months, and the bubbly soaking pools often brim over with other equally eager beavers.

Hot springs and hikes: Umpqua Hot Springs (1) and nearby strolls are located east of Roseburg. Southeast of Eugene near Oakridge, soaks at quiet Wall Creek and popular McCredie (2,3) mix well with hikes in the Waldo Lake and Diamond Peak wildlands. East of Eugene is the ever-popular Cougar (4), with a loop hike in the Three Sisters Wilderness, and nearby Bigelow (5), hidden between hikes along the McKenzie River. Southeast of Portland, a walk to the unique Bagby (6) combines with nearby treks in the Bull of the Woods Wilderness. And south of Bend, on the volcanic east side of the range, comes a hike-in soak on the shores of Paulina Lake (7) and an assortment of hikes in and around Newberry Crater.

Season: All the hot springs can be reached and enjoyed throughout the year except for Paulina, snow-bound through the winter months at 6,300 feet, and Bigelow, submerged during spring runoff. Regardless of weather, Cougar and Bagby see long lines of winter visitors. The hiking season ranges from all year for the low-elevation hikes near Umpqua and Bigelow to summer months only for the higher routes in the vicinity of McCredie, Cougar, Bagby, and Paulina. Summer weather west of the crest can vary from bright sunshine to damp rain clouds (sometimes in a matter of minutes) while the east side around Paulina stays high and dry.

Cascades Area Map

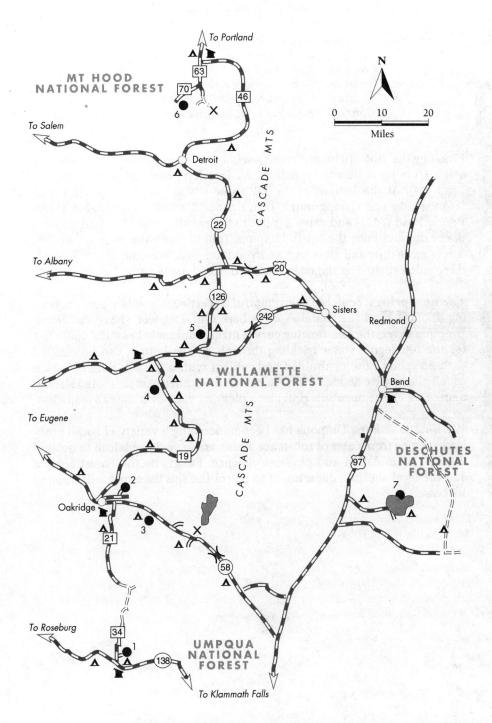

To Portland

MT HOOD
NATIONAL FOREST

63

70

46

6

X

To Salem

N

0   10   20
Miles

Detroit

CASCADE MTS

22

To Albany

20

126

242

Sisters

Redmond

5

WILLAMETTE
NATIONAL FOREST

Bend

4

CASCADE MTS

To Eugene

19

DESCHUTES
NATIONAL
FOREST

2

97

7

Oakridge

3

21

X

58

To Roseburg

34

1

138

UMPQUA
NATIONAL
FOREST

To Klammath Falls

1 Umpqua Hot Springs

General description:	A once grand old soaking pool on a short new path, overlooking a canyon. Keep swimwear handy.
Elevation:	2,640 feet.
General location:	64 miles east of Roseburg.
Map:	Umpqua National Forest.
Contact:	Diamond Lake Ranger District, Umpqua National Forest.

Finding the hot springs: From Roseburg, drive east on State Route 138 about 60 miles to Toketee Junction and turn left on paved Toketee Rigdon Road (34). At the bottom of the hill, bear left at the "Y" and drive past Toketee Lake and Campground. Turn right at 2.3 miles onto graded Thorn Prairie Road (3401) and drive 2 miles to the parking area. The path crosses the bridge and joins the North Umpqua Trail to climb the steep riverbank. A few more dips and rises east and you'll emerge from the woods to see a three-sided shelter on the edge of a bluff. Umpqua is named on the map.

The hot springs: Sculpted from colorful travertine deposits, a pool measuring about 4 by 5 feet perches on a bare cliff 150 feet above the North Umpqua River; the free-flowing curves make a uniquely beautiful container for the 106-degree water trickling through it. The bottom can be cleaned with a syphon hose or drained and refilled with a bucket, both of which usually lie nearby. Shaded from the elements within a shingle-roofed shelter, a sun deck on the open side provides a pleasing view over the canyon below.

Warning to visitors: Umpqua has been undergoing a variety of social problems ranging from cases of substance abuse, arson, and vandalism to isolated cases of intimidation and physical violence. Efforts by the Forest Service and the local sheriff's department to patrol the site have met with limited success.

The shelter at Umpqua Hot Springs faces a broad view over the North Umpqua Canyon.

Umpqua Hot Springs • Clearwater River Trail • Toketee and Watson Falls

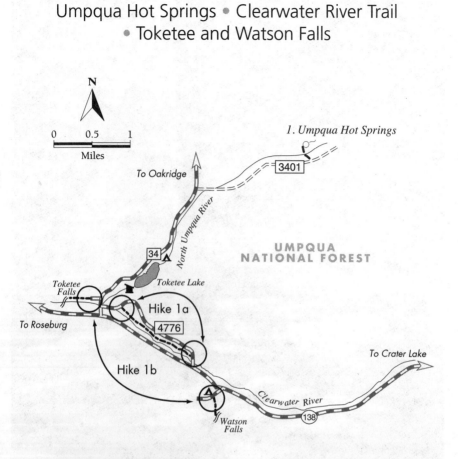

HIKE 1a *Clearwater River Trail*

General description: A riverside walk through an ancient forest, near Umpqua Hot Springs.

Difficulty: Easy.

Distance: 3.4 miles round trip (or 1.7 miles one way).

General location: 60 miles east of Roseburg.

Elevation gain: 200 feet.

High point: 2,640 feet.

Map: Umpqua National Forest.

Contact: Diamond Lake Ranger District, Umpqua National Forest.

Finding the trailheads: At Toketee Junction on State Route 138, take Forest Road 34 to the bottom of the hill. Bear right at the "Y" onto graded FR 4776, the west entrance to Toketee Ranger Station. Drive 0.25 mile to a pullout on the right and the west marker. The east trail sign is found 2 miles farther up the road just before it rejoins the highway.

The hike: Clearwater River Trail meanders through a twilight forest along the riverbank. Shaded by a dense canopy of cedar and Douglas-fir mixed with rhododendrons, alder, and dogwood, it passes lively rapids interspersed with deep pools. The gentle path parallels Toketee Ranger Station Road and can be walked from either end.

HIKE 1b *Toketee and Watson Falls*

General description:	Two short strolls through lush woods, near Umpqua Hot Springs.
Difficulty:	Easy.
Distances:	Toketee Falls, 0.8 mile round trip; Watson Falls, 1.2 miles round trip.
General locations:	60 and 62 miles east of Roseburg.
Elevation gains:	Toketee Falls, 60 feet; Watson Falls, 230 feet.
High points:	Toketee Falls, 2,380 feet; Watson Falls, 2,950 feet.
Map:	Umpqua National Forest.
Contact:	Diamond Lake Ranger District, Umpqua National Forest.

Finding the trailheads: To see Toketee Falls, drive to Toketee Junction on State Route 138 and take Forest Road 34 to the bottom of the hill. Bear left at the "Y" and follow signs to the parking area. To visit Watson Falls, drive 2.2 miles east of Toketee Junction on State Route 138 (or 0.3 mile east of the east entrance to Toketee Ranger Station) and follow signs to the picnic area parking lot (a right turn on FR 37).

The hikes: Toketee Falls, a double waterfall plunging a total of 120 feet, lies at the end of an easy 0.4-mile path along the North Umpqua River near Toketee Lake. At one spot, the river tumbles through a tight gorge filled with water-sculpted pools. Mottled sunlight filters through a colorful grove of Douglas-fir, cedar, maple, and Pacific yew en route to a viewing platform.

Watson Falls, with its 272-foot drop, is the third highest waterfall in Oregon. A steep 0.6-mile trail follows the plunging creek through an ancient forest of Douglas-fir and western hemlock. The understory of ferns, Oregon grape, and salal blends tints of green with the velvet coat of moss draped over the creekside boulders. A footbridge along the way offers an excellent viewpoint, and a side path comes to a stop in the misty spray at the base of the falls.

2 Wall Creek (Meditation Pool) Warm Springs

General description:	A warm soak in a sylvan setting at the end of a short path. Swimwear optional.
Elevation:	2,200 feet.
General location:	50 miles southeast of Eugene.
Map:	Willamette National Forest.
Restrictions:	Trail park pass required.
Contact:	Oakridge Ranger District, Willamette National Forest.

Finding the warm springs: From Eugene, take State Route 58, 40 miles southeast to Oakridge. Turn left to city center, then right on East 1st Street which soon becomes Salmon Creek Road (24). Continue northeast, past Salmon Creek Campground, on pavement. *Campers:* You'll also pass a number of primitive campsites sandwiched between the creek and the main road.

At 9 miles, turn left on a gravel road (1934) signed to Blair Lake. Watch for a pullout on your left in 0.4 mile, now marked with a hiker's symbol and a "No Camping Here" sign. A 0.3-mile path follows Wall Creek to the pool. Wall Creek is labeled simply "warm springs" on the forest map.

The warm springs: A clearing in a virgin forest reveals a pool built directly over the source springs. Bubbles rise gently to the surface in long streamers, heating the water to around 96 degrees. The pool is roughly 10 x 15 feet and oval in shape. It sits on the bank of a small but lively creek surrounded by countless acres of green solitude.

3 McCredie Hot Springs

General description:	A highway pit stop that puts McDonalds and Burger King to shame. As for swimwear, it's a mixed bag.
Elevation:	2,100 feet.
General location:	50 miles southeast of Eugene.
Map:	Willamette National Forest.
Restrictions:	Trail park pass required.
Contact:	Oakridge Ranger District, Willamette National Forest.

Finding the hot springs: From Eugene, take State Route 58, 40 miles southeast to Oakridge. Follow the highway 10 miles farther (0.5 mile past Blue Pool Campground) to a large turnout on the right. A 40-yard path heads upstream to the pools. McCredie is named on the forest map.

Bubbles perk up through the sandy bottom of a pool bordered by age-old trees at Wall Creek Warm Springs.

The hot springs: This soaker-saturated site, sandwiched between Salt Creek and a major highway, offers a variety of soaking pools with temperatures ranging from 95 to 105 degrees. The "party pool" measures about 15 x 20 feet and has a knee-deep bottom that varies in composition from sandy muck to sharp rocks and bits of broken glass.

Any time is party time at McCredie. The social activity varies from mild on weekdays to industrial strength over the weekends. Since it has easy access throughout the year, you're likely to find Winnebago City assembled in the large pullout. A nearby vantage point frequently houses a lineup of truck drivers-cum-birdwatchers.

A few quieter pools are located directly across the broad creek. To reach these with dry feet, drive another 0.5 mile up the highway and take Shady Gap Road across a bridge. Bear right for 0.1 mile to a pullout, then hunt for an overgrown path that follows the creek 0.3 mile back downstream.

Nighttime closure: The Forest Service, long plagued with problems of overuse at McCredie as well as at other sites, such as Cougar (see Hike 4), has posted "Day Use Only" signs both at the hot springs and at all nearby parking areas.

Truck drivers traditionally used the large pullout as an overnight rest stop, but that is now a practice of the past. For those of you with smaller rigs, there are still a few primitive campsites in the nearby woods or full facilities at Blue Pool Campground 0.5 mile down the road.

Early morning steam blankets the "party pool" at McCredie Hot Springs. This is the prime time for a quiet soak here.

Fuji Mountain

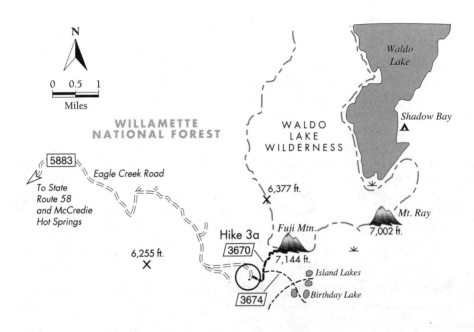

HIKE 3a *Fuji Mountain*

General description:	A brisk climb overlooking a line of volcanic peaks, near McCredie Hot Springs.
Difficulty:	Moderate.
Distance:	3 miles round trip.
General location:	65 miles southeast of Eugene.
Elevation gain:	964 feet.
High point:	7,144 feet.
Hiking quad:	Diamond Peak Wilderness.
Road map:	Willamette National Forest.
Restrictions:	Trail park pass required.
Contact:	Oakridge Ranger District, Willamette National Forest.

Finding the trailhead: Drive 15 miles southeast of Oakridge (5.5 miles past McCredie) on State Route 58. Watch for a train trestle over the highway and turn left just beyond it onto Eagle Creek Road (5883). Follow this gravel road 10.5 miles uphill to a trail sign on the left and a pullout on the right, at 6,180 feet.

The hike: With a peak named Fuji, how can you miss? The short climb is a piece of cake, and the summit offers an overview of no less than th₁ the wilderness areas that now link the Oregon Cascades in an almost unbroken line. The route described here is a short cut to the summit which is overlooked by many hikers.

Fuji Mountain Trail (3674) climbs moderately to a signed junction in 0.25 mile, then traverses along the west side of a ridge. The route weaves upward like a needle through a blue blanket of lupine and aster, backed by tall stands of mountain hemlock and true fir coated with tufts of moss. The last 0.5 mile is a steeper grade eased by switchbacks. Snow patches often obscure the route until mid-July.

As you look south from the summit, snow-capped Diamond Peak presides over the Diamond Peak Wilderness (see Hike 3b). Waldo Lake, framed by a landscape of wooded knolls and ridges, spreads out directly below. Fuji Mountain itself forms the southern boundary of the 39,200-acre Waldo Lake Wilderness. The massive Three Sisters Wilderness lies just beyond it to the northeast; the glacier-capped peaks of the North and South Sisters, along with several other volcanic cones, can be spotted in a straight line fading into the distance.

HIKE 3b *Diamond Creek Loop and Vivian Lake*

General description:	A day hike featuring waterfalls, wildflowers, and a lake in the Diamond Peak Wilderness, near McCredie Hot Springs.
Difficulty:	Moderate.
Distance:	6.5 miles round trip (including a 2.5-mile loop).
General location:	62 miles southeast of Eugene.
Elevation gain:	1,486 feet (loop, 280 feet; 1,206 feet to Vivian Lake).
High point:	5,406 feet.
Maps:	Same as above.
Restrictions:	Trail park pass required.
Contact:	Oakridge Ranger District, Willamette National Forest.

Finding the trailhead: From Oakridge, take State Route 58, 22 miles southeast (12 miles past McCredie) and through the highway tunnel to Salt Creek Falls Viewpoint and trailhead parking.

The hike: A pleasant half-day outing through a shaded forest bursting with rhododendrons leads to waterfalls and a wooded lake. The first mile is part of a loop trail to Diamond Creek Falls. The route described combines the loop with a 2-mile extension south to Vivian Lake.

Diamond Creek Trail (3598) passes the spur to Salt Creek Falls and bridges Salt Creek to a junction. Bear left and begin a gentle climb in a forest of hemlock and Douglas-fir. Thickets of bright pink rhododendrons and the solitary white blooms of beargrass highlight the way. The route

Diamond Creek Loop and Vivian Lake

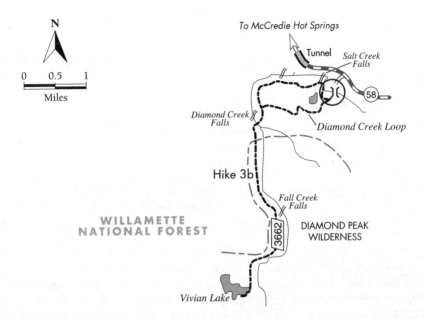

crosses a dirt road in 0.5 mile and once again just before reaching the far end of the loop.

Take the left fork at the junction to reach Vivian Lake. After crossing the same road once more, followed by the Southern Pacific Railroad tracks and then yet another road, you'll welcome the final crossing, the wilderness boundary line! Next, the trail climbs a steep grade beside Fall Creek Falls, then tapers off a bit in the last 0.5 mile along the rushing creek. Thick woods hide the lake until the last minute.

The Diamond Peak Wilderness has expanded to cover 52,337 acres centered on the snow-crowned roots of an old volcano (8,744-foot Diamond Peak) and the 7,100-foot and 7,138-foot lava crags of Mount Yoran. The peaks are flanked by forested ridges, tree-rimmed lakes, and a multitude of lakelets gouged out by glaciers.

Vivian Lake, a relatively small lake marked by an irregular shoreline, sits in a shallow basin walled in by trees. A few tiny clearings offer possible campsites or picnic areas. Looking across the green water, Mount Yoran peeks an angular head above the treetops a couple of miles south.

Retrace your steps to the junction and bear left on Diamond Creek Trail to complete the loop. The path soon reaches a close range overlook of Upper Diamond Creek Falls. The second viewpoint is found via a spur that drops to bridge the creek and returns to the base of the falls. The homeward route offers a few more vistas across the rugged canyon and a short spur to the rhododendron-rimmed shore of Too Much Bear Lake. Be sure to see 286-foot Salt Creek Falls, Oregon's second highest plunge, before leaving the area.

4 Cougar (Terwilliger) Hot Springs

General description:	An idyllic chain of well-known, sometimes too well-known soaking pools on a short path, near Cougar Reservoir. Skinnydippable with discretion.
Elevation:	2,000 feet.
General location:	53 miles east of Eugene.
Map:	Willamette National Forest.
Restrictions:	Trail park pass required.
Contact:	Blue River Ranger District, Willamette National Forest.

Finding the hot springs: From Eugene, drive 41 miles east on State Route 126 to Blue River. Continue 4 miles to paved Forest Road 19 and follow it south along the west side of Cougar Reservoir. At 7.5 miles, you'll pass a lagoon with a waterfall on your right followed by a parking area on the left. Walk back past the lagoon to the trail sign. The well-worn 0.3-mile path hugs the shore, then climbs through a darkening forest to the pools. Cougar isn't marked on the forest map.

The hot springs: Enveloped in the dark hues of a primeval woodland, Cougar is brushed by mottled light filtering down from treetops high above. Five soaking pools spaced apart by giant logs are laid out in steps down a steep ravine. Spring water emerges at 116 degrees and tumbles directly into the uppermost and hottest pool, and cold water flowing down a log flume provides an eye-opening shower.

Each rock and gravel pool is slightly cooler than the one above; they range in temperature from around 108 down to 95 degrees. The moss-coated trunk of one ancient log spanning the cleft plays host to a growth of new ferns.

Some years back, a volunteer group working with the Forest Service built log steps and railings down the slippery bank, replanted the eroded groundcover around the pools, added walkways, built an outhouse up the hill, and had a resident caretaker there to help protect the fragile grounds—a difficult job due to steadily increasing use/abuse problems.

Reminder: If you value a pristine environment, please observe the basics: no soap or shampoo, no glass containers, pack out what you pack in, leave your pets at home, and be kind to the soil by staying on established paths. Cougar needs all the help it can get!

The uppermost pool at Cougar Hot Springs runs too hot for all but the most hardcore soakers.

Nighttime closure: As the crowds at Cougar have kept increasing, so have the difficulties of dealing with the drinkers, dopers, and a few lunatics. The Forest Service has taken over the headache of managing Cougar and come up with a strictly enforced nighttime closure. Signs posted at both the parking area and trailhead read "Day Use Area. Closed Sundown to Sunrise." Camping along the reservoir is limited to very few primitive campsites and a campground near both ends.

Hike 4 *Rebel Creek/Rebel Rock Loop*

General description:	A rugged day hike or overnighter climbing through a lonesome slice of the Three Sisters Wilderness, near Cougar Hot Springs.
Difficulty:	Strenuous.
Distance:	A 12.5-mile loop.
General location:	59 miles east of Eugene.
Elevation gain:	3,271 feet.
High point:	5,311 feet.
Hiking quad:	Three Sisters Wilderness.
Road Map:	Willamette National Forest.
Restrictions:	Trail park pass required.
Contact:	Blue River Ranger District, Willamette National Forest.

Finding the trailhead: Follow the directions above to Cougar and continue south 6.5 miles (14 miles total from State Route 126). The trailhead splits a short way above the parking lot.

The hike: There has been more volcanic activity in the Three Sisters Wilderness during the past few thousand years than in any other part of the entire Cascade range. The Three Sisters are the star attractions in the 285,202-acre Cascade wildland: the striking peaks with their fourteen separate glaciers draw a multitude of climbers, hikers, and sightseers along boot-beaten paths on the east and north, while the western side remains relatively free of crowds.

The Rebel Creek/Rebel Rock Loop offers a quiet route stretching through virgin backcountry. Rebel Creek Trail climbs from creekside greenery and old-growth trees up through meadows. It connects with Rebel Rock Trail, a ridgetop route offering rear balcony views of the Three Sisters and Mount Jefferson before circling back down through more meadows and woods to end at the original trailhead.

It's best to follow Rebel Creek Trail up and Rebel Rock Trail back, as the gain is more gradual this way. Turn left just above the parking loop onto Rebel Creek Trail (3323). Ferns and thimbleberries overgrow the path, and

Rebel Creek/Rebel Rock Loop

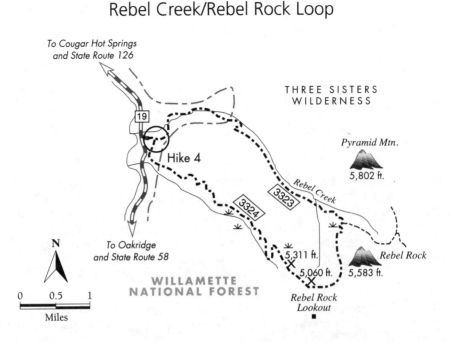

ancient stands of Douglas-fir, cedar, and western hemlock wrap it in many shades of green. It's a gentle climb along the creek, and the only two crossings are on split-log bridges. The trail leaves the creek and begins a moderate 5.7-mile climb to a junction at 4,480 feet.

Take the right fork, Rebel Rock Trail (3324) and climb one more ridge. You'll pass the base of 5,583-foot Rebel Rock while slicing through fields of knee-high flowers. The high meadows are peppered with mountain hemlock and true fir. As the ridgeline route slowly curves, it offers a variety of views en route to a large meadow on a 5,311-foot plateau. From here you can gaze out across the wilderness to several of the highest distant peaks.

It's all downhill from this point. The path plunges through more meadows so overgrown that the route is barely visible until you reach the lower woods. Here, hundreds of invisible spiderwebs span the trail between anchoring trees, ignoring the hiker's right of way. Ferns and thimbleberries choke the path, and the forest closes in overhead.

5 Bigelow (Deer Creek) Hot Spring

General description:	A fern-grotto pool on the McKenzie River, near a paved road. Swimwear advised.
Elevation:	2,000 feet.
General location:	61 miles northeast of Eugene.
Map:	Willamette National Forest.
Contact:	McKenzie Ranger District, Willamette National Forest.

Finding the hot spring: From Eugene, take State Route 126, 57 miles east to Belknap Springs. Continue 4 miles north (midway between mileposts 15 and 14) and turn left onto Deer Creek Road (2654). (*Campers:* There are primitive campsites in the nearby woods and a campground a mile or so up the highway.) Cross the river and park just past the bridge. Follow the lower path a short way downstream to the pool. Bigelow Hot Spring (called Deer Creek by the Forest Service) isn't marked on the forest map.

The hot spring: This little pool, well-camouflaged among the many look-alikes along the riverbank, is a closely-guarded secret. If you were rafting

Bigelow Hot Spring bubbles up from below into a fern grotto pool well hidden along the riverbank.

downstream, it would never catch your eye. Walking right above it on the McKenzie River Trail (see Hike 5a), you wouldn't see the pool through the trees. Even driving across the nearby bridge and looking right at it, there are no telltale signs to give it away unless it's occupied.

With the inlet at the bottom of the bubbly pool, hot water seeps in quietly to provide an optimum soaking temperature of 102 to 104 degrees. Riverside rocks line the outer edge, while the inner side forms a small grotto carved out of the steep riverbank. Luxuriant ferns overhang the pool, and moisture condenses overhead to drip back down on the steaming surface in cool droplets.

Nighttime closure: Following in the footsteps of first Cougar and then McCredie, Bigelow has joined the list of hot springs in Willamette National Forest to institute a night closure. The area around the pool is now officially off limits from sundown to sunrise.

Waking nightmare: *I parked by the bridge. Mine was the only vehicle on a rainy Friday night. It was my first visit to Bigelow in several years. The next morning I awoke to discover the lot rapidly filling to capacity. People were gathering in small clusters and talking with animation. Huge motorhomes pulled in, and more folks piled out.*

I finally squeezed my door open and jokingly asked a lady where the line began. She gave me a blank look and a polite laugh, then hurried off. I finally learned to my great relief that it wasn't Bigelow Hot Spring at all but a running marathon on the McKenzie River Trail that had drawn the crowd!

Hike 5a *McKenzie River National Recreation Trail*

General description: A choice of riverside strolls featuring virgin forests, lava flows and waterfalls, near Bigelow Hot Spring.

Difficulty: Easy.

Distance: Variable.

General location: Beginning 52 miles east of Eugene.

Elevation gain: up to 1,750 feet.

High point: Clear Lake, 3,200 feet.

Map: Willamette National Forest.

Contact: McKenzie Ranger District, Willamette National Forest.

Finding the trailheads: Drive 52 miles east from Eugene on State Route 126 to McKenzie Ranger Station, where you can pick up a free brochure and map listing the many trailheads and exact mileages between points.

The hike: The riverside path above Bigelow Hot Spring is part of the 27-mile McKenzie River National Recreation Trail. Designated as a National Wild and Scenic River in 1988 and listed as a State Scenic Waterway at the same time, the McKenzie is a whitewater river that originates in the high Cascades. Beginning just west of McKenzie Ranger Station and ending near Clear Lake and the river's headwaters, the route is a gentle climb upvalley parallel to State Route 126. There are eleven parking areas along the way that provide a variety of easy access points at signed trailheads.

The lower 8 to 10 miles are usually free of snow year-round. The hiker treads through dim forests of old-growth Douglas-fir mixed with hemlock, cedar, and dogwood. Thick mats of Oregon grape, wildflowers, and salal crowd beneath vine maple and other hardwoods. The upper part passes areas where lava flows once spewed from nearby craters, filling the McKenzie Canyon and forcing the once mighty river through underground channels (see Hike 5b). Tamolitch, a broad valley of lava, remains a dry watercourse except in times of heavy runoff.

Above Tamolitch Valley, the trail passes two impressive waterfalls created by lava. Koosah Falls, a 70-foot drop into a deep pool, is outclassed by magnificent Sahalie Falls, a broad 100-foot plunge over a lava dam followed by a series of cascades that tumble another 40 feet. Clouds of spray billow outward over green banks.

Clear Lake, the next to last stop, was created some 3,000 years ago when a giant lava flow dammed the river and caused the wide valley upstream to fill in. Submerged trees can be seen through the clear surface near the north end, well preserved in the icy, mineral-free water. Springs that average

Graceful log bridges are a common sight along the McKenzie River Trail.

Bigelow Hot Spring • McKenzie River National Recreational Trail • The "Blue Hole" and Tamolitch Falls

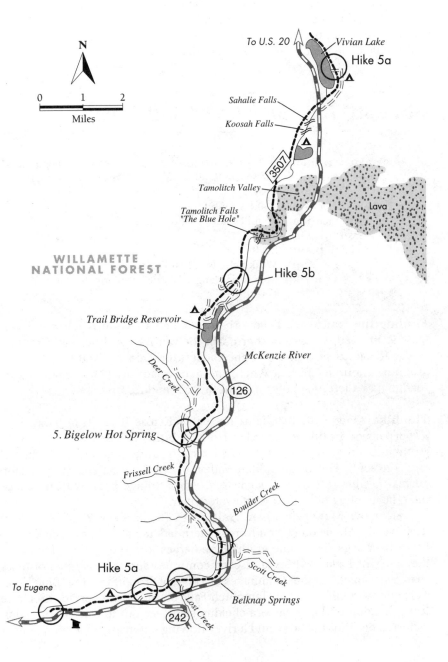

N

0   1   2
Miles

To U.S. 20

Vivian Lake

Hike 5a

Sahalie Falls

Koosah Falls

3507

Tamolitch Valley

Lava

Tamolitch Falls
"The Blue Hole"

WILLAMETTE
NATIONAL FOREST

Hike 5b

Trail Bridge Reservoir

Deer Creek

McKenzie River

126

5. Bigelow Hot Spring

Frissell Creek

Boulder Creek

Scott Creek

Hike 5a

To Eugene

Belknap Springs

Lost Creek

242

43 degrees act as outlets for the buried river and well up from below to feed the lake. Great Springs, one of the largest, can be seen from the trail on the northeast side.

The McKenzie River Trail finally comes to rest near the Old Santiam Wagon Road just north of Clear Lake. This was the historic route over the Santiam Pass that became an early link between the mid-Willamette Valley and the lands in central and eastern Oregon.

HIKE 5b *The "Blue Hole" and Tamolitch Falls*

General description:	A day hike to one of the strangest sights along the McKenzie River Trail, near Bigelow Hot Spring.
Difficulty:	Easy.
Distance:	4 miles round trip.
General location:	66 miles northeast of Eugene.
Elevation gain:	240 feet.
High point:	2,440 feet.
Map:	Willamette National Forest.
Contact:	McKenzie Ranger District, Willamette National Forest.

Finding the trailhead: Follow the directions above to Bigelow and take State Route 126, 5 miles farther north to Trail Bridge Reservoir. Cross the bridge to a junction and bear right (the left fork goes to Trail Bridge Campground). Continue straight where the main road forks right again. As the road makes a left, watch for a small turnout and trail marker.

The hike: One of the highlights on the McKenzie River Trail (Hike 5a) is a spot known locally as the "Blue Hole," a brilliant blue pool of icy water that marks the place where the river rises from its underground channel, near the south end of Tamolitch Valley, to continue its course in a more normal fashion. It's quite a sight to see this strange pool, with no visible inlet, channeling out into a whitewater river.

Follow the McKenzie River Trail north for an easy 2 miles through deep woods. At one point, you'll cross a fern-laden marsh on a curving bridge hewn from logs. The route gradually emerges into the open at Tamolitch, the Valley of Lava. A drier landscape continues across a riverbed of moss-coated volcanic rock that culminates in a 60-foot dropoff into the "Blue Hole." This bone-dry cliff is called Tamolitch Falls on the Forest Service brochure. It would confound any camera-clicking sightseer out to capture one more waterfall on film. But so would a river flowing downstream from nowhere.

The McKenzie River surfaces abruptly from its underground watercourse through the "Blue Hole."

6 Bagby Hot Springs

In the communal bathhouse at Bagby Hot Springs are three handhewn soaking tubs hollowed out from giant logs, the perfect spot for family get-togethers. Photo courtesy of L. Springer, Friends of Bagby.

HIKE 6a *To Bagby Hot Springs*

General description:	A day hike through lush woods to the Shangri-la of hot soaks. No need to pack a swimsuit.
Difficulty:	Easy.
Distance:	3 miles round trip.
General location:	70 miles southeast of Portland.
Elevation gain:	190 feet.
High point:	2,270 feet At Bagby.
Hiking quad:	Battle Ax Green Trails.
Road map:	Mount Hood National Forest.
Contact:	Clackamas River Ranger District, Mount Hood National Forest.

Finding the trailhead: From Portland, take State Route 224 to Estacada and on into Mount Hood Forest. Take a right on Forest Road 46 at 0.5 mile past Ripplebrook Ranger Station, and bear right in 3.5 miles on FR 63. Turn

Bagby Hot Springs

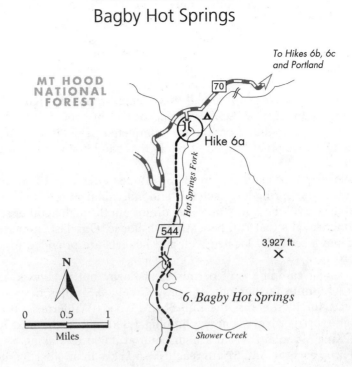

right again in 3.5 miles on FR 70 and drive 6 miles to the trailhead parking lot. You'll pass several campgrounds on the way in. Vandalism has become an increasing problem here, so park close to other vehicles, get your goodies out of sight, and lock up tight. The roads are paved and well marked, and Bagby is named on the maps.

The hike: The 1.5-mile Bagby Trail (544) is a delight in itself as it undulates through a grand old forest of Douglas-fir and cedar with an understory of vine maple. Moss-coated logs litter the way, and the path slices between cross sections with 5-foot diameters. The gentle creekside route passes emerald green pools spaced between rapids. Cross three bridges, then leave the creek behind just beyond the last bridge and climb a short hillside to the springs.

The hot springs: A volunteer group working with the Forest Service has built three rustic bathhouses, fed by two nearby springs, in a sylvan forest setting. The hardworking Friends of Bagby drain and clean the tubs daily and also have added decks with log benches, outhouses, pathways, and landscaping. This unique group welcomes anyone interested in helping them preserve the area. You can send donations or apply for membership to Friends of Bagby, Inc., P.O. Box 1798, Clackamas, OR 97015.

The bathhouse at the upper spring, built in 1983, has a single 6-foot cedar tub enclosed by minimum walls and maximum trees. The ce pure sky. This is the spot for a family or cozy group to enjoy total privacy. A log flume 150-feet long diverts the 135-degree spring water into the tub, and a crude faucet admits cold water.

The communal bathhouse, finished in 1984, is another minimum wall/ maximum tree and sky affair, but on a larger scale. Three huge cedar logs, hollowed out to form long and narrow soaking tubs, are spaced a few feet apart; these rustic log tubs are all that remain from the original bathhouse that burned down in 1979. At one end of the airy room is another 6-foot round tub. An adjoining bathhouse, completed in 1986, is a fully roofed replica of the one that burned; it offers five hand-hewn log tubs in private rooms.

A cleverly designed system of log flumes channels 135-degree water from the lower spring into each tub, and individual gates may be opened or closed to control the flow. Tub water drains out through another set of gates into long troughs that run beneath each house. One last flume feeds cold water into a centrally located well and buckets are provided to carry it to the tubs.

Overnight camping isn't permitted at Bagby but is allowed at Shower Creek 0.25 mile farther on. At Spray Creek, 2.5 miles from the Bagby trailhead, the path enters the Bull of the Woods Wilderness. It continues through more verdant scenery, climbing 1,330 feet in the next 8 miles to Silver King Mountain. From a high point at 4,600 feet along a ridge, you could drop east on Trail 573 to reach Twin Lakes in another 2 miles.

HIKE 6b *Bull of the Woods.*

General description:	A day hike to a lookout in the Bull of the Woods Wilderness, not far from Bagby Hot Springs.
Difficulty:	Easy.
Distance:	7.5 miles round trip.
General location:	76 miles southeast of Portland.
Elevation gain:	883 feet.
High point:	5,523 feet.
Maps:	Same as above.
Contact:	Clackamas River Ranger District, Mount Hood National Forest.

Finding the trailhead: Follow the directions above to the junction of Forest Roads 63 and 70 and continue 2 miles south on FR 63. Turn right on gravel FR 6340 and climb to a three-way junction in 10 miles. A sign on the right marks the trailhead. Park here and put your boots to work.

The hike: The lookout that caps 5,523-foot Bull of the Woods is the logical spot to survey one of Oregon's newer wildlands. The 34,900-acre Bull of the

The lookout tower on top of Bull of the Woods offers an expanse of undulating mountain ranges dotted with volcanic cones.

Woods Wilderness is a spoonful of wooded lakes spread out around the central peak. The small area, which includes the headwaters of the Collawash, Breitenbush, and North Santiam rivers, adds yet another link in the chain of wilderness gems running through the Cascades. The broad view from the summit includes many prominent peaks.

Follow Bull of the Woods Trail (550) on a gentle climb through a forest of Douglas-fir and western hemlock. Rhododendron, bear grass, and lupine brush the path in alternating bursts of pink, white, and purple blue. The route hugs the west side of a ridge topped by North and South Dickey peaks; it's basically one short and sweet traverse with a couple of hairpins at the end that offer previews of coming attractions.

The lookout has expansive open views of glacier-draped peaks from the Three Sisters north to Mount Rainier. Most prominent is the angular white face of Mount Jefferson standing out at 10,495 feet to the southeast. The massive shape of 11,239-foot Mount Hood rises dramatically to the northeast. A pleasant loop may be hiked from the lookout east to the Welcome Lakes (see below).

Bull of the Woods
• Bull of the Woods to the Welcome Lakes Loop

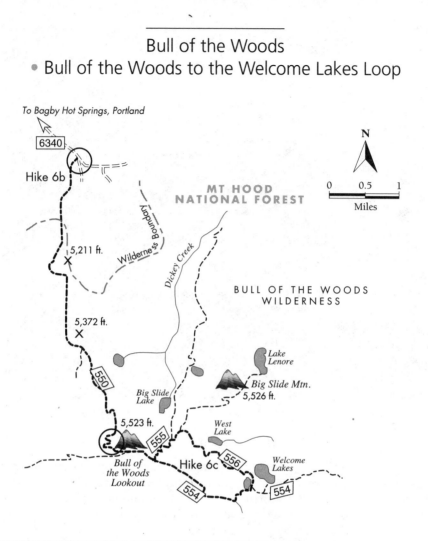

HIKE 6c *Bull of the Woods to the Welcome Lakes Loop*

General description:	A day hike from the lookout to lakes and more views, not far from Bagby Hot Springs.
Difficulty:	Moderate.
Distance:	5 miles round trip (including a 3.3-mile loop).
General location:	80 miles southeast of Portland.
Elevation gain:	1,243 feet (283 feet to start of loop; loop, 960 feet).
High point:	Trailhead, 5,523 feet.
Maps:	Same as above.
Contact:	Clackamas River Ranger District, Mount Hood National Forest.

Finding the trailhead: Follow the route above to Bull of the Woods.

The hike: The Welcome Lakes Loop makes a pleasant side trip from Bull of the Woods Lookout down through a bit more backcountry east of the summit. The 5-mile circuit passes through old-growth timber and open ridges, and it intersects a network of trails en route that could keep a backpacker busy for days.

The route begins by dropping steeply from the lookout through deep woods, then veering east over a rockslide area. A junction is reached in 0.9 mile, 280 feet below the summit, with Schreiner Peak Trail (555) plunging downhill on the left. To follow the loop in a clockwise direction, turn north here and descend tight switchbacks past Dickey Creek Trail branching left down to Big Slide Lake. Continue beyond a pond to a junction with the lower trail to the Welcome Lakes.

Turn right onto West Lake Way (556) and drop gradually through low forest, traversing 250 feet above West Lake, treading through an open rocky area with good views around the scenic basin. The path contours gently downhill along the face of a slope and rounds a corner to arrive at Upper Welcome Lake. Orbit the small lake to intersect the Welcome Lakes Trail at 2.7 miles.

Upper Welcome Lake sits on a ledge a few hundred feet from the trail with a large dry campsite nearby. The surface is brushed in late summer with the yellow blooms of pond lilies. From the viewpoint east of the lake, you can look 240 feet down onto Lower Welcome Lake. An unsigned spur heads down from the Welcome Lakes Trail to the larger lake, adding a mile round trip to the hike.

Turn onto Welcome Lakes Trail (554) for the second half of the loop. The path zigzags up a ridge through meadows and more rockslide areas, passing the Geronimo Trail, which veers off to Elk Lake. The route makes a dip, then rises to follow the crest with views into West Lake Basin and across to Big Slide Mountain to the northeast. Pass the junction with Schreiner Peak Trail, bear right at one last junction 0.2 mile to the west, and retrace your steps back up the mountain.

7 Paulina Lake Hot Springs

The perennial foot warmer at Paulina Lake Hot Springs needs a few buckets of cold water to cool it into the comfort zone.

HIKE 7a *To Paulina Lake Hot Springs*

General description:	A day hike to some "now-you-see-'em, now-you-don't" hot springs on a lake inside a volcanic crater. Carry a swimsuit and shovel.
Difficulty:	Easy.
Distance:	4 miles round trip (or a 7.5-mile loop).
General location:	33 miles south of Bend.
Elevation gain:	180 feet.
High point:	6,520 feet.
Hiking quads:	Paulina Peak and East Lake USGS.
Road map:	Deschutes National Forest.
Restrictions:	Recreational user fee required.
Contact:	Bend/Fort Rock Ranger District, Deschutes National Forest.

Paulina Lake Hot Springs • Paulina Peak

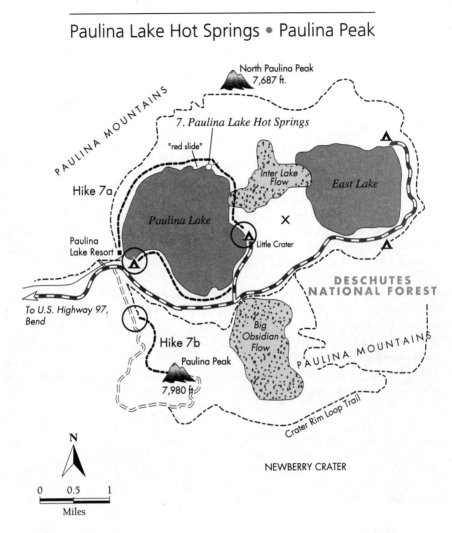

North Paulina Peak
7,687 ft.

PAULINA MOUNTAINS

7. Paulina Lake Hot Springs

"red slide"

Inter Lake Flow

East Lake

Hike 7a

Paulina Lake

Little Crater

X

Paulina Lake Resort

To U.S. Highway 97, Bend

DESCHUTES NATIONAL FOREST

Hike 7b

Big Obsidian Flow

PAULINA MOUNTAINS

Paulina Peak

7,980 ft.

Crater Rim Loop Trail

N

0   0.5   1
Miles

NEWBERRY CRATER

Finding the trailhead: Drive 20 miles south of Bend on U.S. Highway 97, then follow signs 13 miles east to Newberry Crater and Paulina Lake. The springs are on the far shore and can be reached on the Paulina Lake-Shore Loop Trail 2.75 miles from Paulina Lake Campground or 2 miles from Little Crater Campground. Everything here is well signed and easy to find—except the hot springs, which aren't marked at all. Snow blocks the roads in winter, and the prime time for digging a hot pool is said to be June to August.

The volcano: Newberry National Volcanic Monument is a slice of Deschutes National Forest housing much of the lava lands on the east side of the Cascades plus the largest ice-age volcano in Oregon. Several violent eruptions over the past half million years formed the 5-mile-wide caldera called Newberry Crater. Within are two scenic lakes. At one time a single body of water, Paulina and East lakes were eventually split apart by further eruptions.

East Lake has no visible inlet or outlet and is fed, aside from snowmelt, by submerged hot springs bubbling up near the southeast shore. The springs clock in at a staggering 175 degrees, but the heat is instantly lost to the cold lake. Paulina Lake, however, offers an array of usable hot springs on the northeast side in addition to submerged ones along the rocky east coast. Except for snowmelt, their combined flow constitutes the lake's only inlet. Paulina Creek, the outlet, forms the only breach in the rim of the crater.

The hike: Although the round trip to the hot springs from Little Crater Campground is short and sweet, the full loop hike around the lake is well worth the added mileage. The path hugs the photogenic shoreline, leaving it only briefly to climb a prominent landmark known locally as "red slide." Thick forest shades the way without blocking views of Paulina Peak (see below) and the Big Obsidian Flow. The springs can be found between red slide and the Inter-Lake Lava Flow, along a meadow-lined beach.

The hot springs: The springs at Paulina are a tad out of the ordinary. Elusive even after you've found them, they lurk not under water but under gravel. You can walk down the beach, turn and literally watch your footsteps fill with hot water! The challenge is twofold—trying to coax the good stuff out of hiding (that's where the shovel comes in), and then once you've got it, trying to hang onto it long enough for a soak. The springs range from 96 to 113 degrees, so if you stumble onto a live one, a bucket might be in order. (Actually, a sturdy bucket can double for both digging a pool and tossing in lake water.)

I consulted a hydrologist and a geologist, both familiar with Newberry Crater, and was told that the hot springs here bubble up from the depths and simply ride the top layer of the lake's water table. Hot water filters up through the shoreline gravel at the same level as the lake itself. When the lake recedes, the hot water can be tapped, but the trick is to dig deeper than the level of the lake. Then you can sit back and watch it fill, and it will remain filled.

There's a shallow, log-lined soaking pool at 113 degrees over by red slide that appears to be a perennial. It sits on bedrock and can't be deepened, but it should fill up when the lake level's just right. It has a nice platform spanning one end for a seat and some foot dangling. All you need to do is to throw in some cold water.

Paulina Lake Resort offers boat rentals and rustic accommodations under a special use permit from the Forest Service, and the owners keep a sharp eye on the lake, roads, and weather. The summer visitor center at Paulina Lake or the ranger station in Bend can help with other questions.

HIKE 7b *Paulina Peak*

General description:	A day hike to the high point on the rim of Newberry Crater, near Paulina Lake Hot Springs.
Difficulty:	Strenuous.
Distance:	5 miles round trip.
General location:	34 miles south of Bend.
Elevation gain:	1,480 feet.
High point:	7,980 feet.
Maps:	Same as above.
Restrictions:	Recreational user fee required.
Contact:	Bend/Fort Rock Ranger District, Deschutes National Forest.

Finding the trailhead: Follow the directions above to Paulina Lake. Take a right just past the visitor center on a washboard forest road (500) marked for Paulina Peak. Drive 0.8 mile to a pullout and trail sign on your left. The actual trailhead, back by the visitor center, adds an extra mile and 160-foot gain to the hike.

The hike: Although you can drive to the top of Paulina Peak, the road climbs the back side of the mountain. The hiking route contours up the front side and offers views of the lake en route. Crater Rim Loop Trail presents a steady 11 percent grade, but the north-facing slope and thick woods combine forces to shade the way. The lodgepole forest includes a sprinkling of hemlock and ponderosa interspersed with rock and lava slopes. Near the end, a spur trail accesses the craggy summit.

Paulina Lake unfolds below. On the far shore, you can spot red slide, the landmark for the hot springs, as well as the Inter-Lake Lava Flow and Big Obsidian Flow. Beyond the crater rim, the panorama takes in much of the Cascades. The massive cones of Mount Bachelor and South Sister top the northwest horizon. To the southeast is Fort Rock.

HIKE 7c *Other Trips in the Newberry Area*

NEWBERRY CRATER

The crater contains a network of hiking routes to suit every taste. Crater Rim Loop Trail climbs Paulina Peak and then continues around the rim for 20 miles. It can also be entered via the 4.25-mile Lost Lake Trail to provide a 10-mile loop, or via Newberry Crater Trail, bisecting the crater floor from east to west.

Not to be missed are the 0.5-mile Paulina Falls Trail, which offers an exceptional view from the base of the 100-foot plunge, and the 1-mile Obsidian Flow Loop, snaking across frozen cataracts of black volcanic glass. The 1,300-year-old flow is the most recent volcanic eruption in Oregon. The Paulina Peak and East Lake USGS quads cover Newberry Crater, and the Deschutes Forest map handles the roads.

NEWBERRY LAVA TUBES

A lava tube, or lava cave, is a natural underground cavity formerly occupied by lava. It is, in other words, a roofed section of a lava river. Fluid lava streaming underground has created a variety of tubes and complex systems that are fascinating to explore. The Newberry lava tubes are known to be at least 6,800 years old, as they contain ash from the eruption of Mount Mazama, better known as Crater Lake.

Exploring lava caves needn't be a risky endeavor if you simply practice common sense and basic rules of safety, and take appropriate gear. In total darkness, every 100 feet feels like a mile. Experienced cavers carry three sources of light. A good combination is a helmet-mounted light, a powerful flashlight, and a candle for the time when all else fails. Head protection is advisable, as are boots with lug soles. Wear plenty of warm clothes—cave temperatures in central Oregon fall generally in the 35- to 50-degree range.

The Newberry lava tubes lie widely scattered within a crescent-shaped area centered to the east of the crater. The easiest access is via a loop drive on forest roads leaving U.S. Highway 97 just south of Bend and returning at La Pine. (See Area Map.) The most well-known caves are marked on the Deschutes Forest map.

The popular **Lava River Cave,** located near the Lava Lands Visitor Center 10 miles south of Bend, is the longest continuous lava tube in the state. The interpretive trail is 1.5 miles long, of which a full 1.1 miles is underground. One 1,500-foot section has become unstable and is now closed. This is one of Oregon's three commercial caves; with marked paths, stairways over collapsed rubble, and smooth floors, it makes a good introduction to caving.

Boyd Cave is a single lava tube 1,800 feet long. It has a single entrance with a sturdy stairway. The walking is fairly easy over sand and scattered rubble.

Nearby is popular **Skeleton Cave,** a must for the more adventurous. This lava tube is 3,000 feet long and has a fork just beyond the halfway point that can confuse the unwary. The name came from the abundance of Pleistocene-age bones found within. The floor is smooth sand far past the junction room.

The collapsing remains of the **Arnold lava tube system** also are found nearby, including the once famous Arnold Ice Cave. The complex system once extended about 4.5 miles, but most of what's left today is considered either hazardous or difficult scrambling. It's worth a visit just to view the gaping entrance holes.

Lavacicle Cave Geological Area is a narrow, lengthy lava tube with stalagmites of frozen lava. Its two opposing sections total 4,231 feet.

Newberry Area

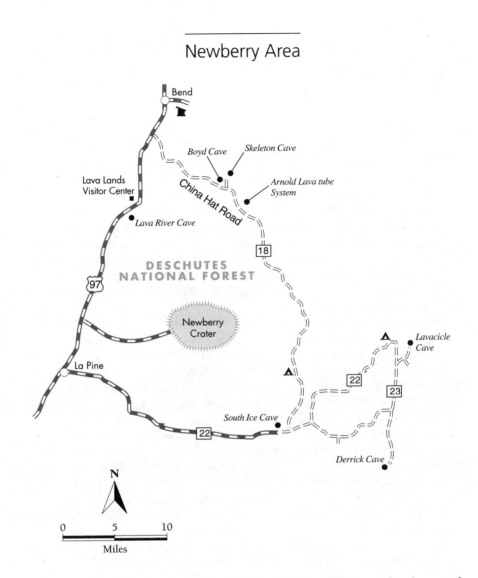

Discovered in 1959, it was badly vandalized before the Forest Service gated the entrance. Contact the Bend/Fort Rock Ranger District for information on access.

Derrick Cave is a complex lava tube 1,200 feet long. The first section is an easy walk to an area where skylights overhead cast eerie rays down the walls. Beyond, it narrows into intriguing and challenging passageways. This cave is on Bureau of Land Management land. The access roads aren't well signed but are well-used and fairly obvious.

South Ice Cave is a high-ceiling cave with permanent ice. It has two sections, one on each side of the ramped entrance; total length of the two caves is 1,000 feet. The cave is managed by the Forest Service as an improved recreation site.

B. THE EASTERN DESERT AND THE OWYHEE RIVER CANYON

OVERVIEW

The southeast corner of Oregon is a land of sagebrush hills, cattle ranches, and high lava plains stretching as far as the eye can see. Of the eleven hot springs listed in this guide, six lie scattered to the west and five line the Owyhee River to the east. Public lands here are administered by the Bureau of Land Management (BLM), with district offices in Burns and Vale.

The desert west of the Owyhee country and south of Burns is a region with a variety of wild hot springs. All six are bordered by either craggy buttes, mountain ranges such as the Steens, lakes, or silvery smooth desert playas. Although vehicle access is long and tedious, all hot springs do have roadside soaking pools.

To the east, the Owyhee carves a rugged canyon through an almost roadless wilderness, draining ultimately into the Snake River. Congress has included nearly 200 miles of the Owyhee and its tributaries in the National Wild and Scenic Rivers System, and many parts are under wilderness study. The state geothermal map lists eight hot springs buried in the canyon. Of these, five are accessible and functional. All but two require a rugged bushwack approach. See Appendix B for an alternate route.

State highway maps don't begin to tell the story here, and forest maps don't apply. Luckily, the BLM prints both a 30-minute series detailing land features and a series of Recreation Guides by Resource Area. The latter maps are more up to date but lack the detail of the 30-minute series. This book uses the most user-friendly road map for each hot spring.

Directions are from the few towns scattered along U.S. Highways 95, 20/26, and State Route 205. The access roads tend to be long and dusty, hiking routes strictly cross-country, campsites primitive and unshaded, and the hot springs, with few exceptions are wild and woolly.

Hot springs and hikes: The desert country to the west of the Owyhee River offers a number of remote roadside hot soaks. Shorter routes to South Harney Lake and Borax Lake (8, 9) are followed by lengthy back roads to Alvord, Mickey, and Willow Creek (10–12). To the east, the rugged Owyhee Canyon makes for challenging cross-country hiking as well as long dusty back roads. Starting upcanyon and south of Jordan Valley at Three Forks (13), we flounder downstream with mad expeditions to Ryegrass (14), Greeley Bar (15), and Echo Rock (16)—accessed along with a companion hike from scenic Leslie Gulch. Farthest north comes a roadside dip at the popular Snively (17) and a nearby desert walk. This area is on BLM land.

Eastern Desert and the Owyhee River Canyon
Area Map

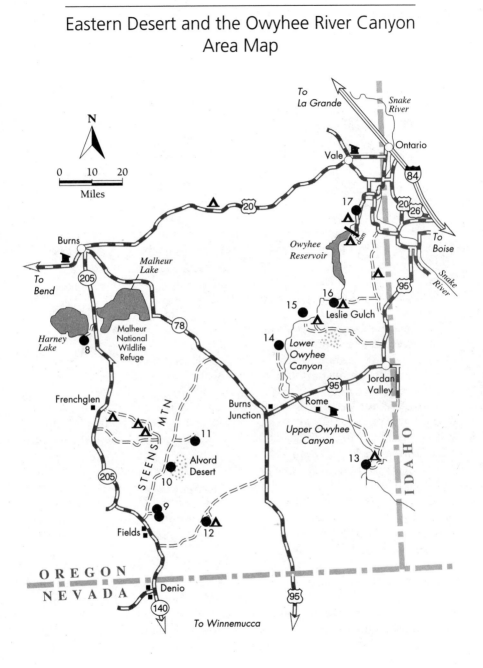

Season: Except for Borax Lake, which is a bit cool for winter use, the soaks west of the Owyhee Canyon are limited only by road access; the final roads to most are nearly impassable when wet. In the Owyhee Canyon, the river level is a second critical factor with all but Snively. Pool temperature restricts Three Forks to warm weather, while summer heat keeps all but "mad dogs and Englishmen" out of the desert. The rafting season, roughly March through mid-June, brings more competition for the hot pools but also more users to keep the algae cleaned out.

Daytime temperatures in the desert often climb to 90 degrees (and sometimes much higher) through the summer months but drop markedly overnight. The weather tends to be dry and clear, and sunscreen replaces raingear as the number one item in the pack.

8 South Harney Lake Hot Springs

General description: Hot pools in a desert meadow near the southeaast tip of Harney Lake. Extremely skinnydippable.
Elevation: 4,100 feet.
General location: 34 miles south of Burns.
Map: Burns District, North half, BLM.
Contact: Burns District, BLM.

Finding the hot springs: From Burns, drive 2 miles east on State Route 78 to the north end of SR 205. Head south 24 miles to the Malheur National Wildlife Refuge. Turn right (west) at an intersection near Milepost 24 where a left turn is marked to Refuge Headquarters.

This seasonal road to Harney Lake deteriorates from gravel to rutted clay and deep powder patches. Watching the dust bounce and swirl on your rear window will remind you of an oversoaped washing machine. Stay on the main track for 8.5 miles, then bear right on a quarter-mile spur that goes past a gate and cattleguard to a grassy flat by the pools. The hot springs are marked on the map.

The hot springs: Water emerges into a source pool at 152 degrees and flows through a marsh lined with tall reeds. Users have dug two soaking pools, about knee deep with silty bottoms, 50 yards apart along this grassy channel. The upper pool is 8 feet square with a temperature range of 104 to 108 degrees. The lower one, closer to 10 feet across, seems to vary from 98 to 103 degrees.

The springs are on a small plot of unposted private land within the wildlife refuge. Camping is allowed at the site, but please pack out what you pack in and respect the landowner's rights.

Geothermal note: The Harney Basin is a broad depression in the high lava plains of eastern Oregon, which covers a major caldera complex. South Harney Lake Hot Springs is the second hottest, and reportedly the only usable soak, out of twenty-five thermal springs and more than thirty-five thermal wells. Bathtub Springs, a few miles to the west, is currently underwater due to the rise in the level of Harney Lake.

9 Borax Lake and Little Borax Hot Springs

A cautious soaker decides to give it a test before trying the waters at Little Borax Hot Springs.

HIKE 9 *To Both Hot Springs*

General description:	A day hike or mountain bike ride to a salty thermal lake and hot pots in a desert valley. Skinnydippable with discretion.
Difficulty:	Easy.
Distance:	8.5 miles round trip.
General location:	5 miles north of Fields.
Elevation gain:	Minimal.
High point:	4,080 feet.
Map:	Burns District, South half, BLM.
Contact:	Burns District, BLM.

Finding the trailhead: The only trick here is finding Fields, which lies in hiding about 111 miles south of Burns on State Route 205 and 97 miles north of Winnemucca via U.S. Highway 95. Fields Station, as the sign reads, does have gas and water (an obligatory pit stop) and a small store/cafe.

Drive north from Fields, bearing right in 1.4 miles onto an all-weather gravel road, known as the Eastside or Alvord Ranch Road, signed to SR 78. Continue 3.6 miles to a grove of trees just off to the right. This is a nice shady spot to park or pitch a tent. The springs are marked on the map.

The hike: The side road continues 3.6 miles to the lake but soon deteriorates into a 4WD track. You can hike, bike, or jeep from here 0.4 mile east to a locked gate, then follow the fenceline 0.7 mile south, a mile east, then north. This route detours around private land. You'll pass a few other roads and two gates which should be left as you found them.

Turn east for the final 1.5 miles, past the north tip of Lower Borax Lake which is also a warm spring but too cold for soaking. The road reaches the lake at the site of an old borax works, where the white powder was once extracted from the water by evaporation and hauled by mule train to Winnemucca.

The hot springs: Superheated, 196-degree water gushes up through vents in the bottom of Borax Lake, cooling as it disperses, to a temperature in the mid-80s that varies in different parts of the lake and times of year. It's a modest lake, only about 300 feet across, and only a foot or so deep until you're well out from shore. The center is quite deep and very pleasant swimming on a warm day. An air mattress or inner tube would ease the trip out.

Little Borax, as it's called by some, refers to the last in a string of small "hot pots" that runs north from Borax Lake. Reach it by following a track 0.7 mile due north from the rusting borax works. The line-up begins just past a third gate, along the right side of the road. The pools, called ephermial vents, come in various sizes and flows. They're all deep, dangerously hot, and subject to occasional sudden surges in temperature.

Borax Lake and Little Borax Hot Springs

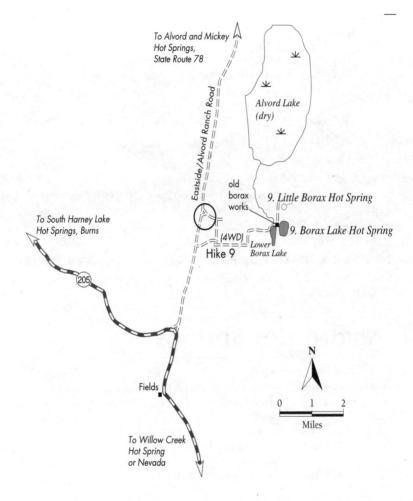

You'll find two narrow pools at the end of the line. The first is lukewarm, in the mid-80s. The last has a temperature that varies from far too hot to barely tolerable. It's about 6 feet deep with a sloping silty bottom and a hole at both ends. It's worth checking out, but do use extreme caution.

Borax Lake and Little Borax are on a private plot owned by the Nature Conservancy but open to the public. The small lake, rimmed by grass, sits in a broad valley just south of Alvord Lake, which is nearly dry. In addition to the salty borax, the water also has a high concentration of arsenic. Be sure you don't ingest it.

At Alvord Hot Springs, this wayfarer opted to give it a try without a test.

10 Alvord Hot Springs

General description:	A roadside shack and hot tanks set between the Alvord Desert and Steens Mountain. Keep swimwear handy.
Elevation:	4,080 feet.
General location:	23 miles northeast of Fields.
Map:	Burns District, South half, BLM.
Contact:	Burns District, BLM.

Finding the hot springs: Follow the directions above to Fields and the Eastside Road. Drive 23 dusty miles northeast, 18 miles past the Borax Lake junction, to a cattleguard and pullout near a crude shack off to the right. The springs, named on the map, are accessible by a short gravel path.

The hot springs: Two adjoining concrete tanks, 10 feet square and 3 feet deep, are recessed into the ground. One is open to the elements while the other is walled in by a boxy bathhouse minus a roof. The walls form a windbreak as well as a sunshade, and the open top promotes nighttime star gazing, a highly recommended activity out here. A changing room with a bench adjoins the shack, and a plank deck with another bench wraps around two sides.

Several springs emerge into the field at a staggering 172 degrees but cool to a mere 125 as the water flows through a ditch. The incoming pipes each have a homemade wooden plug for temperature control; it's crucial to keep them plugged except when draining and refilling the pools. Each tank also has several upside-down spin tubs from old washing machines scattered around for seating and occasional toe-stubbing.

Alvord Hot Springs looks out across the vast satin-finish playa of the Alvord Desert to the east and the silhouette of the rugged Steens to the west. There's a campsite across the road and another with more privacy up Pike Creek, 1.6 miles north. The springs, privately owned but open to the public, are usable year-round. The only thing lacking is a way to keep the cows from using them as well.

11 Mickey Hot Springs

General description:	One modest soaking pool, plus a geothermal display on a very remote desert road. Clothing optional.
Elevation:	4,040 feet.
General location:	40 miles northeast of Fields.
Map:	Burns District, South half, BLM.
Contact:	Burns District, BLM.

Finding the hot springs: Follow the directions above to Fields and the Eastside Road. Drive 34 dusty miles northeast (10.5 miles past Alvord) to a lone tree where the road turns north after heading east for the last mile preceding it. Turn right just past the cattleguard on a seasonal road that soon turns to bumpy dirt.

Stay on the main track as you head east then south to round a hill. Bear left at a fork in 2.6 miles, then continue 4 miles east to a parking area just beyond a low crest. Mickey is named on both the map and the ground. A sign welcomes visitors with a warning of hot springs at near-boiling temperatures and thin breakable crusts.

The hot springs: Mickey is a miniature Yellowstone. It has bubbling mud pots, pressure vents that hiss thin clouds of steam, a boiling geyser that spouts off daily, steamy channels snaking through the grass, and hot pools of all sizes and shapes including a deep-blue bottomless pit 15 feet across. But the really important thing to remember is that Mickey has only one tiny soaking pool. The rest look great, but their temperatures run from 120 to 180 degrees.

A 4 x 8 foot soaking pool with a knee-deep silty bottom collects the cooling runoff from the pit 30 yards away. If you ease your own bottom in gently and manage to keep it suspended, the silt won't stir up. The temperature averages 103 degrees and can be fine tuned by adjusting rocks in the channel.

The geothermal basin is rimmed by rolling hills and Mickey Butte to the north, while a butte to the west is backed by a panoramic shot of the Steens. Camping is permitted in the parking area but not around the springs. Mickey is on a private plot but open to the public and managed by the BLM.

12 Willow Creek (Whitehorse) Hot Spring

General description:	Hot and warm pools back to back, on a far-flung desert road. Definitely skinnydippable.
Elevation:	4,520 feet.
General location:	34 miles east of Fields.
Map:	Vale District, Jordan Resource Area, BLM.
Contact:	Vale District, BLM.

Finding the hot spring: Follow the directions above to Fields and go south on State Route 205 for 8.5 miles. Turn east at the "Y," a junction located 15 miles north of the Nevada border, onto an all-weather gravel road signed to Whitehorse Ranch. Drive 23 dusty miles and look for a hill on your right. Take the dirt road just beyond it. It is the first right after the Willow Creek

At Willow Creek Hot Spring, the day begins with a mug of coffee and a toasty soak.
Bob Westerberg photo.

bridge. Immediately take the left fork, then right at a "Y" (left is the turn for those heading east). Follow the main track back to the south, around the hill and aim for a double hill. Bear right at a stock loading ramp and circle the double hill to the spring.

Westbound travelers will drive 21 miles south of Burns Junction on US 95, then west on Whitehorse Ranch Road for 23.5 miles. Turn left just where the powerline crosses the main road, a few miles past Whitehorse Ranch, and go south at the "Y" past the west exit on the route described above. The spring is named on the map.

The hot spring: Water perks upward at 115 degrees into the hotter of two pools separated by a concrete dam. The temperature averages 104-106 degrees and cools to 80 to 90 degrees in the larger adjoining pool. An anonymous finger has inscribed "Hot" and "Cold" with opposing arrows into the dam, for those with no sense of touch. It's a rare treat, especially in a desert hot spring, to have two temperatures to choose or alternate between.

The hot spring, backed by the rocky double-tipped hill, overlooks a vast expanse of high sagebrush plains. Despite the remote location, Willow Creek is seeing a surprising influx of visitors. Camping is allowed near the spring but must be at least 100 feet away. Quieter campsites are located on the other side of the hill. The BLM has installed a concrete outhouse at the site.

13 Three Forks Warm Springs

HIKE 13 *To Three Forks Warm Springs*

General description:	A day hike to secluded springs and a waterfall pool in the upper Owyhee Canyon. Swimwear optional.
Difficulty:	Easy
Distance:	A 5.5-mile loop.
General location:	35 miles south of Jordan Valley.
Elevation gain:	260 feet.
High point:	4,200 feet.
Hiking quad:	Three Forks USGS.
Road map:	Jordan Valley 30-minute or Vale District, Jordan Resource Area, BLM.
Contact:	Vale District, BLM.

Finding the trailhead: Two gravel roads 15 miles apart travel south from U.S. Highway 95 to Three Forks. Either way, it's a long haul. Travelers coming from Burns Junction continue 30 miles east to a road signed "Three

Three Forks Warm Springs features a warm jacuzzi pool beneath a waterfall.

Forks—35" at Milepost 36. This route has the bonus of passing the Owyhee Canyon Overlook. If you are coming from Jordan Valley, head east, bearing right at a fork in 3 miles. Bear right at the next fork where pavement turns to gravel in 7 miles, just past a school, then right once more at a fork signed "Three Forks 14."

The two roads join up around 30 miles from the highway and 2.7 miles from the canyon rim. The final 1.3-mile stretch to the bottom is quite steep; never attempt it when the road is muddy. Find a place to park at the primitive BLM camp in a grassy flat by the river. The springs are marked on both maps.

The hike: This remote spot, traditionally accessed by fishermen and a few hardy river runners, marks the confluence of three tributaries of the Owyhee River, hence the name Three Forks. The Middle and North forks of the Owyhee come together 0.5 mile to the east and flow into the main fork of the river at the BLM camp and launch site.

A 3-mile jeep road takes a roundabout route from Three Forks Camp to the warm springs. This is the principal access, but when the river level is low, usually from June to October, hike a nice loop by walking up the river canyon to the springs and then following the road back to camp.

The route starts by fording the combined Middle and North forks at the launch site. Jagged walls shadow the deep canyon, and an intermittent

Three Forks Warm Springs

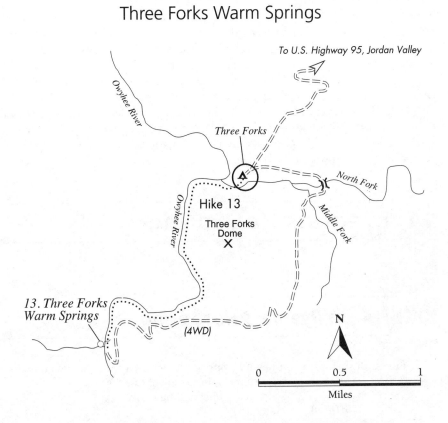

To U.S. Highway 95, Jordan Valley

Owyhee River

Three Forks

Owyhee River

Hike 13

Three Forks
Dome
X

North Fork

Middle Fork

13. Three Forks
Warm Springs

(4WD)

N

| 0 | 0.5 | 1 |

Miles

path reaches the springs about 2.5 miles upstream. To complete the loop, follow the jeep road up the steep bank and swing east to breathtaking views of the gorge. The track curves around a hill at the high point on the hike, then dips across a sagebrush valley and drops to ford the Middle Fork.

The North Fork is bridged, and the rocky gorge upstream makes an inviting side trip. The road improves in the short distance back to camp, tempting the unwary driver to try it, but it offers some surprises and almost no place wide enough to turn around when you change your mind.

The warm springs: Clusters of 95-degree springs are located on both sides of the river, and the rugged Owyhee Canyon forms a magnificent backdrop. There's a camping area along the east bank where several warm streams snake through tall grass to the river. Above are two tiny pools, each with a sit-down shower provided by a length of pipe. But the best is yet to come.

On the opposite bank, several thermal waterfalls pour into the river at 3,750 liters per minute, all emanating from Warm Springs Canyon. You may spot a rope descending from a boulder above the largest falls. That's your target. But don't aim for it during the spring runoff or you'll likely end up downstream at Rome.

Ford the cold river and climb to a large soaking pool enclosed between boulders. This gem is a good 3 feet deep and has a gravel bottom. The scouring action of three cascades pouring into it keeps it clean as a whistle; the resulting warm Jacuzzi is delightful. There's another pool or two upstream, but beyond the source the side canyon is dry. With the cold river and a luke-warm soak, Three Forks should be saved for a hot day.

Note: The springs are located on unposted private land. Please pack out what you pack in, observe fire restrictions, and respect the landowner's rights. Also, as the springs are within the Wild and Scenic River corridor, no development of any kind is allowed.

14 Ryegrass Hot Spring

HIKE 14 *To Ryegrass Hot Spring*

General description:	A day hike or overnighter to a spring known only to river runners, in the lower Owyhee Canyon. Swimwear: a hat and bug juice.
Difficulty:	Moderate.
Distance:	8 miles round trip.
General location:	24 miles north of Rome.
Elevation gain:	440 feet.
High point:	Trailhead, 3,560 feet.
Hiking quad:	Lambert Rocks USGS.
Road maps:	Crooked Creek and Skull Spring 30-minute, BLM.
Contact:	Vale District, BLM.

Finding the trailhead: Take U.S. Highway 95 to Rome, the launch site for raft trips down the lower canyon. Go 4 miles west (0.2 mile east of Milepost 58) and watch for a stop sign on the north side of the highway at the crest of a low hill. Nothing else marks the spot. Whatever you do, don't take this seasonal road if the ground is at all damp. You'll never make it.

Drive 3.5 miles north to a ranch on Crooked Creek. The gravel ends at the doorstep. Back up and take the obscure right fork past the ranch. Be sure to leave the gate as you found it or as the signs request. **Note:** There's a classic early season swimming hole in the creek at the bottom of the hill. See the story at end of this description.

The route, a boundary road for Wilderness Study Areas on each side, continues north and roughly parallels the Owyhee Canyon just visible

At Ryegrass Hot Spring (formerly Unnamed Hot Spring No. 1), hikers can enjoy a plunge in the river as well as a hot-water soak.

Ryegrass Hot Spring

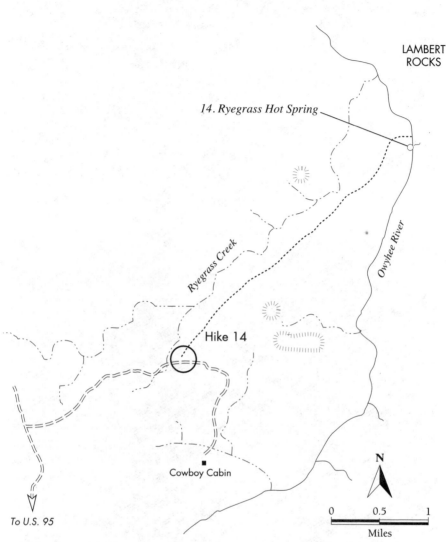

LAMBERT ROCKS

14. Ryegrass Hot Spring

Owyhee River

Ryegrass Creek

Hike 14

N

Cowboy Cabin

0   0.5   1
Miles

To U.S. 95

to the east. It's slow going over rocks, potholes, and sandy washes. You'll eventually cross a plateau strewn with lava rocks and drop into the broad valley of Ryegrass Creek.

Watch for a "Y" in the road about 15 miles from the fork at the ranch. Bear right and park after a mile or so. The hot spring isn't marked on either the hiking quad or the roadmap and misplaced to the north on the state geothermal.

The sensible approach: As is true for the following two hot springs, the most logical route is by raft (See Appendix C). In this case, downstream from the BLM launch site in Rome. What follows is an alternative for the self-motivated adventurer.

The hike: The route itself is a gentle downhill grade; the trick is to keep track of key landmarks on the enclosed trail map. The banks of Ryegrass Creek are visible across the valley, and the route parallels the canyon. Notice a rounded hill close to a long low one. Make sure you keep those hills on your right, or you'll end up in another drainage.

Strike out in a northeast direction between the creek canyon and the rounded hill and work your way over a grassy desert floor scattered with sagebrush and lava rocks. Soon you'll see a pyramid-shaped hill over by the creek. At a point midway between the two hills, the canyon veers north. Continue straight, aiming for a peninsula across the river. A faint drainage system, named Ryegrass Creek on the BLM map, will lead you eastward to the easiest route down the rocky bank. The spring is located a short distance upstream, at 3,120 feet.

The hot spring: Water emerges from the ground at 110 degrees, and several steamy channels lined with orange algae flow down the bank into one or two small pools hidden in the tall grass at the river's edge. The pools get some TLC and cleaning during the float season, roughly March through June, but at low water you'll have them all to yourself. If you decide on a soak, you'll need a bucket to cool them down with river water. But the river may look a lot more inviting on a hot summer day.

The river runners' camp is a grassy beach near the big bend downstream. A colorfully banded rock formation known as Pruitt's Castle stands out to the north at the true outlet of Ryegrass Creek. Across the river, a jeep track winds down the steep peninsula by Lambert Rocks.

Note: The spring lies within the Wild and Scenic River corridor in a wilderness study area, so no development of any kind is allowed. Please treat it with respect and practice low-impact camping techniques.

Midsummer madness: *I stopped on the return drive at the large pond in Crooked Creek just outside the ranch gate. This desert oasis, hidden on a dead-end road with no tire tracks on it but my own, turned out to be the ideal retreat for the Fourth of July.*

I managed to escape the mad holiday weekend, parked smack dab in the middle of the road, stark naked for three blissful days, enjoying both the backwaters of the surging currents of humanity and the eddies of the creek swirling out of a culvert through a swimming hole guaranteed to match any you can conjure up from childhood memories!

15 Greeley Bar Hot Spring

This cliff is the landmark for the river crossing to Greeley Bar Hot Spring.

HIKE 15a *To Greeley Bar Hot Spring via Twomile Spring*

General description:	A "you-gotta-be-crazy" day hike or overnight jeep and bushwhack to a soak you could have rafted to, on the far side of the lower Owyhee Canyon. Swimwear superfluous.
Difficulty:	Strenuous, plus a major river crossing.
Distance:	5-mile round trip.
General location:	41 miles northwest of Jordan Valley (8 miles of four-wheel-drive road).
Elevation gain:	-340 feet.
High point:	Trailhead, 3,100 feet.
Hiking quads:	The Hole in the Ground and Jordan Craters North USGS.
Road maps:	Skull Spring and Sheaville 30-minute, BLM.
Contact:	Vale District, BLM.

Finding the trailhead: From Jordan Valley, drive 8 miles north on U.S. Highway 95. Turn left on what starts out an all-weather gravel road marked "Jordan Craters 24." In dry conditions, most high-clearance passenger cars can make it all the way to Jordan Craters; in damp weather, forget the whole idea (see Hike 15b for an alternate route to the hot spring). The Birch Creek junction (see below), marked "Owyhee River 6" to the right, is approximately 24 miles from US 95.

To reach Twomile Spring, take the left fork to a junction in 1.5 miles marked "Jordan Craters 1." This is the best spot to park a passenger car with the possible exception of the Jordan Craters parking area. Proceed by jeep or mountain bike on the unmarked right fork, continuing straight at the 4-way intersection at 2.2 miles, and right at 2.4 miles on a track that leads to Hole in the Ground, reaching the canyon rim 0.7 mile later. Stash your bike here unless you're a glutten for punishment.

The primitive track drops over the canyon edge and gets even rougher on the final approach. Watch for a spring in a patch of green below the road, about 2.5 miles from the rim, and park wherever you can find room. There's barely enough room to pull over, much less camp, but the short cut down from here saves two rocky road miles to the bottom, without lengthening the hike. The hot spring is not marked on any map and is misplaced several miles downstream on the state geothermal.

The sensible approach: As with Ryegrass and Echo Rock Hot Springs, the only sane approach to this extremely remote site is by raft. In this case, a 45-mile trip downstream from the BLM launch site in Rome (See Appendix C). A lengthy voyage, to be sure, but not as far-fetched as what follows.

Greeley Bar Hot Spring

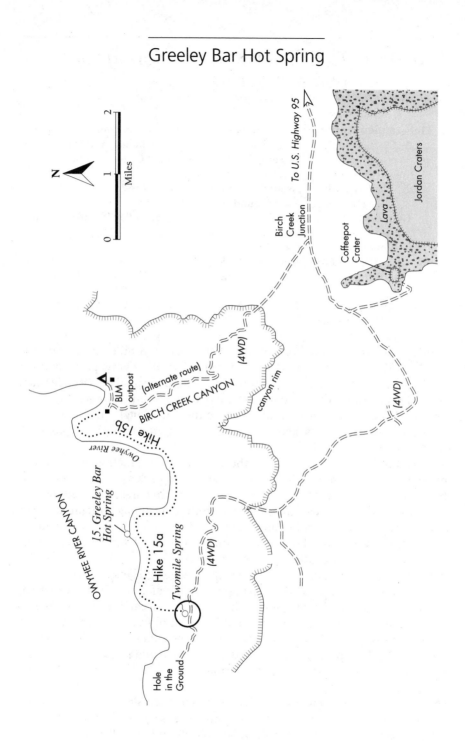

N

0   1   2
Miles

To U.S. Highway 95

Birch Creek Junction

Jordan Craters

Lava

Coffeepot Crater

(4WD)

canyon rim

(4WD)

(4WD)

BIRCH CREEK CANYON

(alternate route)

BLM outpost

Hike 15b

Owyhee River

OWYHEE RIVER CANYON

15. Greeley Bar Hot Spring

Hike 15a

Twomile Spring

Hole in the Ground

The challenge: Without a raft, the next best "craft" would be a jeep since the final 8-mile stretch of access road beyond Jordan Craters junction is a rough 4WD track. If you do not have a jeep, the next choice is a mountain bike, which could easily cover the 5.3 miles to the canyon rim if not the full 8 miles to the trailhead at Twomile Spring.

The hike: The cross-country route from Twomile Spring to the river is less than a mile. Route finding is just a matter of following the drainage downhill, picking whatever way seems least difficult over grassy slopes dotted with sagebrush. An isolated butte stands out above the far bank.

The shoreline route downstream is a short but very tiring boulder-hop over lava rocks choked with cockle burs and poison ivy. In some areas you can short cut across the slope above, but beware of rattlesnakes in the tall grass in warm weather. Watch for a distinctive cliff above a lava-strewn hillside on the far bank. The jagged wall's outline rises from left to right. This is the landmark you need to locate the hot spring lying hidden in the marsh below.

In order to cross the river, which at this point is broad, smooth, and quite deep, you might find an inner tube or air mattress (with a life jacket) useful. Launch a bit upstream. I managed to ford the river, but it was waist deep in spots even in mid-September, when the level is really low. There isn't a right time to go or an easy way to cross, and by late season, no guarantee of a soak.

The hot spring: Those who make it will find a source pool at 110 degrees tucked away in the tall reeds. In early summer mix the river into it by moving a rock or two in the dam. The pool may be stranded on the bank as the river recedes, with no way to cool it off unless you have a bucket. Greeley Bar is a popular stop during the float season; the boaters who stop to soak keep the algae cleaned out. In the non-float season however, you can count on having the pool, as well as the cleaning responsibility, all to yourself.

Note: The spring lies within the Wild and Scenic River corridor; no development of any kind is allowed. Remember to practice low-impact camping techniques.

Hike 15b *Greeley Bar Hot Spring via Birch Creek*

General description:	An alternate route, possibly a tad less insane, to the hot spring described above.
Difficulty:	Moderate, plus a major river ford.
Distance:	9-miles round trip.
General location:	37 miles northwest of Jordan Valley, including 4 miles of four-wheel-drive road.
Elevation gain:	Minimal.
High point:	Greeley Bar, 2,760 feet.
Maps:	Same as above.
Contact:	Vale District, BLM.

Finding the trailhead: An alternate route to Greeley Bar Hot Spring that is recommended by the BLM is via a maintained jeep road down Birch Creek Canyon to the Owyhee River. Follow the directions above as far as the Birch Creek junction and take the right fork 1.4 miles to the canyon rim. The final 4-mile stretch is a steep four-wheel-drive plunge ending at a manned BLM outpost with a campground, launch site for rafts, and a historic ranch.

The hike: The bushwhack upstream to the hot spring from Birch Creek Camp follows an abandoned jeep track for the first mile, then an intermittent cattle path for the reamining 3.5 miles. It stays on the south bank of the Owyhee Canyon all the way until the major river ford described above.

Although the expedition from both directions verges on madness, the Birch Creek route has a few advantages over the Twomile Spring route. The overall mileage from Jordan Valley is a bit less. The final four-wheel-drive stretch is in somewhat better shape and is half the length; also, it's patrolled on a regular basis. The hike is said to be easier going and the gain minimal. In addition, there's both a campground and a manned BLM station at the trailhead. The only disadvantage is the longer hike, 9 miles as opposed to 5 miles, round trip. See the previous hike and the enclosed trail map for a comparison of routes.

16 Echo Rock Hot Spring

Echo Rock Hot Spring (formerly Unnamed Hot Spring No. 2) echoed this soaker's whoops of joy against the rock wall on the opposite side. NOEL COLLAMER PHOTO

HIKE 16a *To Echo Rock Hot Spring*

General description:	A trailless day hike or overnighter to a hot shower enjoyed by river rats, on the Owyhee Reservoir. Wear what you normally shower in.
Difficulty:	Strenuous.
Distance:	10 miles round trip.
General location:	43 miles northwest of Jordan Valley.
Elevation gain:	+400 feet, -320 feet.
High point:	3,000 feet.
Hiking quads:	Rooster Comb and Diamond Butte USGS.
Road map:	Sheaville 30-minute or Vale District, Malheur Resource Area, BLM.
Contact:	Vale District, BLM.

Finding the trailhead: From Jordan Valley, take U.S. Highway 95, 18 miles north. Turn left onto an all-weather gravel road signed to Succor Creek State Park. Follow signs to Succor Creek for 10 miles, then turn left on a gravel road marked "Leslie Gulch—15." This road twists down a canyon marked by vertical towers and pinnacles jutting from steep slopes (see Hike 16b). Even without the hot spring, it's worth the drive just to see and experience Leslie Gulch. The road ends at a boat ramp on the reservoir, where rafts running the lower canyon can take out. The hot spring is marked but nameless on the maps.

The sensible approach: As is true of the two previous soaks, the easiest route to Echo Rock is by raft. In this case, there's even a shortcut. You can put in at the BLM launch site at Leslie Gulch and simply paddle straight up the reservoir. Barring that option, what follows is the least complicated alternative.

The challenge: Reach this remote spring on foot by following the reservoir's shoreline upstream from Leslie Gulch, but only when the water level is low, usually from July to November. The shoreline's one major obstacle is a rock outcrop attached to a huge hill that blocks the start upstream. The route described here is a shortcut best suited to bighorn sheep that traverse the face of the hill with a relatively modest gain of maybe 400 feet in a mile.

The hike: Walking upstream from the boat ramp, you'll notice a faint path that angles up a meadow, then climbs steeper slopes to disappear just above the outcrop. This lofty route is only one of many engineered by the bighorn sheep of Leslie Gulch, which currently number over two hundred. All in all, they do a decent job of maintenance. Their lives depend on it. The dropoff is awesome, but the path, 10 inches on the average, is wider than it appears from below and well packed. The ascent is strenuous but short.

After crossing above the first pinnacle and rounding a bend, the track continues. It undulates across the face and passes above several more outcrops before finally dropping steeply to the river at Spring Creek. From here, the going shouldn't be too tough when the water level is low. Just follow the long reservoir 3 miles upstream, tracking the bends with those on the map. When you think you're closing in, watch for a few rivulets of warm water crossing your path and follow them to their source.

The hot spring: Well hidden on the bank above, you'll discover a niche in the rocks with an ingeniously rigged shower pipe usually in place. Out gushes a lovely stream of 103-degree water. Follow the steamy flow farther uphill, past a tentsite on a sagebrush flat, and find a soaking pool, which sports a healthy growth of algae by late summer. It's usually in cleaner shape during the rafting season, from March through mid-June, but you can't go too early in the year or the shoreline route will still be underwater. It's a narrow window.

Note: This hot spring, due to its location on the shoreline of the reservoir, is administered by the Bureau of Reclamation (BOR). The agency is concerned about protecting sensitive natural resources associated with the spring. Indian Hot Spring (as it's called by the BOR) is definitely a resource worth preserving, so please treat it with care.

The primitive route to Echo Rock Hot Spring climbs high above the Owyhee River Canyon at the start.

Echo Rock Hot Spring • Juniper Gulch

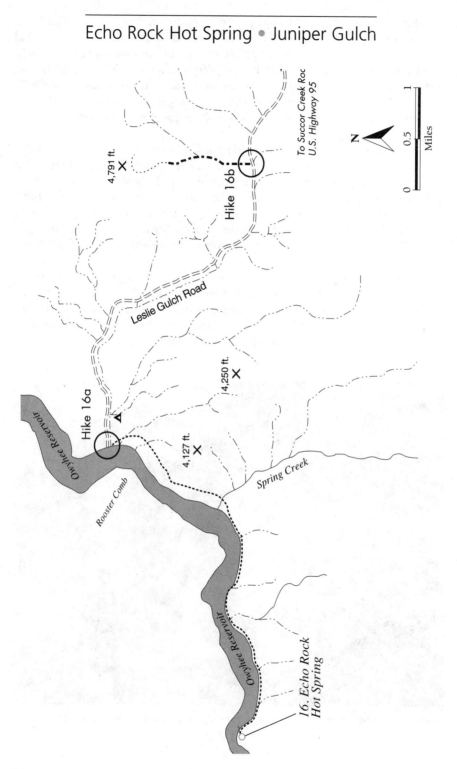

4,791 ft.

To Succor Creek Roc
U.S. Highway 95

N

Miles

0   0.5   1

Hike 16b

Leslie Gulch Road

Hike 16a

4,250 ft.

4,127 ft.

Owyhee Reservoir

Spring Creek

Rooster Comb

Owyhee Reservoir

16. Echo Rock
Hot Spring

HIKE 16b *Juniper Gulch*

General description:	A day hike up a side canyon in Leslie Gulch, not far from Echo Rock Hot Spring.
Difficulty:	Easy.
Distance:	3 miles round trip.
General location:	40 miles northwest of Jordan Valley.
Elevation gain:	1,200 feet.
High point:	4,600 feet at the crest.
Maps:	Same as above.
Contact:	Vale District, BLM.

Finding the trailhead: Follow the directions above to Leslie Gulch and drive about midway between the overlook point and the boat ramp at the end. Watch for a prominent pullout on the north side of the road 0.5 mile west of a cabin. You'll find restrooms, garbage cans, and a Wilderness Study Area sign near the trail.

The hike: Leslie Gulch is a moonscape of bizarre rock formations capping steep hills. Of igneous origin, the talus slopes are said to be an ash flow tuff from volcanic eruptions 15 million years ago, with a harder core of more erosion-resistant rhyolite, which forms the spires. Side canyons offer access

The spires at Leslie Gulch have a honeycomb effect caused by trapped gases in the cooling lava.

but with few exceptions are too vertical to be feasible routes. Juniper Gulch, however, provides easy access up slot canyons into a land of Swiss cheese rocks and eerie shapes. The hike culminates at an eagle-shaped spire perched on the crest, with an 800-foot gain in the final 0.5 mile.

A well-defined path follows Juniper Gulch north between high walls that gradually converge. Early on, you'll pass a huge Cheshire cat grinning down at you. Bear left into a second slot canyon 0.5 mile up and you'll soon see the eagle rock standing tall on a skyline of convoluted shapes up ahead. Using care, it's possible to scramble all the way up to stand beside it. From the crest, you can enjoy a face-to-face confrontation with the towering bird as well as a panoramic view of Leslie Gulch.

Note: Leslie Gulch, including all of its side canyons, is an Area of Critical Environmental Concern (ACEC) administered by the BLM. Activities are limited to day use, and camping is permitted only at Slocum Creek Campground near the boat ramp.

17 Snively Hot Spring

General description:	An all-too-popular roadside and riverside attraction at the lower end of the Owyhee Canyon. Swimwear essential when standing up.
Elevation:	2,280 feet.
General location:	30 miles south of Ontario.
Map:	Mitchell Butte 30-minute or Vale Disctict, Malheur Resource Area, BLM.
Contact:	Vale District, BLM.

Finding the hot spring: From Ontario, head 20 miles south on U.S. Highway 20/26, followed by State Route 201, to Owyhee Junction. Follow signs south toward Lake Owyhee State Park. From a prominent pipeline spanning the mouth of the canyon, continue 1.5 miles. If you miss the concrete standpipe on your left, where spring water boils up from the bottom at 135 degrees, you can't mistake the BLM sign announcing Snively Hot Spring Recreation Site and Campground. The spring is named on both maps.

The hot spring: Scalding 150-degree water flows from the standpipe through a ditch into one large shallow pool dammed by rocks. The result is a startling swirl of hot and cold currents as the source and the river mix. The hot floats on top of the cold, so you'll have to keep stirring it up to stay comfortable. The overall temperature is adjustable by shifting the riverside rocks.

Unfortunately, Snively exhibits strong symptoms of overuse/abuse disease. This is due mainly to its easy access via paved roads. As a result, evenings, especially in the summer, tend to be boisterous parties; mornings

Snively Hot Spring has a scenic backdrop that's hard to beat.

are usually a peaceful scene marred only by the beer cans and other litter from the night before.

The setting is nothing short of spectacular. Red rock cliffs and graceful cottonwoods line the deep canyon on both sides. Snively can be reached and enjoyed year-round, as the upstream dam controls the flow of the river and partially protects the pool during spring runoff.

HIKE 17 *"Henry Moore" Rock*

General description:	A day hike and bushwhack up a desert wash, near Snively Hot Spring.
Difficulty:	Moderate.
Distance:	5.5 miles round trip.
General location:	30 miles south of Ontario.
Elevation gain:	1,040 feet.
High point:	3,320 feet.
Hiking quad:	Owyhee Dam USGS.
Road map:	Same as above.
Contact:	Vale District, BLM.

Snively Hot Spring • Henry Moore Rock

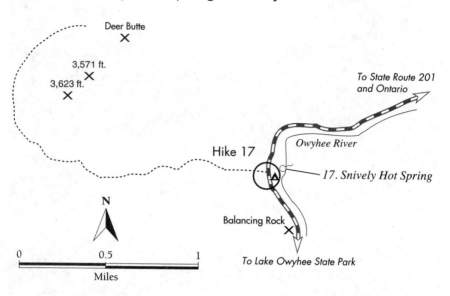

Finding the trailhead: Follow the directions above to Snively. The unmarked route starts by the fence across the road.

The hike: The Owyhee River Canyon between Snively and the Owyhee Reservoir offers cross-country routes up any number of side canyons or ridges. This is one that follows an intermittent stream around the west side of a prominent butte to a hidden amphitheater in the rock walls.

Climb the gate near the cattleguard and follow the wash due west through a desert valley alongside Deer Butte, aiming for a low wall of rocks a mile away. As you draw near, the wall becomes a jumble of gigantic boulders that seem to block the tiny canyon. Watch for a route over them on the right.

Around the next few bends are two short pouroffs that you must climb over; after this the route opens up again. Sagebrush dots the rolling hills, while tamarisk and tall grasses hug the streambed. The wash curves north around the end of the butte to reach one more fence about 2 miles up.

Step across the gate and continue on the northeastward curve that leads into a three-sided amphitheater with colorful walls of banded layers of rock. In the center of this gallery, standing on a tall pedestal, is a rock statue with a tiny head that looks for all the world like a sculpture by the twentieth century British artist Henry Moore.

Washington Locator Map

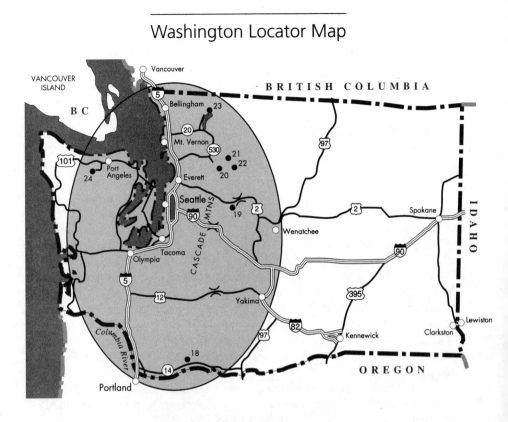

Washington

AN OVERVIEW

The Evergreen State has surprisingly few hot springs on public land that are both accessible and functioning. The seven springs on the Washington Locator Map are all in magnificent hiking country. They are all guaranteed great soaks, and, with the exception of Sulphur and Gamma, are all fairly easily accessible. Although they don't form a chain like those in Oregon or convenient clusters like those in Idaho, Washington's scattered springs are worth a visit.

The hot springs are located in two highly scenic areas—one gem in the Olympic Mountains, the range that forms the jagged core of the Olympic Peninsula, and the rest in the northern Cascade Range, with its many sharply sculpted glacial peaks. Both areas abound in craggy summits that rival the Swiss Alps, alpine meadows bursting with wildflowers, shrouded rain forests, and seething rivers with waterfalls that thunder into vast canyons. Opportunity here is limited only by the hiker's imagination.

This guide gives directions from major towns along State Route 14, Interstate 5, and U.S. Highway 101. As a general rule, the access roads are paved and well signed, the campgrounds heavily used, and the hiking trails maintained and teeming with avid hot springers during the short summer months.

Other wild hot springs: This is a list of springs marked on the state geothermal that have been tracked down but, due to a variety of glitches, sadly, did not qualify for this guide.

Packwood—Alive, contrary to official report, but not well. A 70-degree trickle, on bedrock with no usable pool, often submerged by the Cowlitz River, no approach path, and accessible only by private road. In Gifford Pinchot National Forest.

Deception Creek—A mere 70 degrees, no usable pool,and no approach path. In Gifford Pinchot National Forest.

Orr Creek—Again, only 70 degrees, no usable pool, and a nasty bushwhack. In Gifford Pinchot National Forest.

Ohanapecosh—Boggy seeps of historical interest only, on Hot Springs Nature Trail at Ohanapecosh Visitor Center, in Mount Rainier National Park.

Lester—Reportedly great soaks but no public access. Managed by Tacoma Watershed. On the Green River and almost in Mount Baker-Snoqualmie National Forest.

Goldmeyer—Fantastic pools in a sylvan setting, but privately operated and at last report charging $20/day or more. Surrounded by Mount Baker-Snoqualmie National Forest and the Alpine Lakes Wilderness.

Swift Creek—Buried under a huge landslide in the late 1970s. Unreachable anyway due to trail bridge washouts. In Mount Baker-Snoqualmie National Forest.

Hot springs and hikes: We start at the Columbia Gorge with a soak at Wind River (18) and hikes to waterfalls and views. Southeast of Everett comes a hike-in soak at Scenic (19) and a nearby alpine climb. Forest roads out of Darrington access the hiker's soaking box at Kennedy (20), an ideal base for high-country treks, as well as hunting expeditions for hidden pools at Sulphur and remote Gamma (21, 22). Baker (23), northeast of Mount Vernon, has an easy access dip and a companion climb to glacier views. And on the Olympic Peninsula, soaks at Olympic (24) mix well with alpine rambling in Olympic National Park.

Season: Although summer and fall are the prime times for hot springing, some pools are accessible and usable in the off-season. Winter road closures and deep snow impede access to Baker, Kennedy, and especially to Sulphur and Gamma. Spring runoff won't bury the tub at Scenic or the uppermost pools at Olympic, and you can access both through the winter months on cross-country skis. The low-elevation springs at Wind River can

Washington Area Map

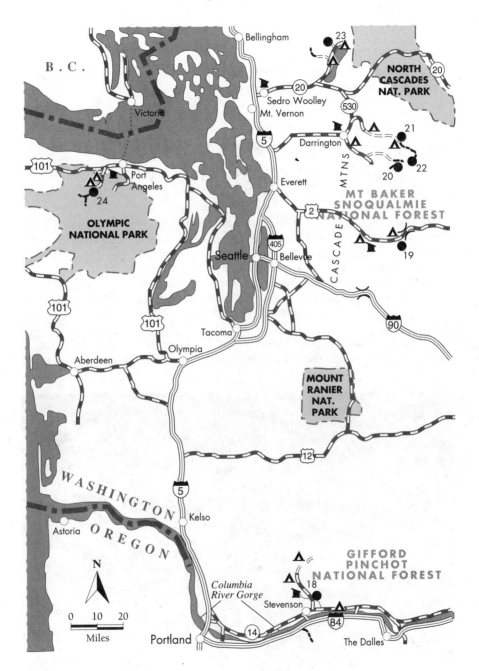

be reached on foot all year, but the pools are submerged during high water.

Hiking trails in the Columbia Gorge are enjoyable all year, but the high-country hiking season doesn't get comfortably underway until late July, and even then you can't be sure you'll get blue skies. In an average year, the mountains west of the Cascade crest are cloud-free one day out of every six. The months of November through April bring torrents of rain to the lowlands and snow to higher elevations. Intermittent storms are common through June and likely to return by early September.

18 Wind River Hot Springs (St. Martins on the Wind)

General description:	Riverside pools on a 0.75-mile path, near the Columbia Gorge. A swimsuit/birthday suit mix.
Elevation:	160 feet.
General location:	7 miles northeast of Stevenson.
Map:	Gifford Pinchot National Forest.
Contact:	Wind River Ranger District, Gifford Pinchot National Forest.

Finding the hot springs: Follow State Route 14 along the Columbia River Gorge, 5 miles east of Stevenson or 15 miles west of Hood River

Downstream travelers often drop in for a warm-up at Wind River Hot Springs.

Wind River Hot Springs

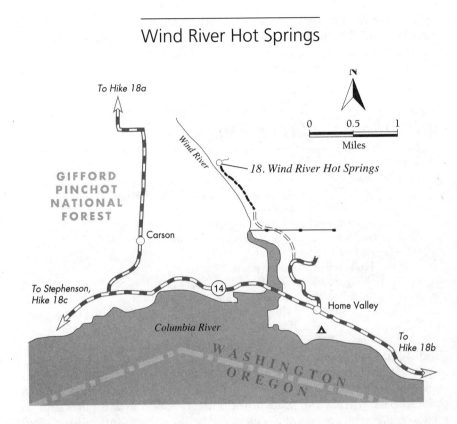

To Hike 18a

GIFFORD
PINCHOT
NATIONAL
FOREST

Wind River

18. *Wind River Hot Springs*

0   0.5   1
Miles

Carson

To Stephenson,
Hike 18c

14

Columbia River

Home Valley

To
Hike 18b

WASHINGTON
OREGON

to Home Valley. Take Berge Road a mile north, then go left on Indian Cabin Road. The road twists between the legs of a power pole tower, then turns to gravel and follows the powerline down to the river. The road-end parking lot, 2.5 miles from the highway, is privately owned. You'll find a notice to visitors and a box where the owner collects a small fee. Camping is discouraged, but there's a county campground in Home Valley.

The walk starts on a wooded path, thick with poison oak, along an eroded and slippery bank and then drops down to a riverside scramble over slick boulders. When a small waterfall upstream comes into view, you've reached the first pool. The hot springs aren't marked on the forest map.

The hot springs: Wind River Hot Springs consist of two soaking pools nestled between riverside boulders. 107-degree water bubbles up from bedrock through a sandy bottom; its ample flow keeps the pools clean. You can lower the temperature by adjusting rocks at the river's edge.

The downstream dip is smaller, right at water level, and registers a few degrees cooler. The upper pool sits a tad higher on the bank and enjoys a longer season of use. Users often dig a gravel pool at one end to mix the outflow with river water for a cooler soak. A third spring nearby has dried up beneath a pool of stagnant water.

Thick forest borders the river, and the upstream view includes Shipherd Falls. A proposed study would include the Wind River within the National Wild and Scenic River system. If this plan comes to pass, it may safeguard a very special place.

HIKE 18a *Falls Creek Falls*

General description:	A day hike to a triple waterfall, near the Columbia Gorge and Wind River Hot Springs.
Difficulty:	Easy.
Distance:	3.5 miles round trip.
General location:	20 miles northeast of Stevenson.
Elevation gain:	600 feet.
High point:	2,000 feet.
Hiking quad:	Wind River Green Trails or USGS.
Road map:	Gifford Pinchot National Forest.
Contact:	Wind River Ranger District, Gifford Pinchot National Forest.

Finding the trailhead: Follow State Route 14 along the Columbia Gorge, 3 miles east of Stevenson or 2 miles west of Home Valley if you are coming from Wind River Hot Springs. Turn north on Wind River Road and go through Carson. Pass the road to the ranger station at 8.5 miles and the turnoff to Mineral Springs at about 14 miles. Take a right in a mile on gravel Forest Road 3062. Bear right in another 2 miles on a road signed Lower Falls Creek Falls-Trail 152A. You'll soon reach the road-end trailhead, a total of 17 miles from State Route 14.

The hike: For connoisseurs of waterfalls, this one is a must. A broad cascade pours over cliffs high above, churns over a shelf partway down, then another shelf, and reaches the bottom in a total of 250 feet in three graceful tiers. Clouds of spray billow out across the narrow canyon. If you're taking pictures, afternoon's the best time to catch sunlight on the falls.

Trail 152A wanders through a forest of Douglas-fir, hemlock, and larch along the south bank of Falls Creek. It bridges the creek at the halfway point, then climbs above the north bank at a moderate grade. Shortly after you cross a boulder-strewn ravine, watch for a view of the upper and middle tiers just before the final viewpoint across from the middle and lower descents.

Falls Creek Falls

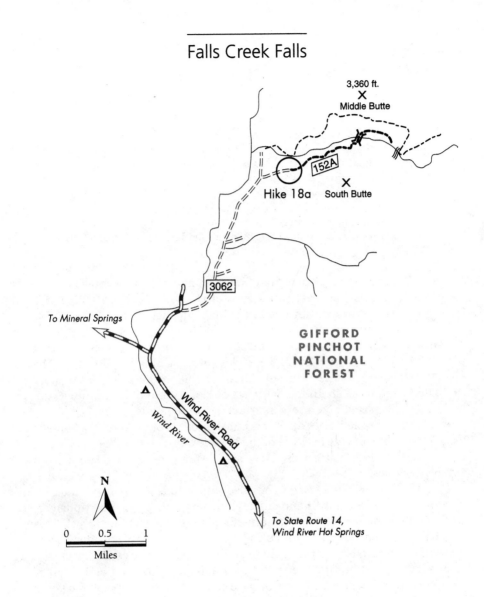

HIKE 18b *Dog Mountain*

General description:	A day hike climbing to views of the Columbia Gorge, near Wind River Hot Springs.
Difficulty:	Strenuous.
Distance:	5 miles round trip.
General location:	9 miles east of Stevenson.
Elevation gain:	2,340 feet.
High point:	2,500 feet.
Hiking quad:	Trails of the Columbia Gorge.
Road map:	Gifford Pinchot National Forest.
Contact:	Wind River Ranger District, Gifford Pinchot National Forest.

Finding the trailhead: Follow State Route 14 along the Columbia Gorge 9 miles east of Stevenson or 11 miles west of Hood River. The parking area and trail sign are on the north side of the highway just west of Milepost 54.

The hike: Open slopes bursting with over two hundred species of spring wildflowers coupled with a bird's-eye view of the Columbia Gorge are the hiker's reward for a short but stiff climb to the site of a former lookout cabin perched on the south-facing flanks of Dog Mountain. A rerouted trail both eases the ascent and offers intermediate viewpoints.

Prime time for the flower display is mid-March through May. The route is usually passable all year because of the low elevation, but it's a hot climb in the summer unless you get an early start. Watch out for poison oak on the lower slopes.

Dog Mountain Trail 147 switches back up a hillside where ponderosa pine mixes with Douglas-fir and alder. Here along the gorge, one finds vegetation typical of both the dry eastern climate and the wet northwest. This unusual coexistence is made possible by the unique sea level corridor carved through the Cascades by the Columbia River. The path contours up the front side to pass the first viewpoint at a mile and a second at 1.5 miles. Enjoy a taste of what's to come as you gaze across flowered slopes to the gorge below. At 2.5 miles, you'll reach a shelf dug from the hillside where the lookout cabin once stood.

Here the ground comes alive with color. Purple daisies and asters blend with blue penstamon and lupine, while golden buttercups and sunflowers vie with flaming red paintbrush. And here the broad blue green band of the Columbia River bisects the surrounding uplands in its journey to the sea. Look down at Wind Mountain to the west and across the channel to the white tip of Mount Hood jutting above cliffs that have turned green from waterfall spray.

If all this isn't enough, you can take the loop trail up to the 2,948-foot summit. The 3 miles round trip and 450-foot gain are offset by a

Dog Mountain

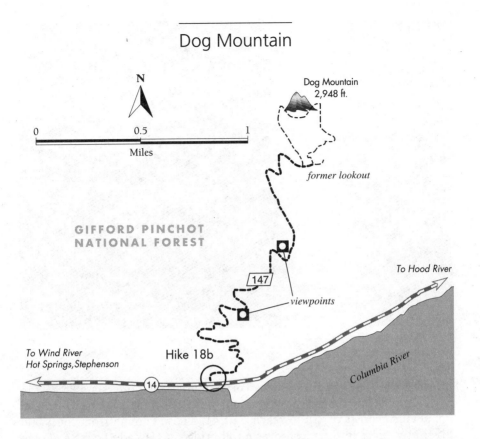

panoramic view. The uppermost slopes of Dog Mountain are blanketed with balsamroot and tiny pink spreading phlox, and massive Mount Hood dominates the southern skyline at 11,225 feet.

HIKE 18c *Eagle Creek Trail*

General description:	A popular day hike or overnighter to waterfalls on the Oregon side of the Columbia Gorge, near Wind River Hot Springs.
Difficulty:	Easy.
Distance:	12 miles round trip.
General location:	7 miles south of Stevenson.
Elevation gain:	+1,080 feet, -320 feet.
High point:	1,200 feet.
Hiking quad:	Same as above.
Road map:	Mount Hood National Forest.
Restrictions:	Trail park pass required.
Contact:	Columbia Gorge Ranger District, Mount Hood National Forest.

At Tunnel Falls, the trail disappears behind the cascade. BOB WESTERBERG PHOTO

Finding the trailhead: From the Portland area, take Interstate 84 east to Eagle Creek Park (Exit 41). Westbound travelers must make a U-turn at Bonneville Dam (Exit 40) to reach Exit 41. Those coming from the Wind River area cross into Oregon over a toll bridge at Cascade Locks and continue west as outlined above (12 miles total). Follow signs past the campground to parking for Eagle Creek Trail 440.

The hike: The Oregon side of the Columbia Gorge is famous for its profusion of waterfall hikes, and the Eagle Creek Trail into the Columbia Wilderness ranks as one of the finest. It gets the heaviest use in summer, but low elevation makes it enjoyable during the off-season as well. Highlights include a verdant forest backed by cliffs, views from high bridges, and a succession of waterfalls along narrowing canyon walls. A variety of loops can constitute a longer trip, but the sheer drop of Tunnel Falls at the 6-mile mark makes a good destination for a day hike.

Eagle Creek Trail 440 meanders through old-growth woods above the glacially carved canyon of Eagle Creek and soon traverses a railed section carved from rock. A spur at 1.5 miles leads to a distant view of Metlako Falls, and another drops to Lower Punch Bowl Falls. The main trail comes to the upper falls at 2.1 miles. Punch Bowl Falls may be a bit modest as waterfalls go, but it's exquisitely graceful. It forms a perfect punchbowl in its delicate descent, spilling over rimrock into a circular pool below. Nearby benches offer a pleasant overlook.

Eagle Creek Trail

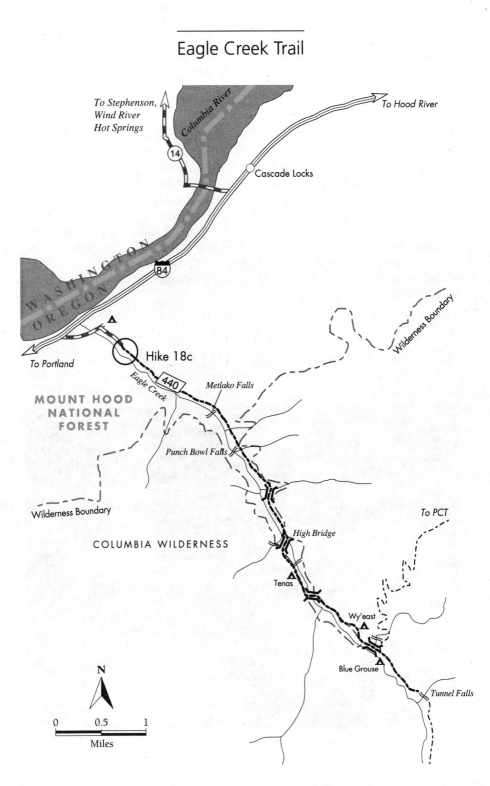

To Stephenson,
Wind River
Hot Springs

Columbia River

To Hood River

14

Cascade Locks

WASHINGTON

OREGON

84

Wilderness Boundary

To Portland

Hike 18c

Eagle Creek

440

Metlako Falls

MOUNT HOOD
NATIONAL
FOREST

Punch Bowl Falls

Wilderness Boundary

COLUMBIA WILDERNESS

High Bridge

To PCT

Tenas

Wy'east

Blue Grouse

Tunnel Falls

N

0   0.5   1

Miles

Next, the route spans two lush side canyons on high steel bridges. At 3.3 miles, it crosses the now narrow gorge of Eagle Creek itself, a full 80 feet below, on High Bridge. The route soon passes Tenas Camp, then bridges the gorge once again to pass more tentsites at Wy'east Camp.

At 5 miles, just beyond the wilderness boundary, reach the junction with the Eagle-Benson Trail, which climbs 2,900 feet in 3 miles to the Pacific Crest Trail (PCT) and Benson Plateau. Pass another waterfall nearby, then Blue Grouse Camp at 5.3 miles, the last stop before Tunnel Falls.

The route past Tunnel Falls actually slices a 25-foot tunnel through sheer rock behind the falls. Spray drifts across the side canyon to shower anyone nearby, and the roar reverberates from nearby walls. Seen from across the ravine, hikers approaching the plunge resemble a trail of ants.

Beyond are more waterfalls, views, and remote camps. Side trails offer tempting choices. A backpacker could loop back via Eagle-Tanner and Tanner Butte trails or continue on to join the PCT at Wahtum Lake, returning across beautiful Benson Plateau or perhaps down quiet Herman Creek to Government Cove.

19 Scenic Hot Springs

Much creative design and labor went into the improvements at Scenic Hot Springs.
WALTER DIETRICH PHOTO

HIKE 19a *To Scenic Hot Springs*

General description:	A short but stiff day hike to a well-named gem, near the Cascade crest. Naked bodies welcome.
Difficulty:	Strenuous.
Distance:	4 miles round trip.
General location:	60 miles southeast of Everett.
Elevation gain:	1,140 feet.
High point:	Hot springs, 3,500 feet.
Hiking quad:	Stevens Pass Green Trails or Scenic USGS.
Road map:	Mount Baker–Snoqualmie National Forest.
Contact:	Skykomish Ranger District, Mount Baker–Snoqualmie National Forest.

Finding the trailhead: From Everett, take U.S. Highway 2, 50 miles southeast to Skykomish. Continue 10 miles to Scenic, the service depot for the Burlington-Northern Railroad's Cascade Tunnel. Cross the highway bridge that spans the tracks and watch for a parking area on the north side of the highway 0.3 mile east of Milepost 59. Walk 0.1 mile back to a jeep track on the south side. The springs aren't marked on any map.

The hike: Tucked away high on a hillside overlooking Windy Mountain and the broad canyon just west of Stevens Pass, Scenic Hot Springs lives up to its name. User-built soaking boxes collect the flow, and evergreen branches frame the view. Locals and a few wintertime ski buffs are the primary users. It's bordered by Mount Baker-Snoqualmie Forest and the northern tip of the Alpine Lakes Wilderness. The springs and access route are on a plot of private land within the forest; the owners don't object to visitors as long as visitors continue to show respect for the property.

The rocky track climbs a steep 0.5-mile slope to a string of powerlines, then gets steeper and rockier as it turns to follow them eastward. The towers have number plates. After you pass No. 5, look for a faint path to the right that contours uphill in a 0.5-mile arc leading to the springs.

The hot springs: Four wooden soaking boxes collect the flow from the springs via a system of hoses that runs between them. According to a nearby sign, the average temperatures are 108 in the "lobster pot" and 103 degrees in the "bear's den." The combined outflow from these tubs is piped to the "gazebo" (106 degrees), which in turn feeds the "monster" (99 degrees).

You can vacuum the tubs with a syphon hose or drain and refill them with a bucket; the hose and bucket usually lie nearby. There are stairways and decking with rails and benches covering the treacherously steep slopes around the springs.

These elaborate improvements were crafted by a volunteer group who

Scenic Hot Springs • Surprise Lake

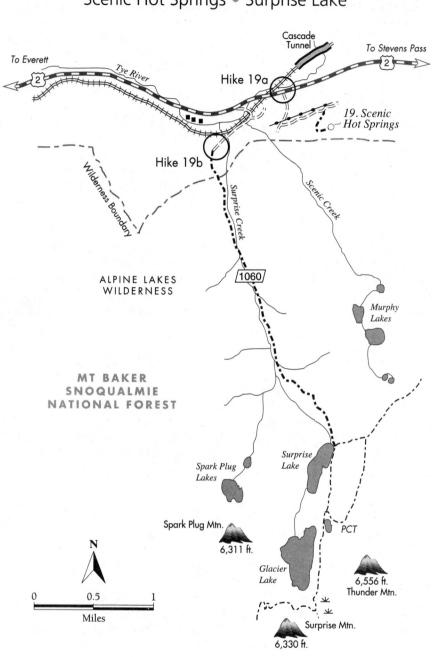

To Everett

Tye River

Cascade Tunnel

To Stevens Pass

Hike 19a

19. Scenic Hot Springs

Hike 19b

Wilderness Boundary

Surprise Creek

Scenic Creek

ALPINE LAKES WILDERNESS

1060

Murphy Lakes

MT BAKER SNOQUALMIE NATIONAL FOREST

Spark Plug Lakes

Surprise Lake

Spark Plug Mtn.
6,311 ft.

PCT

6,556 ft.
Thunder Mtn.

Glacier Lake

N

0   0.5   1
Miles

Surprise Mtn.
6,330 ft.

call themselves the Friends of Scenic Hot Springs. If you'd like more information or want to make a donation, reach them at P.O. Box 268, Skykomish, WA 98288.

HIKE 19b *Surprise Lake*

General description:	A day hike or overnighter to the first in a group of secluded lakes in the Alpine Lakes Wilderness, near Scenic Hot Springs.
Difficulty:	Moderate.
Distance:	8 miles round trip.
General location:	60 miles southeast of Everett.
Elevation gain:	2,300 feet.
High point:	4,500 feet.
Maps:	Same as above.
Restrictions:	Trail park pass required.
Contact:	Skykomish Ranger District, Mount Baker–Snoqualmie National Forest.

Finding the trailhead: Follow the road access above to Scenic. At 0.7 mile east of Milepost 58, turn right on an unmarked road that bridges the Tye River and drops down to cross the train tracks and intersect a side road. Turn right again and drive 0.25 mile to the parking area and trail sign.

The hike: An image of evergreenery walled in by white granite is mirrored in the glassy surface of Surprise Lake. Three tiny islands near the outlet stipple the reflection. The oblong lake lies at the end of a brisk 4-mile climb, which soon joins the Pacific Crest Trail (PCT) and leads on to other alpine delights.

Surprise Creek Trail (1060) starts by swinging away from the creek in a moderate climb up an open hillside but swings back at 0.5 mile to enter cool woods along Surprise Creek. Soon shrouded under a canopy of age-old trees, it hugs the creek banks in a gentle 2.5-mile stretch upvalley past waterfalls and blue pools. Rocky walls gradually converge as the canyon narrows.

The final mile is a steep climb up the headwall in a series of tight hairpins that parallels the cataract of the rushing stream below. The old route of the PCT branches off to twist straight up the east canyon wall just before the path reaches the north tip of the lake at 4 miles.

Surprise Lake, nestled in a hanging valley flanked by cliffs, makes a delightful spot to enjoy a picnic lunch. For a longer trip, follow the trail 0.7 mile south to the PCT and on up to Glacier Lake, lying in a bowl of granite at the base of Surprise Mountain. Grassy campsites tempt the visitor to stay and explore the alpine basin or to climb the 6,330-foot peak for an overview of other lakes and mountains in the magnificent 305,407-acre Alpine Lakes Wilderness, Washington's third largest wildland.

Darrington Area Map

MT BAKER/SNOQUALMIE NATIONAL FOREST

20 Kennedy Warm Spring

HIKE 20a *To Kennedy Warm Spring*

General description:	A day hike or multi-day backpack featuring a soaking box in the Glacier Peak Wilderness. No need to pack a swimsuit.
Difficulty:	Easy.
Distance:	11 miles round trip.
General location:	67 miles northeast of Everett.
Elevation gain:	+1,100 feet, -100 feet.
High point:	Kennedy, 3,300 feet.
Hiking quad:	Glacier Peak Green Trails.
Road map:	Mount Baker–Snoqualmie National Forest.
Restrictions:	Trail park pass required.
Contact:	Darrington Ranger District, Mount Baker–Snoqualmie National Forest.

The "standing room only" cedar box at Kennedy Warm Spring can accommodate a crowd of vertical soakers, including many who find their toes dangling in space.

Finding the trailhead: To reach this alpine hideaway from Interstate 5, take State Route 530, 32 miles east to Darrington. Turn right onto the Mountain Loop Highway (20) and drive 10 miles south along the Sauk River. Turn left onto White Chuck Road (23) and drive 11 dusty miles east to the road-end parking area and trail sign. Kennedy is named on both maps but misleadingly called *hot*.

The hike: Remember Badfinger singing "You'd better hurry 'cause it's going fast"? Well, Kennedy Warm Spring, currently down to 92 degrees, has been dropping about a degree every year according to one oldtimer who can remember when it was once 102. Despite the lukewarm temperature and a yellowish cast from iron oxide deposits in the water, Kennedy remains a favored goal for day trippers as well as a popular stopoff for longer distance trekkers on the nearby Pacific Crest Trail (PCT).

The Glacier Peak Wilderness surrounding Kennedy fills 576,865 prime acres of the North Cascades and forms the largest wildland in the state of Washington. Measuring 35 miles long by 20 miles wide, it offers 450 miles of hiking trails. Most of the passes are not snow-free until mid-August, but this varies from year to year. The PCT snakes through the heart of the wildland as it swings around Glacier Peak, Washington's fourth highest and most remote volcanic cone.

The White Chuck Trail (643), probably the most popular walk in the Glacier Peak area, winds gently up the canyon of the White Chuck River. An understory of ferns and vine maple flourishes under a ceiling of ancient cedar and Douglas-fir. You can hear the river constantly through the trees but rarely see it. Side streams cross the path in a headlong rush to join the cascade below. At one point, the route drops to river level along a gravel beach; at another, it passes beneath pumice rockslides and cliffs of volcanic tuff.

Kennedy Ridge Trail branches left at 5 miles to climb up beside alpine meadows and glaciers (Hike 20b). The main trail soon bridges Kennedy Creek, intersects the spur branching right to the spring, then ends in 1.5 miles at a junction with the PCT. You can ramble south from this point through Glacier Peak Meadows and on over White Pass in another 10 miles, or travel north to Kennedy Ridge past glaciers and tumbling streams to cross Fire Creek Pass and on to Gamma Hot Springs (see Hike 22).

The short spur to the spring passes many campsites along and above the river; a cold spring at the guard station provides good drinking water. The path bridges the river to a junction: the right fork leads to more campsites, then shoots up to Lake Byrne (Hike 20c) and beyond; the left fork follows the river a short way upstream to reach Kennedy Warm Spring in a total of 5.5 miles.

The warm spring: The extraordinary soaking box here consists of a 4- x 5-foot cedar box recessed into the ground. Since the water depth is over 5 feet, the strategy is to do your soaking in a vertical position. A surprising

Kennedy Warm Spring • Glacier Creek Meadow
• Lake Byrne

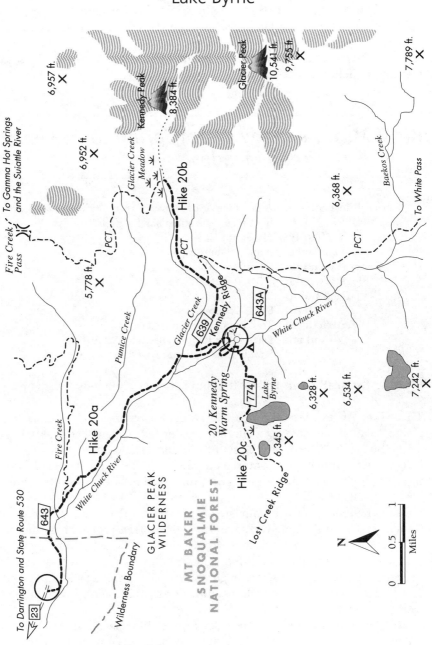

6,957 ft.
X

Kennedy Peak
8,384 ft.

Glacier Peak
10,541 ft.
9,755 ft.
X

7,789 ft.
X

To Gamma Hot Springs
and the Suiattle River

Baekos Creek

6,952 ft.
X

Glacier Creek
Meadow

Hike 20b

To White Pass

Fire Creek
Pass

6,368 ft.
X

Fire Creek

5,778 ft.
X

PCT

PCT

PCT

Pumice Creek

Glacier Creek

Kennedy Ridge

639

643A

White Chuck River

Hike 20a

774

Lake
Byrne

6,328 ft.
X

6,534 ft.
X

7,242 ft.
X

White Chuck River

20. Kennedy
Warm Spring

Hike 20c

6,345 ft.
X

643

GLACIER PEAK
WILDERNESS

MT BAKER
SNOQUALMIE
NATIONAL FOREST

Lost Creek Ridge

To Darrington and State Route 530

23

Wilderness Boundary

N

0   0.5   1
Miles

number of bodies can squeeze into the small box in this unusual fashion, either standing up, if they're tall enough, or by just gripping the sides with toes suspended.

Spring water filters in through the rocky bottom and rises in warm bubbles to the surface. A small platform borders the box; there is a handy rack nearby for clothes and towels. Nestled into the bank between the milky river and a wall of trees, Kennedy's magic bubble box offers highly scenic therapy for aching muscles.

HIKE 20b *Kennedy Warm Spring to Glacier Creek Meadow*

General description:	A day hike or overnighter from the warm spring to high meadows and glacial icefalls.
Difficulty:	Moderate.
Distance:	9 miles round trip.
General location:	72 miles northeast of Everett.
Elevation gain:	+2,450 feet, -100 feet.
High point:	5,650 feet.
Maps:	Same as above.
Restrictions:	Trail park pass required.
Contact:	Darrington Ranger District, Mount Baker–Snoqualmie National Forest.

Finding the trailhead: Follow the route above to Kennedy Warm Spring.

The hike: An exhilarating side trip from the warm spring climbs to an alpine meadow bisected by a gurgling glacier-fed stream. The grassy banks along the creek make an idyllic spot to sit and dangle hot toes in icy water, enjoy a picnic lunch, and contemplate the world around you. Head farther upvalley, if you can tear yourself away, for a face-to-face confrontation with nearby glaciers.

From Kennedy, retrace your steps 0.5 mile to the point where White Chuck Trail meets Kennedy Ridge Trail (639). Tree roots across the path form randomly spaced steps as the route climbs 875 feet in 2 miles to join the Pacific Crest Trail at 4,150 feet. Continue up the ridge where you will have more frequent glimpses through the trees to silvered glaciers and peaks. The PCT emerges into the lush meadow bordering Glacier Creek (at 5,650 feet) in another 2 miles.

The heather meadow bursts with lupine and glacier lilies. Marmots stare down from rocky castles, and tiny birds sing out from invisible perches. Glacier Creek ripples down the slope in rocky steps to form small pools between cascades. A campsite bedded in a plush, green carpet lies just downstream from the path. The dark moraine above Kennedy Glacier juts into view at the head of the long meadow.

For a view of distant peaks and a close-up of two glaciers, leave the trail behind and follow the creek up beyond the valley. A faint climber's route leads up the side of a moraine and follows the rocky crest ever closer to the glistening 10,541-foot cone of Glacier Peak. Scimitar Glacier can be seen to the southeast, and the double tongue of Kennedy Glacier looms before you. Ribbons of water emerge from the base of the icefall to twist and braid their way downhill over glacial debris.

HIKE 20c *Kennedy Warm Spring to Lake Byrne*

General description:	A day hike climbing from the warm spring to an alpine lake and panoramic vistas.
Difficulty:	Strenuous.
Distance:	5 miles round trip.
General location:	72 miles northeast of Everett.
Elevation gain:	2,250 feet.
High point:	5,550 feet.
Maps:	Same as above.
Restrictions:	Trail park pass required.
Contact:	Darrington Ranger District, Mount Baker–Snoqualmie National Forest.

Finding the trailhead: Follow the route described to Kennedy Warm Spring.

The hike: The bubble box at Kennedy makes the ultimate base for yet another outing, more demanding but every bit as rewarding as the climb to Glacier Creek Meadow above. Lake Byrne, nestled in a rock basin directly across the deep canyon of the White Chuck from Glacier Peak, offers a close view of the massive pyramid, if the curtain of clouds parts far enough to let you look across. The short climb is a real backbreaker, but the spectacular scenery is worth the price.

The Lake Byrne Trail begins at the bridge by Kennedy. A relentless series of tight switchbacks drags the path straight up the canyon wall; luckily, the route is shaded by an obliging forest. At 1.5 miles, the path levels off long enough to pivot southwest and then north around a sharp knoll, passing a heather-dappled meadow at the first open views across the canyon. The final stretch of hairpins is open to both the sun's rays and increasingly broad panoramas. The path fords the gushing outlet to reach the northern tip of Lake Byrne at 2.5 miles.

Fragile meadows fringe one side of the oblong lake while scattered clusters of subalpine fir cling to outcrops of rock on the far side. Ice can often coat the deep blue lake and snow obscure the trail until mid-August. Camping is banned within 0.25 mile of Lake Byrne, but there are two good campsites north of the outlet.

Looking east from Lake Byrne, see the massive cone of Glacier Peak across the canyon of the White Chuck River.

Experienced scramblers can roam the steep ridges that wall the lake. The high knob at the south end offers one of the finest views in the North Cascades. Looking due east, 10,541-foot Glacier Peak fills the foreground. On a clear day, you can see the distant white cones of Mount Baker (see Hike 23) and Mount Shuksan to the northwest. Tree blazes, boot treads, and the lure of cross-country travel can lure the more adventurous traveler westward from Lake Byrne to a chain of lakes and meadows along Lost Creek Ridge.

21 Sulphur Warm Springs

HIKE 21 *To Sulphur Warm Springs*

General description:	A daunting hunt for seeps hiding in a primeval forest in the Glacier Peak Wilderness. Swimwear superfluous.
Difficulty:	Moderate.
Distance:	3.6 miles round trip.
General location:	75 miles northeast of Everett.
Elevation gain:	+480 feet, -120 feet.
High point:	2,040 feet.
Hiking quads:	Lime Mountain and Downey Mountain USGS.
Road map:	Mount Baker–Snoqualmie National Forest.
Restrictions:	Trail park pass required.
Contact:	Darrington Ranger District, Mount Baker–Snoqualmie National Forest.

Note: Save this one for late summer when the water level is down, the creek safer to cross, and any pool more likely to have surfaced. Also, check with the Forest Service on current road and trail conditions.

Finding the trailhead: From Interstate 5 north of Everett, take State Route 530 about 40 miles east and north, past Darrington, to the Suiattle River Road (26). Drive 21 dusty miles east to Sulphur Creek Campground, near the road-end trailhead for the following hike to Gamma. The springs are named on both maps but misleadingly called *hot*.

The hike: In this neck of the woods, Sulphur Warm Springs ranks second only to Gamma for sheer elusiveness. It's pinpointed on the maps on the edge of Sulphur Creek at the 1,920-foot contour line and listed by the Forest Service as located across the creek from a point precisely 1.8 miles up Trail 793, but stumbling across it on the ground is another matter.

Sulphur Creek Trail 793 begins across the road from the campground, climbs the bank and contours past gullies through a dimly lit forest. As it finally drops, you'll enter a wildland of fallen logs and rushing water.

The trick is to gauge the 1.8-mile point, beyond which the trail fades into a fishermen's route, and then watch for a faint track angling downhill to a haphazard line of footlogs crossing the torrent. If you've picked the right track and managed to balance your way over the right logs, the springs should be lurking close by.

Sulphur Warm Springs

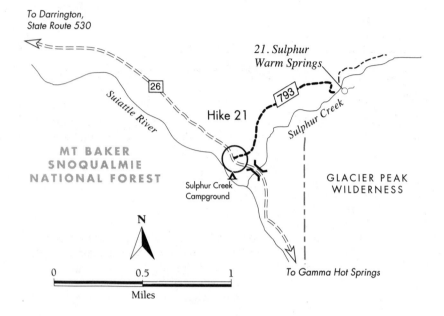

The warm springs: One guidebook stated: "Several hot springs seep and flow down a heavily vegetated slope from the south into Sulphur Creek. The main spring issues from a crack in the bedrock immediately adjacent to the creek bank. There is a pool that will accommodate two people comfortably dug into the bank." The flow was listed at 10 gpm and the temperature as 98 degrees.

The Forest Service printout had this to say: "The springs consist of small colored pools, smelling of hydrogen sulphide gas, and are not large enough to take a dip in." The temperature listed was a mere 80 degrees. The district ranger states: "The springs (about the size of a quarter) seep out of the ground, and the landmarks are not established because the creek washes all signs away."

I also met a ranger from Gifford Pinchot National Forest who claimed that he'd not only found a pool at the described location but that he had actually soaked his bones in it. When he was pressed for a description, a secretive smile crossed his lips as he simply replied "not too bad."

And what did your fearless reporter discover firsthand after zigzagging back and forth across every log in sight at least twice, and bushwhacking for hours through primeval ooze armed with machete, magnifying glass, divining rod, and infrared scanner? Nothing. Not even a two-bit seep.

Conclusion? If some industrious elf has gotten there ahead of you and dug a cozy little soaker, and perhaps heated it up a few notches, then, if you're persistent and lucky enough to find it, you might possibly end up with something to write home about. But, come to think of it, maybe "the one that got away" makes a better story.

22 Gamma Hot Springs

The shallow pool at Gamma Hot Springs can be greatly improved with the help of a shovel and a tarp. DAN LAFOE PHOTO.

HIKE 22 *To Gamma Hot Springs*

General description:	A challenging expedition, for hard-core fanatics only, to hot springs buried deep in the Glacier Peak Wilderness. Swimwear? You gotta be kidding!
Difficulty:	Strenuous.
Distance:	33 miles round trip.
General location:	76 miles northeast of Everett.
Elevation gain:	+5,800 feet, -1,200 feet.
High point:	6,300 feet.
Hiking quads:	Lime Mountain and Gamma Peak USGS.
Road map:	Mount Baker–Snoqualmie National Forest.
Restrictions:	Trail park pass required.
Contact:	Darrington Ranger District, Mount Baker–Snoqualmie National Forest.

Finding the trailhead: Refer to the note and directions above to Sulphur Creek Campground. Continue another mile southeast to the Suiattle River trailhead at the road end, 22 miles from State Route 530. Gamma is named on both maps.

The call: First, conjure up a pristine hot spring emerging from bedrock at the head of a canyon framed by jagged peaks, light years from the nearest outpost. Then, fit your humble body into the scene, boldly going where no one has gone before and seeking out secret soaks.

This vision is known as the call of the wild hot spring, and the only cure is to follow it. But treatment can be risky unless proper precautions are taken. Check with the Forest Service on current conditions. Get a weather forecast and travel prepared. Go late in the summer when the streams are low.

The hike: This expedition, in addition to nearly 12 miles to reach Gamma Ridge, involves a series of steep switchbacks up the ridgeline trail followed by a bushwhack down Gamma Creek to reach the goal. **Note:** One shouldn't be tempted to consider Gamma Creek as an alternate route up. It's an extremely steep canyon, and those who have tried it report deadfalls and impassable waterfalls. Another approach not recommended is that of attempting to follow the 5,000-foot contour line across to the hot springs from Gamma Ridge Trail.

The well-traveled route up the Suiattle River follows an abandoned road past the wilderness boundary. After a mile, Milk Creek Trail branches right to climb to Fire Creek Pass. The Suiattle River Trail (784) dips and rises along the bank, skirting side streams through an ancient forest. Finally climbing the bank, it reaches several campsites and a footbridge at Canyon Creek at 5.8 miles.

The route offers glimpses through the trees of mountains on the far side of the broadening valley. In another 3 miles it passes the Miners Ridge Trail. The path then dips and rises past Miners Creek and comes to an end when it intersects the Pacific Crest Trail (PCT) at 11.2 miles.

Take the right fork downhill on the PCT and cross Skyline Bridge. Here you'll leave the Suiattle River and head south up a gradual slope across the valley. From this point, one could conceivably do a double dip by following the PCT up over Vista Ridge and Fire Creek Pass and then down to Kennedy Warm Spring (Hike 20a), some 26 highly scenic miles away.

Approaching Gamma Ridge, you'll leave the PCT and the last vestiges of civilization behind and forge your way into true wilderness. Turn left on Gamma Ridge Trail (791) and zigzag up toward Gamma Peak. The route is extremely steep in places and very tiring with a heavy pack. There's a campsite near the base of Gamma Peak, a hundred feet or so below the ridge.

You can scramble from camp directly down the Gamma Creek drainage on a web of goat trails. About 750 feet down the hill you'll cross a feeder creek on your right and continue down Gamma Creek on a track maybe 50

Gamma Hot Springs

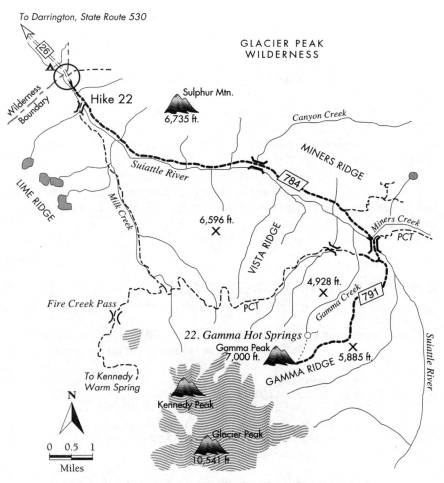

feet up the bank. Take great care in this stretch, as the ground is very steep and crumbly. As you approach the springs you'll spot an obvious dirtslide around the stream.

The hot springs: Scalding water seeps up at 140 degrees through rock fractures and flows through a tiny pool into the glacier-fed stream. The slope is quite steep, which makes any user-built pool or dam difficult to maintain without a tarp. The pool temperature is a bit on the toasty side, but you can channel water in from the creek with the aid of small logs and a little ingenuity.

In 1996, one group was rumored to have brought in a hand drill, rebar and a tarp to build a wall of logs to create a pool, which they then lined with the tarp. It made an excellent pool, 2 feet deep. Without the tarp it dwindled to about 8 inches, but could still be caulked up with sand, dirt, twigs, and other debris.

At last report, there was a register tucked into a nearby tree. It's a 6-inch piece of PVC pipe with end caps, and it holds some good stories. Sign it if you can find it. And if you happen to do the scramble to the top of Gamma Peak, you may find one up there as well, a film canister tucked into a rock cairn at the summit.

The deep canyon is sandwiched between serrated ridges, and the hot springs nestled in the shadow of the 7,000-foot peak. A bit beyond, Gamma Ridge slices a jagged line between two massive glaciers on the north flanks of 10,541-foot Glacier Peak.

Note: I've been suffering from the Gamma bug for years, but all attempts at a cure have been foiled to date. This write-up is not based on my own experience but on a detailed report from a fellow fanatic who actually managed to get there.

23 Baker Hot Springs

General description:	A pool that is often brimming with bathers, framed by evergreens at the end of a short path. Swimwear recommended.
Elevation:	2,000 feet.
General location:	56 miles northeast of Mount Vernon.
Map:	Mount Baker–Snoqualmie National Forest.
Restrictions:	Trail park pass required.
Contact:	Mount Baker Ranger District, Mount Baker–Snoqualmie National Forest.

Finding the hot springs: From Interstate 5 near Mount Vernon, take State Route 20 about 20 miles east. Bear left at Milepost 22 on Baker Lake Road and follow it up the west side of the lake. Turn left at Baker Lake Resort on gravel Forest Road 1144 and climb 3.2 rough miles to a large turnout. A primitive 0.3-mile path through the woods emerges into a clearing at the pool. Baker Hot Springs isn't shown on the forest map.

The hot springs: Users have dug a shallow pool at Baker out of a sandy bank. The pool varies from 4 to 10 feet across and is seldom more than a foot and a half deep. Natural mineral water bubbles up from the bottom at 104 degrees and cools as it disperses. The water is often a bit murky and has a slight mineral odor, but that doesn't faze the aficionados who come for a soak. Unless you feel like sharing your cozy cocoon, try the early mornings or the off-season months.

Warning: Lab tests show high bacteria counts in the water during periods

Baker Hot Springs

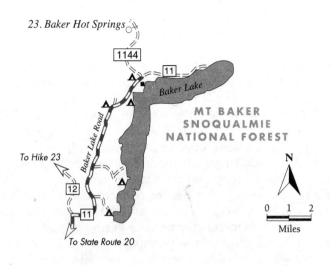

23. Baker Hot Springs

1144

11

Baker Lake

MT BAKER
SNOQUALMIE
NATIONAL FOREST

Baker Lake Road

To Hike 23

12

11

To State Route 20

N

0   1   2
Miles

of heavy use.

Background: At one time, the Forest Service developed the area as a designated recreation site. They built a boardwalk to span muddy stretches and installed a wooden tub over the springs. The tub was later taken out due to bacteria brewing in the cedar walls. The boardwalk was also removed.

Management problems associated with increasing public use have brought about a change in policy, and as the current user-built pools become excessive in size, they will periodically be filled in.

HIKE 23 *Park Butte*

General description:	A day hike or backpack featuring alpine meadows and close-up views of Mount Baker, not far from Baker Hot Springs.
Difficulty:	Strenuous.
Distance:	7 miles round trip.
General location:	45 miles northeast of Mount Vernon.
Elevation gain:	+2,180 feet, -80 feet.
High point:	Lookout, 5,450 feet.
Hiking quad:	Hamilton Green Trails.
Road map:	Mount Baker–Snoqualmie National Forest.
Restrictions:	Trail park pass required.
Contact:	Mount Baker Ranger District, Mount Baker–Snoqualmie National Forest.

Finding the trailhead: Follow the directions above and drive 12 miles up Baker Lake Road. Turn left just beyond a bridge on Forest Road 12 and follow signs to Mount Baker National Recreation Area and Schriebers Meadow. You'll reach a camping area and the trail sign in another 9 miles. The trailhead is a 20-mile drive from Baker Hot Springs.

The hike: This short climb in the Mount Baker National Recreation Area is a hard one to beat for wall-to-wall alpine views. Snow-draped peaks rim the horizon, and the awesome sight of Mount Baker's Easton Glacier steals the foreground. Lush meadows and tiny lakes are cupped between rocky knolls, and tumbling streams carve clefts between ridges and glacial moraines. Fat marmots announce your arrival with piercing cries.

Park Butte Trail (603) begins by bridging Sulphur Creek and undulating through Schriebers Meadow, where heather and huckleberries choke the open spaces and Mount Baker glistens between scattered stands of cedar and fir. Beyond lies a moonscape of rock and rushing streams. Volcanic mudflows and meltwater from the massive Easton Glacier have sliced free-ways through the forest here; you'll probably have to boulder-hop a bit to cross the channels, especially on warm summer afternoons.

The path gradually becomes wrapped in cool woods and gains 800 feet in a long steep mile to Lower Morovitz Meadow. Western hemlock gives way to mountain hemlock en route. Western redcedar yields to a strange looking cousin, the Alaska cedar, whose needles hang in long chains from drooping limbs. The off-white, shaggy bark peels off in long strips as if a bear had used the tree as a sharpening post for giant claws.

The grade tapers on the way to Upper Morovitz Meadow where you'll find superb picnic sites amid alpine scenery. The main trail goes across the meadow past a junction. Spectacular panoramas increase as it climbs the last mile above Pocket Lake to the summit. The lookout cabin, maintained by Skagit Alpine Club of Mount Vernon, is available to the public on a first-come, first-served basis when not being used by its maintenance crew.

Park Butte, ringed by peaks far and near, will take your breath away just when you stop to catch it. The 10,778-foot white cone of Mount Baker dominates the view. Its satellite peaks, the Black Buttes, jut above the Deming Glacier in sharp contrast. Looking westward, you'll see the ser-rated crests of the Twin Sisters range. To the south are Loomis Mountain and Dock Butte, backed in the far distance by Mount Rainier. To the east and southeast rise other distant cones including snow-clad Glacier Peak (see Hikes 20a-c).

Returning to the junction in the upper meadow, there's another direction to go that's well worth exploring. Take Railroad Grade Trail (603.2) north to-ward Baker Pass and ramble a mile northeast to intersect the long rocky spine of Railroad Grade. Pick your way along the tip of this knife-edged ridge, a moraine built up by the nearby Easton Glacier.

You can gaze eastward across the giant cleft to the massive glacier and barren landscape below the ice or look up to the gleaming white volcanic

Park Butte

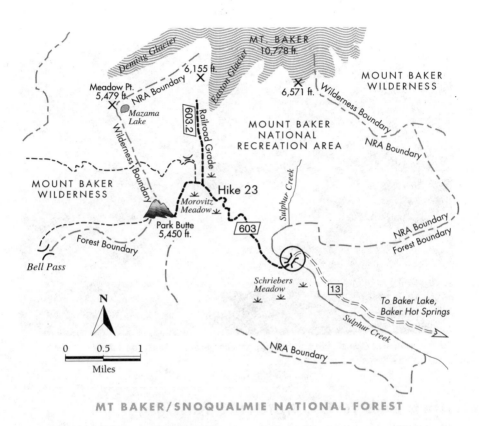

MT BAKER/SNOQUALMIE NATIONAL FOREST

cone of Mount Baker. Clusters of subalpine fir speckle the high meadows west of Railroad Grade, and other cross-country routes beckon.

There's also an alternate, hiker-only route, which is considerably longer, that travels into the high country. The 6-mile Scott Paul Trail (603.1) begins 100 feet up the Park Butte Trail, swings upward to the northeast, then returns westward to end at Upper Morovitz Meadow. It crosses the terminal moraine of Squak Glacier as well as Railroad Grade, providing spectacular views of glaciation at work.

24 Olympic Hot Springs

The largest pool at Olympic Hot Springs mirrors a canopy of evergreens on a quiet summer day.

HIKE 24a *To Olympic Hot Springs*

General description:	A day hike or overnighter to popular soaking pools in Olympic National Park. Skinnydippable with discretion.
Difficulty:	Easy.
Distance:	5 miles round trip.
General location:	18 miles southwest of Port Angeles.
Elevation gain:	260 feet.
High point:	Hot springs, 2,060 feet.
Hiking quad:	Mount Carrie USGS.
Road map:	Olympic National Park brochure.
Contact:	Olympic National Park.

Finding the trailhead: Drive 8 miles west of Port Angeles on U.S. Highway 101. Take Olympic Hot Springs Road 10 miles south and west on pavement, past Elwha Ranger Station, to a roadblock and parking area at the signed trailhead. The springs are named on the USGS quad.

Olympic Hot Springs • Appleton Pass • Boulder Lake

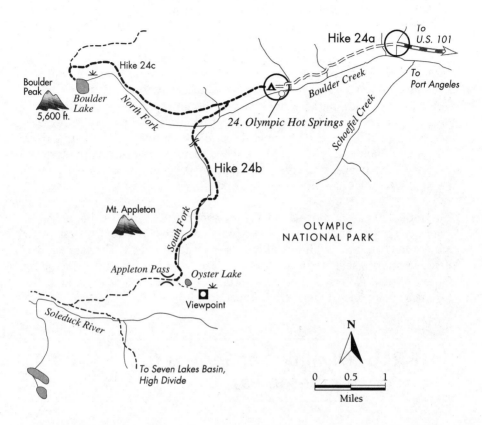

Background: Geologists believe that surface water here percolates downward until it reaches the earth's interior. Then, through cracks in the rock, steam and heated water rise back to the surface.

A more poetic explanation is the Native American legend that tells of two dragon-like fish who fought a mighty battle here long ago. Neither was able to win, so they crawled into caves where both shed hot, bitter tears. These tears still provide hot water at Olympic and nearby Sol Duc Hot Spring, a modernized historic resort. The tears at Olympic range from lukewarm to 118 degrees.

In more recent times, a famous resort at Olympic Hot Springs met a spectacular demise when an electrical short simultaneously ignited a fire and turned on the organ. The resort burned to the ground to the strains of Beethoven's Funeral March.

The hike: Nowadays, the Park Service has barred the final stretch of the access road to motor vehicles in an attempt to curb overuse of the fragile soaking pools and also because of the instability of the road surface. The end of the original road was constructed on fault surfaces and continues to slump.

Walk the last 2.2 miles of crumbling pavement, a gentle grade through deep woods, and set your pack down at Boulder Creek backcountry camp. At one time this site was fully developed with flush toilets and piped water, but it has been transformed into a primitive camp for backpackers. The short path to the springs drops down to bridge Boulder Creek, then meanders downstream passing one soaking pool after another.

A variety of side paths wriggle down the grassy bank and up into the forest. Some hit the jackpot while others just circle around in a maze reinforced by the steady tread of hopeful feet. Perseverance mixed with a dash of logic and luck will lead you to the more secluded pools. A popular destination for day trippers, it's also the stepping-off point for longer trips into the high Olympics (see the following hikes).

The hot springs: Without a doubt the hot spot of the Olympics, this cluster of steaming springs and pools lies sandwiched between a lush forest of fir and hemlock and the whitewater rapids of Boulder Creek. There are a total of seven bubbly soakers in a variety of sizes and temperatures, including one by a small waterfall. The most skinnydippable pool, at the end of the trail, is an easy one to miss when unoccupied.

HIKE 24b *Olympic Hot Springs to Appleton Pass*

General description:	A day hike or overnighter from the hot springs to alpine meadows and views, in Olympic National Park.
Difficulty:	Strenuous.
Distance:	10.5 miles round trip.
General location:	20 miles southwest of Port Angeles.
Elevation gain:	+2,920 feet, -120 feet.
High point:	5,000 feet.
Maps:	Same as above.
Contact:	Olympic National Park.

Finding the trailhead: Follow the route above to Olympic Hot Springs.

The hike: Olympic Hot Springs makes a great base for a side trip to Appleton Pass. This deservedly popular route climbs up through a moss-coated primeval forest to an awesome view across High Divide. Wave after wave of snow-capped peaks recedes southward to the horizon like whitecaps on a stormy sea. Mount Olympus, at 7,965 feet, rides the highest crest. Airy campsites dot the pass, and a tempting extension of the route could be made

Avalanche lilies carpet the viewpoint just east of Appleton Pass, and the jagged peaks along High Divide are seen to the south.

from here across to Seven Lakes Basin and High Divide.

Appleton Pass Trail begins at the upper end of Boulder Creek backcountry camp and winds through twilight woods to a junction with Boulder Lake Trail at 0.7 mile (see Hike 24c). The gentle grade continues until the path bridges the North Fork of Boulder Creek. Now the work begins as the route shoots up the canyon of the South Fork of Boulder Creek. Two short spurs a short distance apart lead to cascading falls and a small campsite apiece while the main trail bridges the creek and climbs on.

Crunch your way along a path littered with the small cones of western hemlock and Douglas-fir mixed with a dash of cedar. Log walkways aid the traverse over fragile marshy areas to a large campsite at 2.5 miles. The route crosses several rockslides spaced between stands of subalpine fir and a wavy tangle of slide alder.

Cross the South Fork twice and eventually emerge into a steep meadow in a high basin just below the pass. A thick mat of summer wildflowers competes with huckleberry, willow, and other bushy plants in the waist-deep grass. The humid fragrance is intoxicating. Watch for fat marmots sunbathing on rocky outcrops as you work your way up the trail.

Catch your breath and prepare for the last nine switchbacks up a precipitous slope that's often deep in snow until midsummer. An ice axe is well advised for early season hikers; a far easier snow climb from here crosses past tiny Oyster Lake up a long valley to a viewpoint 0.5 mile east of Appleton Pass.

Views from the pass itself are limited to tantalizing glimpses through the trees, so it's well worth the extra 0.5 mile and 300-foot gain to follow the ridgeline path east to the unnamed viewpoint. Tiny dwarfs of subalpine fir dot the plush green carpet spread out here, and the view unfolds in all directions. See the glaciers of Mount Olympus directly behind the foreground ridge of High Divide.

Snow Joke: *My fingers and toes were half-frozen from kicking one precarious step after another into crusty snow on the final steep pitch to Appleton Pass. My knees shook every time I made the mistake of glancing back down the slick wall. Concentrating instead on looking up, I began to see a sight that made me doubt my senses. A volley of snow-white balls was arcing through the blue sky above me, coming from some source just out of sight.*

As I hauled my stiff body onto the crest, I beheld a talented snowball juggler practicing his art, wearing only faded cutoffs and sturdy boots. He paused long enough to share a precious quart of milk, then gathered up a handful of white avalanche lilies which he promptly consumed for dessert. Then, with a cheerful wave, he leaped over the edge. I blinked twice and peered down just in time to see him disappear far below in a graceful glissade, using only his boots for skis.

HIKE 24c *Olympic Hot Springs to Boulder Lake*

General description:	A day hike or overnighter from the hot springs to a lake and high views, in Olympic National Park.
Difficulty:	Moderate.
Distance:	7 miles round trip.
General location:	20 miles southwest of Port Angeles.
Elevation gain:	2,150 feet.
High point:	4,350 feet.
Maps:	Same as above.
Contact:	Olympic National Park.

Finding the trailhead: Follow the route described to Olympic Hot Springs.

The hike: Another pleasant outing from the hot springs, not as spectacular as that to Appleton Pass (see above) but less demanding, climbs to a small lake nestled in a wooded basin. The snowfields and cliffs of Boulder Peak rise 1,250 feet above the southwest shore, offering a challenge rewarded by excellent views.

Start toward Appleton Pass from Boulder Creek backcountry camp and branch right in 0.7 mile onto Boulder Lake Trail. The route is a traverse climbing steadily above the North Fork of Boulder Creek, with a forest of Douglas-fir giving way to graceful western hemlock. Beyond Halfway Creek, the trail passes rockslide areas followed by stands of cedar and fir, crosses two rushing creeks, and finally levels into a meadow at the head of the valley. Subalpine firs line the last short rise.

Boulder Lake has a level campsite near the small peninsula on the north shore. The short climb from the lake to the 5,600-foot summit of Boulder Peak is steep but not difficult. The panoramic view includes Mount Appleton, nearby to the southeast, which almost eclipses massive Mount Olympus in the distance, and 7,000-foot Mount Carrie crowning the eastern end of High Divide.

British Columbia Locator Map

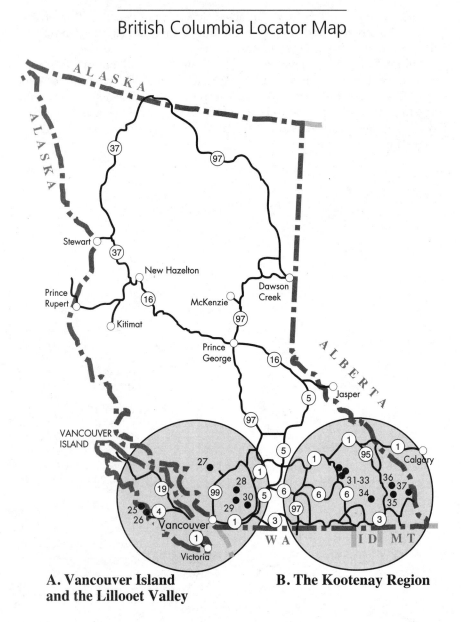

**A. Vancouver Island
and the Lillooet Valley**

B. The Kootenay Region

British Columbia

Beautiful British Columbia has her fair share of wild hot springs. The ones described here are concentrated in the southwest and the southeast corners of the province. The southwest area covers both Vancouver Island and the Lillooet Valley on the adjacent mainland. The southeast corner, commonly known as the Kootenays, includes dips on both the west and east sides. The reader will find a total of thirteen hot springs, all temptingly close to the U.S. border, marked on the B.C. Locator Map.

The hot springs in the southwest corner see the highest use. This isn't too surprising when you consider that roughly 75 percent of B.C.'s population is located here, concentrated mainly in metropolitan Vancouver, the largest city, and in Victoria, the capital. The soaks in the Kootenays, on the other hand, remain nearly as lonesome as those in Idaho.

A. VANCOUVER ISLAND AND THE LILLOOET VALLEY

AN OVERVIEW

The west side of Vancouver Island is a maze of inlets, channels, and islands. The rugged coastline boasts two hot springs, 8 miles apart, accessible only by boat or plane. Several companies at the road-end town of Tofino offer scheduled service in addition to charters; the two springs can be combined for a double dip.

On the nearby mainland, hot spring fans will find no less than four soaks scattered within weekend range of the greater Vancouver area, in a line stretching the length of the Lillooet Valley northwest from Harrison Lake to the upper Lillooet River, bordered by ranges of high peaks in spectacular Garibaldi Park and the remote and sparsely developed Coast Mountains.

Hikers in these parts will discover driftwood-strewn beaches interspersed with tidal pools on the big island. In contrast, the high country on both sides of the Lillooet Valley offers day trippers and backpackers alike such enticements as twilight forests and glacial streams, jagged peaks, a broad range of alpine delights at popular Garibaldi Park, and up-close glacier views at a more remote park.

Directions in this guide follow from towns on highways 4, 99, 7, and a variety of back roads. As a general rule, the forest roads are long and dusty

Vancouver Island and the Lillooet Valley Area Map

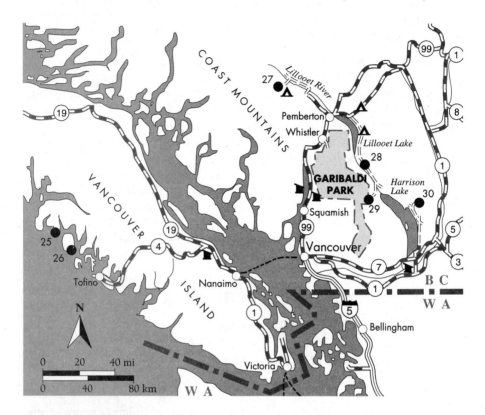

from excessive use by logging trucks, backwoods campsites are undeveloped, hiking trails are primitive outside of the parks, and the soaking pools are well-used on weekends despite somewhat cumbersome access.

Hot springs and hikes: On the west coast of Vancouver Island, hops by sea or air will drop you at popular Hot Springs Cove and little-known Ahousat (25, 26). Back on the mainland, a remote road up the Lillooet River northwest of Pemberton reaches five-star soaks at Meager Creek (27) followed by a trek in magnificent Garibaldi Park. A drive southeast of town accesses a glacier hike en route down the Lillooet River to a dip in St. Agnes Well (28). Farther downstream is a hike to Sloquet Creek Hot Springs (29). And last, a dusty drive up the east side of Harrison Lake leads to a hike-in soak at Clear Creek (30).

Season: The springs on Vancouver Island can be accessed and enjoyed virtually all year thanks to scheduled transportation and a mild maritime climate. The Lillooet Valley soaks are best in early summer through fall, as winter road closures make access difficult. Spring runoff buries the pools at

Vancouver Island Area Map

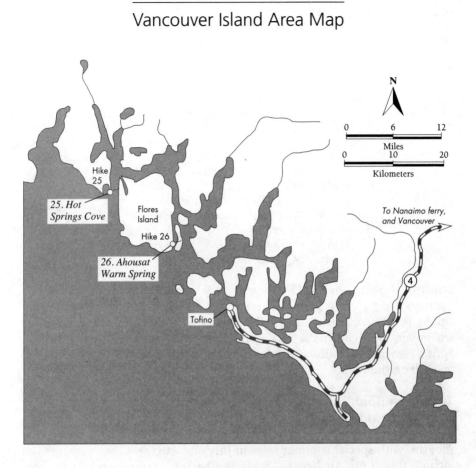

Sloquet and possibly at Clear Creek, but most pools at Meager stay high and dry.

Hikers in the coastal area can expect cool but sunny summers and mild winters with heavy rains. The hiking season on the mainland is limited to summer months only for the higher routes, with cold winters and heavy snows on west-facing slopes.

25 Hot Springs Cove

HIKE 25 *To Hot Springs Cove*

General description:	A popular boardwalk stroll to tidal hot pools in a marine park. Swimwear advised.
Difficulty:	Easy.
Distance:	2.5 mi/4 km round trip.
General location:	West coast of Vancouver Island.
Elevation:	Sea level.
Map:	Provincial Parks of Vancouver Island.
Contact:	BC Parks, Strathcoma District.

Finding the Trailhead: On Vancouver Island, take Highway 4 west to the road-end town of Tofino. The springs at Sharp Point are on the tiny Openit Peninsula, 20 mi/32 km to the northwest, and can only be accessed by sea or air. One can make arrangements to stop over at Ahousat Warm Spring (see below), halfway up the coast to Sharp Point. The hot springs are marked on the map.

Transportation: Visitors can take a scheduled sea bus from Tofino, a scenic one-hour ride leaving twice a day all summer, or fly Pacific Rim Airlines, offering year-round scheduled flights twice a day from Port Alberni, with special summer rates in July and August. Charter companies include Tofino Air, Air Nootka, Seaforth Charters, Inter-Island Excursions, Chinook Charters, and the Whale Centre. Contact the Tofino Infocentre for an update on transportation choices and general information about the hot springs.

The hike: Visitors are deposited at Government Wharf, the site of an abandoned fish cannery where, until the summer of 1991, a floating house at the dock offered homemade food, hot coffee, and other goodies for sale. The Park Service doesn't expect it to return, but who's to say if another party may take it up. Look for sun starfish at low tide, and the sea anemones that grow profusely from the logs of the wharf.

Maquinna Park was named after a famous Nootka chief in an area where habitation can be traced back more than 5,000 years. The tiny park offers no facilities, but you can pitch a tent nearby or camp for a fee in the adjacent reserve.

The boardwalk trail spans a marshy area and heads south from the wharf to the rocky tip of the Openit Peninsula. The hot springs are located near the end. Beyond, you can explore the shoreline and observe the abundance

Hot Springs Cove

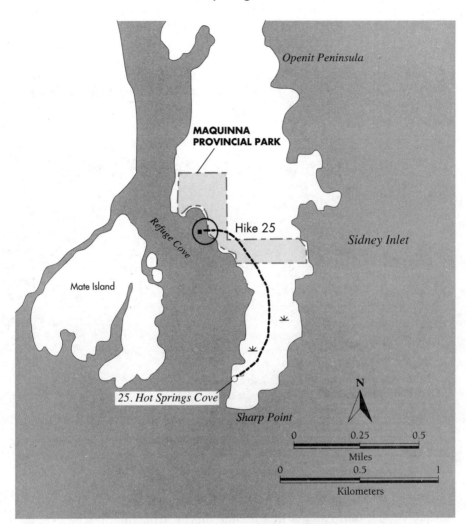

of fascinating marine life at low tide.

The hot springs: Water issues from bedrock at 129 degrees F/54 degrees C, cascades over a 12-feet/3.6-meter waterfall, and eventually drains into three tidal pools the size of bathtubs. Icy ocean waves swirl through the pools with the incoming tide, which dilutes the scalding water to a more comfortable temperature. The uppermost pool offers the most relaxing soak and a great view of the sea.

Magnificent Hot Springs Cove has become quite a tourist attraction in recent years. Access is no longer a major obstacle, and in the prime summer months, July through September, as many as one hundred people or more may flock to the springs in a single day. The best odds of getting a quiet soak would be on weekdays or during the off-season.

A nautical boardwalk: Ship's name graffiti is known the world over as sailors record their ports of call. At Hot Springs Cove, this graffiti has taken a different twist. Rather than paint their names and deface local landmarks, sailors regularly engrave, burn or chisel their ship's name into a plank and then nail it into the boardwalk. Some even bring their plank already prepared. Others add the date of each successive visit. The boardwalk is becoming a lesson in Who's Who of coastal yachting, not to mention a testament to the artistry of visiting seamen.

26 Ahousat (Flores Island) Warm Spring

HIKE 26 *To Ahousat Warm Spring*

General description:	A stroll to a warm pool on an island, not far from Hot Springs Cove. Swimwear recommended.
Difficulty:	Easy.
Distance:	2 mi/3.2 km round trip.
General location:	Off the west coast of Vancouver Island.
Elevation:	Sea level.
Map:	Same as above.
Contact:	BC Parks, Strathcoma District.

Finding the trailhead: On Vancouver Island, take Highway 4 west to the road-end town of Tofino. The warm spring is located at the south end of Flores Island, 12 mi/19 km northwest, and can be accessed only by sea or air. Hot spring fans can get in a double dip by arranging to stop here en route to Hot Springs Cove (see above). The spring isn't marked on the map.

Transportation: See above.

The hike: Charter boats to Flores Island drop people off at Ahousat, where there's a dock and a tiny general store. Trails are poorly defined, but you can follow the B.C. Hydro power poles south from the shoreline of Matilda Inlet to the spring. Skirt or cut across the small bay mentioned below, depending on the tide. Private boats can cruise right by Ahousat and head for the dock, if it's still afloat, on the tidal flat by the pool.

Visitors can also be deposited at Marktosis. A faint trail heads south through a dense groundcover of salal, salmonberry bushes, and ferns, to-

Ahousat Warm Spring

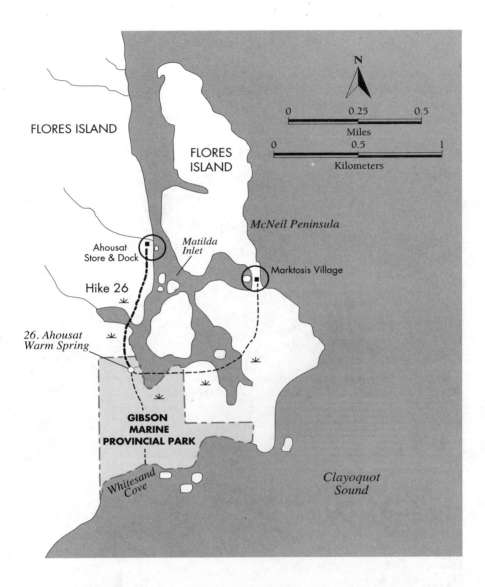

ward a line of power poles at Matilda Inlet. At the halfway point, it reaches the bay and follows the poles and shoreline west to the spring. At low tide the water is only 6 inches/15 centimeters deep, and you can cut across the head of the inlet. The distance is the same from both trailheads.

The warm spring: A concrete swimming pool, 8 x 20 feet and 4 feet deep/ 2.4 x 6 x 1.2 m, collects the flow. The pool has a magnificent setting on a beach at the southwest tip of Matilda Inlet in tiny Gibson Marine Park. The

Upper Lillooet Valley Area Map

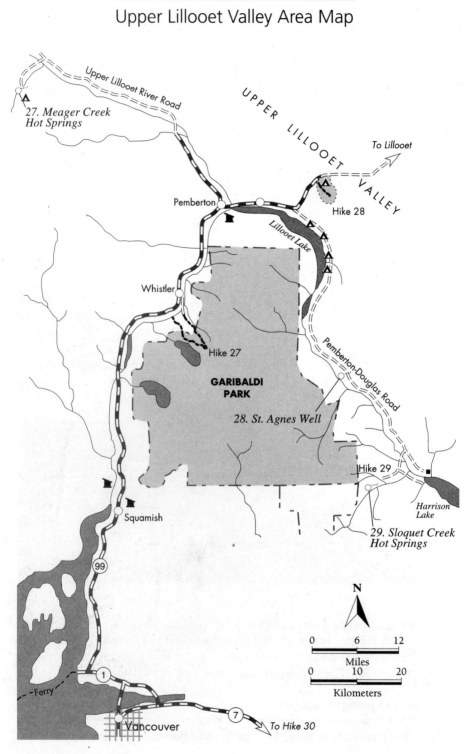

27. Meager Creek Hot Springs

Upper Lillooet River Road

UPPER LILLOOET VALLEY

To Lillooet

Pemberton

Hike 28

Lillooet Lake

Whistler

Hike 27

GARIBALDI PARK

Pemberton-Douglas Road

28. St. Agnes Well

Hike 29

Squamish

Harrison Lake

29. Sloquet Creek Hot Springs

99

1

Ferry

Vancouver

7

To Hike 30

N

| 0 | 6 | 12 |
Miles
| 0 | 10 | 20 |
Kilometers

only drawback is a soaking temperature that hovers around 77 degrees F/25 degrees C, well below the optimum range except during hot weather.

If you have a little time to spare, there's an outstanding side trip nearby. As you near the spring, an old boardwalk path branches south. The scenic route leads to a sandy beach on the south end of the island at Whitesand Cove. Tiny islands dot the ocean view, and Vargas Island is visible to the southeast across Clayoquot Sound.

27 Meager Creek Hot Springs

General description:	A Shangri-la of soaking pools, near a remote road in the Coast Mountains. Swimwear seems the norm.
Elevation:	2,400 ft/732 m.
General location:	Upper Lillooet Valley.
Map:	Squamish Forest District.
Contact:	BC Forests, Squamish Forest District.

Finding the hot springs: From Vancouver, take scenic Highway 99 north past Whistler (see following hike) and on to Pemberton. Go north to Pemberton Meadows, about 17 mi/27 km up the Lillooet River. Beware of log trucks and turn right on Hurley River Road. The gravel road bridges the river to a fork in 5 mi/8 km where it turns uphill. Bear left on the rougher

The upper pool at Meager Creek Hot Springs features a submerged bench for relaxed soaking.

Meager Creek Hot Springs

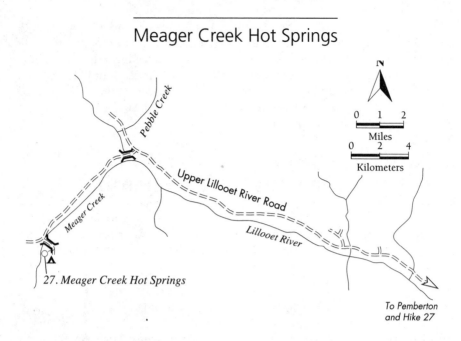

27. *Meager Creek Hot Springs*

To Pemberton
and Hike 27

Lillooet River Road and continue to the Mile-24 log truck sign. Take the left fork here and bridge the river. Follow Meager Creek Road 7 mi/11 km upstream to the springs. Meager, a total of 47 mi/75 km from Pemberton, is signed on the ground and named on the forest map.

The way it was: Logging opened the way to Meager Creek in the late 1970s and brought with it a few hardy hot springers. B.C. Hydro took an active interest for a time, exploring the springs' potential as an alternate energy resource. The specs were impressive: the largest springs in the province, a temperature range of 101-129 degrees F/38-54 degrees C, and a volume of 347 gal/min/1,526 l/min. But the project was eventually abandoned as unfeasible and the springs left to nature.

Then, on Thanksgiving weekend of 1984, Nature stepped in and dealt a harsh blow. Heavy rains brought down a monstrous mud slide that covered the valley floor and flooded areas as far away as Pemberton. The hot springs were demolished, vehicles buried, and the surviving bathers evacuated by helicopter.

The hot springs today: The Squamish Forest District, after years of hard work mending the damage, has developed the area into a designated recreation site. The grounds, maintained by a caretaker, were planned to accommodate large numbers.

Two huge cedar pools have been constructed as well as ample decks and cabanas for clothes, all tastefully designed to blend into the environment. The parking lot and campground sit on terraces high up the bank, and stairways ease the descent. An age-old forest spreads a green canopy,

The lower pool at Meager is a unique example of a primitive spring that's been elaborately developed.

and ferns border the causeways that span marshy spots below.

The uppermost pool measures a full 15 x 20 ft/4.5 x 6 m and has a submerged bench along one side. Clocking in at 110 degrees F/43.3 degrees C at the time I was there, it sorely needed some means of channeling cold water from the creek. The lower gem, known as "sky pool," is even longer and about neck deep when standing up. It registered just 90 degrees F/32.2 degrees C, but it was definitely a five-star soak on a midsummer day.

There is also a creekside pool built of mortared rock. This one's easy enough to cool with a few splashes from the glacier-fed stream. Also nearby is a small rock pool beside a sauna shed. Winding paths connect all the soaks, and the forest provides both shade and privacy.

Meager Creek Hot Springs has indeed come a long way. Nowadays, visitors are said to pour in by the hundreds on long weekends. Let's just pray the numbers don't grow too much larger and bring the abuse problems common to overused hot springs in the states, or the Forest Service may live to regret the paradise they've developed here.

HIKE 27 *Singing Pass via the "Musical Bumps"*

General description:	A point-to-point day hike or overnighter featuring alpine views and a high meadow pass, en route to Meager Creek Hot Springs.
Difficulty:	Moderate.
Distance:	10.5 mi/17 km one-way.
General location:	Between Vancouver and Pemberton.
Elevation gain:	+1,640 ft/500 m, -3,770 ft/1,150 m.
High point:	6,720 ft/2,050 m.
Hiking quad:	Cheakamus and Fitzsimmons Garibaldi Park 92J/2E.
Road map:	Garibaldi Park brochure or Squamish Forest District.
Contact:	BC Parks, Garibaldi/Sunshine Coast District.

Finding the trailheads: Take Highway 99 to Whistler Village and go east following signs toward Blackcomb Mountain Ski Area. Watch for a dirt road veering right, signed "to Singing Pass." Drive 3 mi/4.8 km uphill to Fitzsimmons Creek trailhead and leave a car here.

Return to Highway 99, and hop south to the Gondola exit. Drop a second vehicle off at the Gondola Base parking lot and ride the gondola, followed by Red Chair, to the "high start" trailhead at the Round House on the north side of Whistler Mountain. The trails aren't marked on the Whistler quad.

The hike: The high route to Singing Pass is a favorite among connoisseurs of alpine vistas. After a brief initial climb, it glides along a ridge capped by three knolls: Piccolo, Flute, and Oboe. Hikers ride the "musical bumps," as they are affectionately called, on a descending scale, each bump lower than the previous one, to Singing Pass. Here, the Fitzsimmons Creek Trail lets you continue the downhill glide back to the shuttle car.

The advantages of the point-to-point route versus a round trip on Fitzsimmons Creek Trail are the nonstop panoramic views plus a good 330-ft/100-m less gain. The only drawbacks are the required car shuttle between trailheads and the need to take ski lifts. Call the Whistler Infocentre to make sure the lifts are running.

From the Round House, an unofficial path works its way south to the top of the T-bar, then on up a narrow basin between the summits of Whistler and Little Whistler. Try to avoid the ice fields near the lower summit as you traverse steep slopes to the crest. The climb places you 820 ft/250 m above the Round House, encircled by lofty views of Garibaldi Park.

Here you turn your back on Whistler Mountain and begin a southeasterly route along the knobby spine. Sail over 6,560-ft/2,000-m Piccolo Summit, dip and rise over Flute, then bob to Oboe. Look straight down at Cheakamus Lake, ahead to nearby Fissile Peak, and across Fitzsimmons Valley to a multitude of peaks in the Spearhead Range to the northeast.

Singing Pass via the Musical Bumps

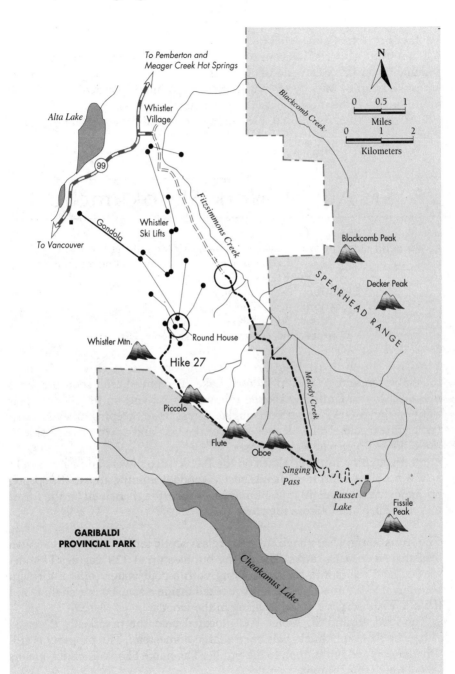

Coast down flowered slopes to Singing Pass, nearly 500 ft/150 m below Oboe, where tiny wildflowers blanket broad subalpine meadows. From Singing Pass itself, a side trip beckons. The 1.2-mi/2-km path to Russet Lake crosses a ridge that adds an extra 820-ft/250-m gain to the hike but offers yet another horizon of snow-clad peaks.

The route down Fitzsimmons Creek begins with a brief view of mountains on the west side of the main valley below which you can see from the head of Melody Creek. It then drops into old-growth forest. You continue down the musical scale as you skirt the side canyons of Oboe and Flute Creeks, then finally cross Harmony Creek a short way from the trail's end.

28 St. Agnes Well (Skookumchuck)

General description:	Roadside hot tanks by the Lillooet River, seasonally frequented by locals and man-eating mosquitoes. Keep swimwear handy.
Elevation:	400 ft/122 m.
General location:	The Lillooet Valley.
Map:	Squamish Forest District.
Contact:	BC Forests, Squamish Forest District.

Finding the hot spring: From Vancouver, take Highway 99 north to Pemberton and go east to Lillooet Lake. The paved road soon branches up and away to Duffey Lake (see following hike) and on to Lillooet. Bear right on the gravel Pemberton-Douglas Forest Road, keeping an eye peeled for logging trucks. Follow it the length of the lake and down the east side of the Lillooet River past Rogers Creek.

Start watching number plates on the B.C. Hydro towers and hang a right at Tower 682. A short track heads past a wooded camping area to the spring. St. Agnes Well, about 40 mi/64 km from Pemberton, is named on the forest map but misplaced across the road.

The hot spring: Users have cut a fiberglass septic tank in half to create two oval-shaped soaking tanks. The spring bubbles up at 129 degrees F/54 degrees C and feeds into the tubs, along with a cold water source, through sections of PVC pipe. One tank is squeezed inside a ramshackle shelter, and the other sits across a small clearing in the woods.

The land around St. Agnes Well, located near the practically deserted village of Skookumchuck, was once a large homestead. The property is still privately owned but is open to the public. The name Skookumchuck means "good water" in Chinook.

The best part about St. Agnes is that it breaks the long drive to Sloquet Creek Hot Springs (see below). Popular with folks from as far off as Vancouver,

St. Agnes Well • Sloquet Creek Hot Springs

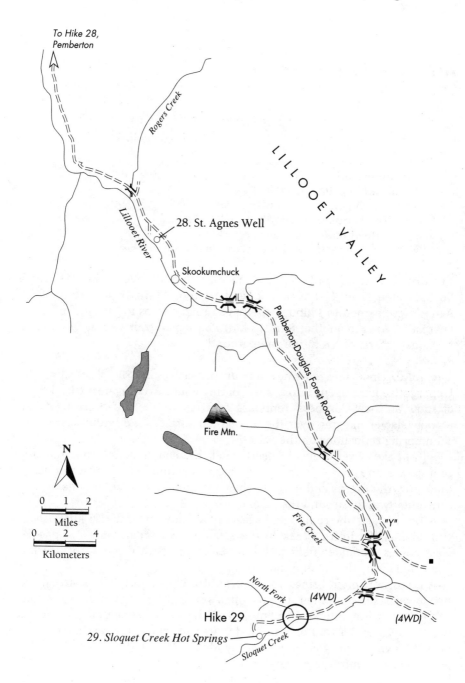

To Hike 28, Pemberton

Rogers Creek

LILLOOET VALLEY

Lillooet River

28. St. Agnes Well

Skookumchuck

Pemberton-Douglas Forest Road

Fire Mtn.

N

0 1 2
Miles

0 2 4
Kilometers

Fire Creek

"Y"

North Fork

(4WD)

(4WD)

Hike 29

29. Sloquet Creek Hot Springs

Sloquet Creek

it periodically gets some heavy-handed treatment. Piles of empty beer cans and other garbage greeted me, and clouds of hungry mosquitoes kept my visit short.

HIKE 28 *Joffre Lakes*

General description:	A day hike or overnighter to glacier-fed lakes and alpine views, on the way to St. Agnes Well.
Difficulty:	Moderate.
Distance:	7 mi/11 km round trip.
General location:	The Lillooet Valley.
Elevation gain:	1,200 ft/366 m.
High point:	5,300 ft/1,615 m.
Hiking quad:	Duffey Lake 92J/8 NTS.
Road map:	Squamish Forest District.
Contact:	BC Parks, Garibaldi/Sunshine Coast District.

Finding the trailhead: Follow the directions above to Duffey Lake Road, located 11 mi/18 km east of Pemberton or 29 mi/47 km north of St. Agnes Well. Signed to Lillooet, the paved road climbs to tiny Joffre Lakes Recreation Area in another 8 mi/13 km. The signed trail, not shown on the NTS quad, starts off from the campground.

The hike: Good things come in small packages, and the short climb to Upper Joffre Lake opens into a world of tiny wildflowers against a backdrop of snow and ice. Climbers' tents are dwarfed by the broad snout of the Matier Glacier hanging over the blue green surface, and white peaks cast shimmering reflections on the water.

Joffre Lakes Trail begins in deep woods but soon emerges to a magnificent view of the glacier from the lower lake. Continuing in forest through a thick growth of ferns and berry bushes, the improved track does its best to skirt muddy areas around the lake.

After the lake, the route climbs steeply for the next mile/1.6 km, zigzagging high above Joffre Creek in the shade of tall cedars and Douglas-fir. Next comes a boulder field to cross before the path drops to bridge the creek and circle the small middle lake.

A final short pitch brings you to beautiful Upper Joffre. The size of the two lower lakes combined, Upper Joffre's roughly triangular shape is convoluted with tiny inlets and peninsulas. Clusters of subalpine fir dot the rocky slopes, and a wall of scree and talus rises above the far shore to the ragged tongue of the glacier, backed by Mount Matier.

For a close confrontation with glacial magnificence, take the rocky path beyond the lake and follow the inlet stream to the camping area. A cairned route climbs over talus to a ridge overlooking the lake and mountains beyond,

Joffre Lakes

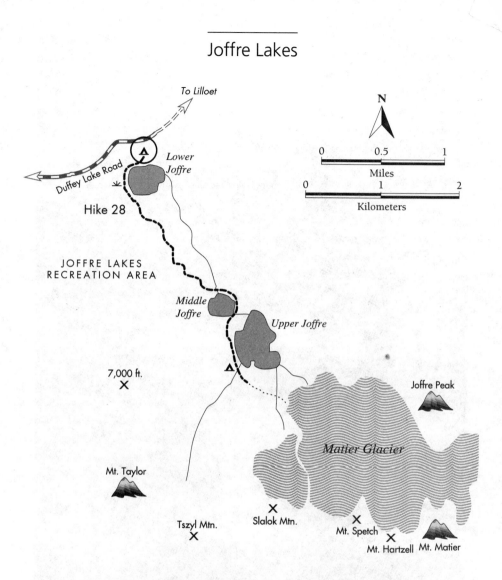

and the short climb adds a gain of around 700 ft/213 m to the hike. Look directly across the lake to Joffre Peak. A few more steps brings you face to face with the icefalls of the Matier Glacier.

In the dark: *Since I planned an early start for the climb, I broke camp and started morning coffee in the dark, disdaining the aid of a flashlight. Who needs light to do a simple task performed every day? Not me. No problem finding the pot and the water bottle. No problem filling the pot and starting up the stove. The problem came a few minutes later when the horrible smell of burning plastic told me the one item I hadn't found, my breakfast bowl stashed inside the pot!*

Joffre Lakes Trail starts with a preview of the Matier Glacier seen from the lower lake.

Sloquet Creek Hot Springs offers the ultimate in secluded soaking close to nature.

HIKE 29 *To Sloquet Creek Hot Springs*

General description:	A day hike to remote creekside hot pools in the Coast Mountains. Swimwear advised if others present.
Difficulty:	Easy except for a major stream ford.
Distance:	4 mi/6.4 km round trip.
General location:	Lower Lillooet Valley.
Elevation gain:	+200 ft/61 m, -60 ft/18 m.
High point:	760 ft/232 m.
Hiking quads:	Glacier Lake 92G/16 and Stave River 92G/9 NTS (optional).
Road map:	Squamish Forest District.
Contact:	BC Forests, Squamish Forest District.

Finding the trailhead: Follow the directions above to St. Agnes Well and continue down the Lillooet River to a "Y" at 20 mi/32 km. Bear right and cross the river, then go left to bridge Fire Creek. Drive 2 mi/3.2 km down the west side of the river to a rough road on the right just before the bridge over Sloquet Creek. The Sloquet Creek Road has some rocky spots that demand a high-clearance vehicle and very few places to park, much less turn around. If in doubt, you can park below and walk the final 5.5 mi/8.8 km.

At 3.5 mi/5.6 km, the road dives beneath the North Fork Sloquet Creek. There's ample room to park or pitch a tent nearby. The pullout is a total of around 64 dusty mi/102 km from Pemberton. The springs are marked without a name on the forest map and omitted on the Stave River quad.

The hike: Fording the North Fork Sloquet Creek would be suicide during the spring runoff; it's still a good 2 feet deep (0.6 m) in midsummer. The water is icy cold and the current moves along at a good clip. Beyond the creek, a jeep track continues 2 mi/3.2 km west through deep woods well up the bank and eventually drops down to end beside the stream. There's a good tentsite or two in the grassy clearing, and a short path leads downstream to the pools.

The hot springs: The main spring, one of the hottest in B.C. at 154 degrees F/68 degrees C, cascades into a source pool hot enough to cook eggs. Downstream, steamy water from other springs flows through a chain of shallow pools in the bedrock bank. Closest to the source, the largest pool registers nearly 113 degrees F/45 degrees C. The temperature drops to a toasty 105 degrees F/40.5 degrees C in the creekside pools. Cold water can be admitted for a cooler dip.

The soaking pools are enclosed on one side by a tangle of undergrowth and overhanging trees and hemmed in on the other by the rushing torrent of Sloquet Creek. Shafts of sunlight filter through the treetops, and the stream ripples right past your nearly submerged nose. How close to heaven can you get?

Road note: Just for the record, the river road does continue down the west side of Harrison Lake all the way south to Highway 7, but it's reported to be quite rough—four-wheel-drive only. The 60-mi/97-km drive is reported to take six to ten hours. So, unfortunately, there is no easy link between the hot springs here and those down at Clear Creek (see below).

30 Clear Creek Hot Springs

HIKE 30 *To Clear Creek Hot Springs*

General description:	A day hike or mountain bike ride to hot tubs on the east side of Harrison Lake. Swimwear is anyone's guess.
Difficulty:	Easy.
Distance:	5 mi/8 km round trip.
General location:	Lower Lillooet Valley.
Elevation gain:	1,000 ft/305 m.
High point:	2,500 ft/762 m.
Hiking quad:	Mount Urquhard 92H/12 NTS (optional).
Road map:	Chilliwack Forest District.
Contact:	BC Forests, Chilliwack Forest District.

Finding the trailhead: From Vancouver, take Highway 7 east to the Kent district. Go north on Highway 9, passing Harrison Hot Springs Resort and Sasquatch Provincial Park. Beware of log trucks as you continue on the gravel Harrison East Forest Road up the east side of Harrison Lake.

After passing a logging camp, stay on the main road, which veers left at Cogburn Creek. In another few miles you pass Big Silver log sort and enter Big Silver Road. Stay on this main road to 4.3 mi/7 km. Turn right on Clear Creek Road, which is in good 4WD condition, and continue 3.7 mi/6 km, to the trailhead. If you don't have a jeep, you could do the last stretch on a mountain bike. Park at the designated parking area and dig out your walking shoes. The springs aren't marked on either map.

The hike: The trail is an old logging road now closed to vehicle traffic in order to protect Clear Creek, a valuable fish habitat, from environmental damage. The track is bordered by stately trees and is a pleasant walk. There are a couple of streams to navigate. Camping is rustic and unmanaged, so pack out your garbage.

The hot springs: At last count, Clear Creek sported four soaking tubs perched on rocks at waterline, a wooden tub 6 ft/1.8 m in diameter, a plywood box that would hold about the same volume if it didn't leak, and two garden-variety bathtubs. The spring bubbles out of the bank at 95 degrees F/35 degrees C, and lengths of PVC pipe transport water to the tub of your choice.

Clear Creek Hot Springs

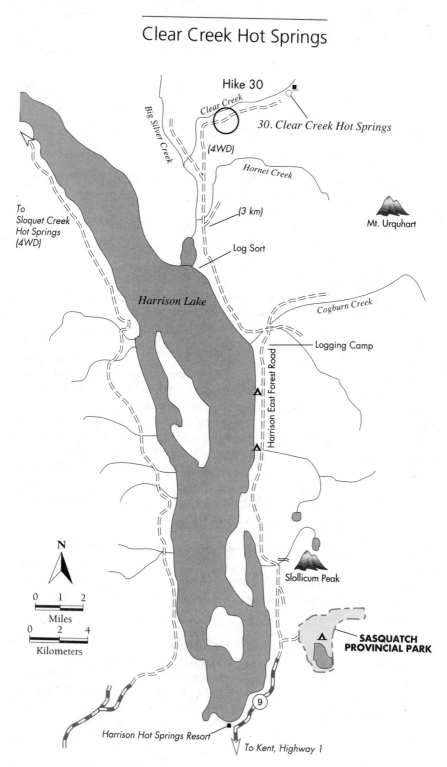

Hike 30

Clear Creek

30. Clear Creek Hot Springs

Big Silver Creek

(4WD)

Hornet Creek

To
Sloquet Creek
Hot Springs
(4WD)

(3 km)

Mt. Urquhart

Log Sort

Harrison Lake

Cogburn Creek

Logging Camp

Harrison East Forest Road

N

0   1   2
Miles
0   2   4
Kilometers

Slollicum Peak

SASQUATCH
PROVINCIAL PARK

9

Harrison Hot Springs Resort

To Kent, Highway 1

Nearby, there's a cabin and a swimming pool built of cedar logs by a woman prospector back when the road was first opened. The pool wastes away collecting silt and algae. Although she still has mining claims, the land is publicly owned.

You'd expect this far-flung spot to be one of the quieter soaking grounds in the province, but unfortunately that isn't the case. Remote as it may be, Clear Creek is still the closest wild dip to the metropolitan Vancouver area. It's normally accessible and usable from April through September, but visitors on summer weekends must come prepared to wait awhile for a tub.

B. THE KOOTENAY REGION

AN OVERVIEW

The Kootenays encompass an area of fertile river valleys and narrow, glacially carved lakes sandwiched between mountain ranges, with Kootenay Lake running north to south down the center. To the west, three hot springs are clustered above a long lake in the rugged Selkirk Range; to the east, four more are spread out across the southern Rocky Mountain Trench. All are tucked away in sylvan settings, yet most are accessible in short walks.

Hikers enjoy trails that meander through age-old forests to the many scenic lakes in the area or climbs to high overlooks. In addition to the routes in this guide, national parks such as Glacier and Banff and a variety of provincial parks offer a wide range of alpine destinations.

Directions follow out of Nakusp on Highways 6 and 23 and out of Cranbrook on Highways 95A, 93/95, and 3. Back roads and hiking routes

Kootenay Region Area Map

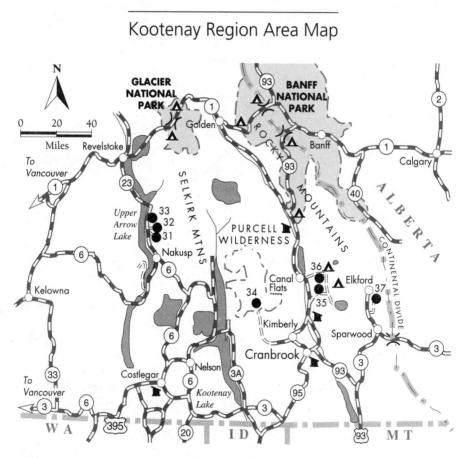

The West Kootenays Area Map

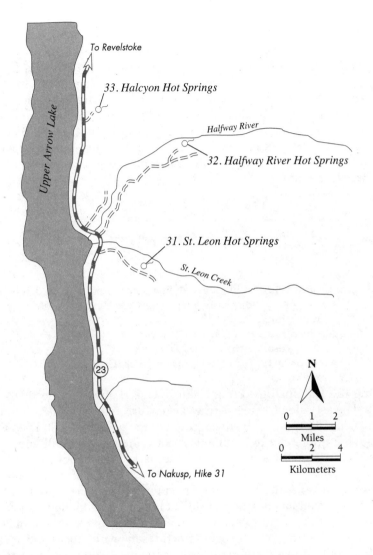

run the gamut from short and well maintained to long and poorly defined. Campsites vary from developed to primitive, and the bubbly soaking pools generally have room to spare.

Hot springs and hikes: In the West Kootenays, Highway 23 north of Nakusp leads to easily accessed yet secluded soaks at St. Leon, Halfway River, and Halcyon (31–33) near Upper Arrow Lake; hiking options include a climb to an overlook of the lake. In the East Kootenays, the remaining four springs fan out north of Cranbrook. A remote road northwest of town accesses a trek to Dewar Creek Hot Springs (34) in the Purcell Wilderness. North of town, a loop drive combines roadside soaks at popular Ram Creek and Lussier (35, 36) with hikes in nearby parks. To the northeast, logging roads access a stroll to Fording Mountain Warm Springs (37).

Season: Although early summer through fall is the best time, the soaks in the West Kootenays are accessible in the winter from the highway by cross-country skiers. They should not be affected by the spring runoff. In the East Kootenays, access to all but Lussier hinges on seasonal road closures.

The hiking season is normally late July through mid-September for high routes such as Saddle Mountain and the viewpoints above Fish Lake. Prime time for the trek to Dewar Creek is mid-August. Summer weather generally brings hot days with occasional thunderstorms. Expect cold nights at higher elevations.

31 St. Leon Hot Springs

General description:	A unique soak in a cedar forest well hidden below a dirt road. Keep swimwear handy.
Elevation:	2,200 ft/670 m.
General location:	The West Kootenays.
Map:	Arrow Forest District.
Contact:	BC Forests, Arrow Forest District.

Finding the hot springs: From Nakusp, take Highway 23 north 14 mi/23 km up the east side of Upper Arrow Lake. Turn right 1.5 mi/2.4 km past a rest area onto St. Leon Forest Road (south of the bridge over St. Leon Creek) and climb 2 mi/3.2 km to a pullout. A path plunges downhill and reaches the pool at 0.25 mi/0.4 km. St. Leon isn't marked on the forest map.

The hot springs: A clearing in the forest reveals a concrete pool with free-flowing curves and a smooth and sloped bottom. The kidney-shaped pool, built by a highway crew, is a good 15 ft/4.6 m long and 2.5 ft/0.8 m deep in the center. The springs emerge from fractures in nearby rocks and are piped into the pool to provide a blissful soak averaging 103 degrees F/39 degrees C. There is also a small pool in the rocks above.

St. Leon Hot Springs is on private property but open to the public. A hotel dating back to gold rush days once stood nearby, as at nearby Halcyon, but both hotels burned down in the 1950s and no trace remains today. The forest is magnificent, and the gourmet sampler of wild dips would be hard pressed to improve on the present user-built pool.

The unique pool at St. Leon Hot Springs, with curves in the shape of a guitar, sets a new standard in creative design.

HIKE 31 *Saddle Mountain Lookout*

General description:	A day hike to a lookout with sweeping views of the Arrow Lakes and surrounding mountains, not far from St. Leon Hot Springs.
Difficulty:	Strenuous.
Distance:	6 mi/9.7 km round trip.
General location:	The West Kootenays.
Elevation gain:	2,243 ft/684 m.
High point:	7,643 ft/2,330 m.
Hiking quad:	Nakusp 82K/4 NTS.
Road map:	Arrow Forest District.
Contact:	BC Forests, Arrow Forest District.

Finding the trailhead: From Nakusp, drive 12 mi/20 km south on Highway 6 and take the ferry across Arrow Lake. Turn right on Saddle Mountain Road and drive 6 mi/10 km up the far shore. Take a left on the lookout road and climb 5 mi/8 km to the road-end parking area. The trailhead is 23 mi/37 km from Nakusp.

Saddle Mountain Lookout

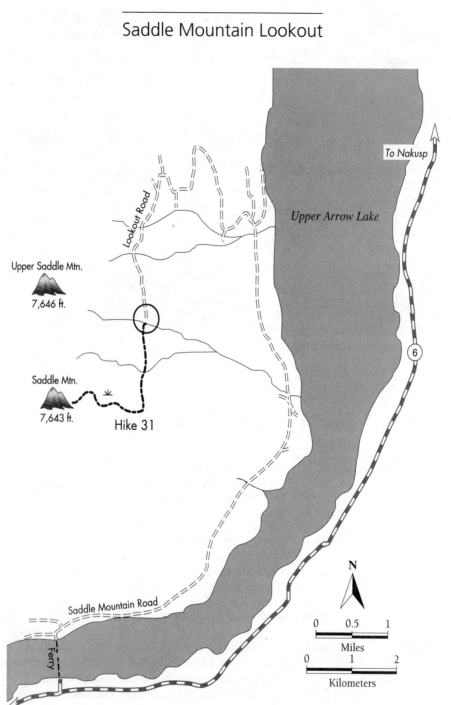

Upper Arrow Lake

To Nakusp

Lookout Road

Upper Saddle Mtn.
7,646 ft.

Saddle Mtn.
7,643 ft.

Hike 31

6

N

Saddle Mountain Road

Ferry

To Vernon

0   0.5   1
Miles

0   1   2
Kilometers

The hike: Saddle Mountain Trail begins near the top of a large clearcut but is soon wrapped in a forest of hemlock and cedar as it climbs the east-facing flank. You'll pass an old cabin on the way, then travel past stands of spruce and balsam, and eventually reach alpine meadows dotted with tiny wildflowers giving way to rocky slopes near the summit.

The lookout is a great spot to enjoy the sight of Upper and Lower Arrow Lakes stretched out below. Look west to views of the Monashee Range and east to the southern Selkirks. Scalping Knife Mountain looms across the lake canyon to the south. But don't lose track of time, or you'll find yourself watching the last ferry of the day depart without you.

32 Halfway River Hot Springs

General description:	Steamy soaking boxes hiding in the woods below a dirt road. Skinnydippable with discretion.
Elevation:	2,000 ft/610 m.
General location:	The West Kootenays.
Map:	Arrow Forest District.
Contact:	BC Forests, Arrow Forest District.

Finding the hot springs: From Nakusp, drive north 15 mi/24 km up the east side of Upper Arrow Lake on Highway 23, past the St. Leon Creek bridge. Turn right on an old logging road just south of the Halfway River bridge and follow it 6.5 mi/10.4 km uphill. Drop over the edge on a track that ends at a fire ring. A path plunges down the bank to reach the springs in 0.25 mi/0.4 km. The springs aren't marked on the forest map.

The approach: The first clue is a small sign nailed to a tree that reads: "There's no place anything like this place anywhere near this place, so this must be the place!" Thanks to volunteer work, the site is now complete with a secluded camping area and outhouse in addition to the soaking boxes. The next sign welcomes the visitor, gives a bit of background, and provides a few pointers on enjoying a comfortable soak. A notice warns about poison ivy, which flourishes along the path and surrounds the springs.

The hot springs: Around the bend is the coup de grâce, a plywood soaking box 7 ft/2 m square with an adjoining box half the size. A pipe channels water from the 141-degree F/60.5-degree C spring, and a valve regulates the flow. The recommended technique is to leave it at just a trickle, otherwise it gets far too hot. A bucket has been provided for adding river water.

The three-sided shed offers a dry spot for clothes, and decking covers the muddy ground around the springs. A path leads to the nearby river where those so inclined can take an ice cold plunge between soaks. A lush cedar forest wraps the area in total privacy.

Just for the record: In 1973 Forest Service employees were fighting a forest fire and discovered a second hot spring on the Halfway River. It is reported to lie another 7 mi/11 km upstream in a rocky gorge. Unfortunately, the terrain isn't conducive to making a pool, as the spring flows down a rockslide of boulders. Logging roads follow both sides of the river, and the road on the north bank continues up the broad valley into the high country.

Mirage: *We spent the afternoon bushwhacking in vain up both sides of the river, finally found the path, and decided on one last try. Expecting an algae-coated puddle at best, we were dumbfounded to find the user-built facilities, and stood gawking at a group in the pool sipping wine from long-stemmed glasses and nibbling snacks from a well-stocked cooler. If we'd only known in advance, we could have saved ourselves the effort and stopped at the Travel Infocentre in Nakusp. Apparently they have an album on display with color photos, full specs, and directions to all three "wild" dips in the area.*

33 Halcyon Hot Springs

General description:	Roadside hot soaks overlooking a lake. Nudity common despite heavy use.
Elevation:	2,000 ft/610 m.
General location:	The West Kootenays.
Map:	Arrow Forest District.
Contact:	BC Forests, Arrow Forest District.

Finding the hot springs: From Nakusp, follow Highway 23 north 20.5 mi/ 33 km up the east side of Upper Arrow Lake, or 6 mi/9.6 km north of the Halfway River bridge (see above). A dirt road on the right goes uphill and soon reaches the springs, but it's easier to park at the bottom and walk up. Folks camping overnight usually try to park above the springs. Neither Halcyon nor the turnoff are marked on the forest map.

The hot springs: Several patched-together soaking boxes lined with plastic nestle into a grassy hillside a short distance apart. The springs range from 116-123 degrees F/46.5-50.5 degrees C. Lengths of pipe carry water from the source to the tubs, and the pipes can be diverted for a cooler soak. The springs have a high lithium content, and many visitors fill bottles of the stuff to take home.

Halcyon is on private land but open to the public. Like St. Leon, it's the site of a hotel dating back to gold rush days. No sign remains of past use, but there's talk of possible future development. The soaking boxes here are frequently filled to capacity, and the area shows some signs of abuse. The best feature at Halcyon is the sweeping view of the Monashee Mountains across the long expanse of Upper Arrow Lake.

Travelers heading farther north could try the 1.5-mi/2.5-km stroll to tiny Pingston Lake or climb the steep 3.7-mi/6-km Mount Begbie Trail to the toe of the glacier. Crossing the icefall to the summit requires mountaineering skills. A chain of lakes west of the peak is accessible by an alpine route. Both of these hikes are located near Highway 23 on the stretch between Shelter Bay and Revelstoke and are administered by the Revelstoke Forest District. Or you could save your energy for a choice of hikes in Mount Revelstoke or Glacier National Park.

Those traveling south could drive up to Nakusp Hot Springs, a city-owned plunge, and take either a scenic 0.5-mi/0.75-km-loop stroll on the Cedar Trail or a strenuous 2.5-mi/4-km trek to Kimbol Lake. A good option farther south is the climb to Saddle Mountain (Hike 31). The Arrow Forest District in Castlegar administers this area. The Travel Infocentre in Nakusp, open on weekends, can also shed light on local trails as well as on all three hot springs.

The East Kootenays Area Map

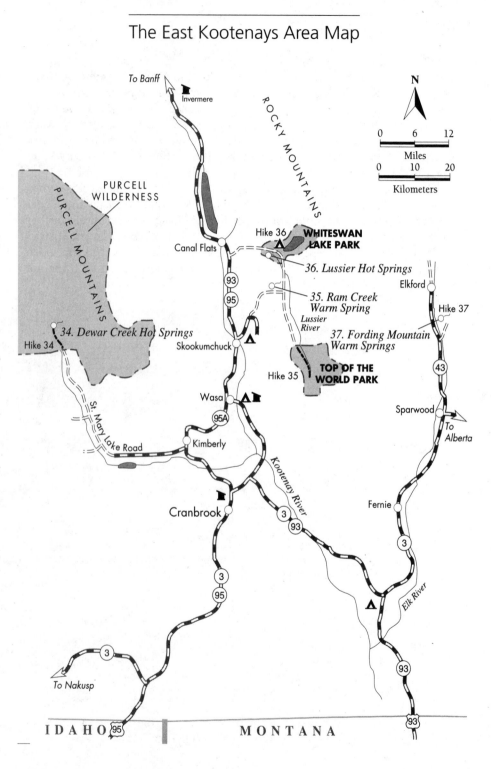

To Banff

Invermere

PURCELL WILDERNESS

PURCELL MOUNTAINS

ROCKY MOUNTAINS

N

0   6   12
Miles

0   10   20
Kilometers

Canal Flats

Hike 36

WHITESWAN LAKE PARK

36. Lussier Hot Springs

93

95

35. Ram Creek Warm Spring

Lussier River

34. Dewar Creek Hot Springs

Hike 34

Skookumchuck

37. Fording Mountain Warm Springs

Elkford

Hike 37

TOP OF THE WORLD PARK

Hike 35

43

St. Mary Lake Road

Wasa

95A

Sparwood

To Alberta

Kimberly

Kootenay River

Cranbrook

3

93

Fernie

3

3

95

Elk River

To Nakusp

3

IDAHO   95

MONTANA

93

93

34 Dewar Creek Hot Springs

At Dewer Creek Hot Springs, one side of me sizzled while the other side froze.

HIKE 34 *To Dewar Creek Hot Springs*

General description:	A remote day hike or overnighter to geothermal wonders and a dicey dip in the Purcell Wilderness. Extremely skinnydippable.
Difficulty:	Moderate.
Distance:	12 mi/19.3 km round trip.
General location:	The East Kootenays.
Elevation gain:	200 ft/61 m.
High point:	Hot springs, 4,800 ft/1,463 m.
Hiking quads:	Kaslo 82F/15 and Dewar Creek 82F/16 NTS.
Road map:	Cranbrook Forest District.
Contact:	BC Parks, East Kootenay District.

Finding the trailhead: From Cranbrook, take Highway 95A north to Marysville, which is one stop before Kimberly. Turn left on St. Mary Lake

Road and head west past the lake, where pavement turns to gravel. The main road follows the St. Mary River, curving northwest past a side road at Redding Creek.

When you reach another road branching left signed "West Fork St. Mary Road," 35 mi/56 km from Marysville, bear right on Dewar Creek Road. Head north up the main valley on a deteriorating surface that peters out in 5 mi/8 km in a meadowed camping area. Neither the path nor the hot springs are marked on the maps.

The challenge: The geothermal display at Dewar Creek is guaranteed to take your breath away. Both the steaming springs and the wild setting are visually stunning. But the access to this remote fairyland can be a different story, as is the problem of blending temperatures for a proper soak.

Both the roads and the trail are subject to spring washouts, and visitors should check with the Park Service before setting out. The roads get progressively rougher even when intact; it's also a bit of a navigational challenge to follow them. The path isn't too difficult in dry weather but becomes a quagmire when damp.

The hike: The Dewar Creek Trail into the Purcell Wilderness Conservancy can be found west of the clearing. The path plunges into a twilight forest of Douglas-fir and Engelmann spruce dotted with stands of aspen and birch. You'll soon cross a major stream on a footbridge, then continue through woods along the east bank of Dewar Creek. Many small side streams intersect the route, and the ground tends to stay damp. Huge puddles of ankle-deep mud alternate with meadows laced with blue lupine and pale pink paintbrush. The path eventually emerges onto a broad promontory opposite the climber's route to Leaning Towers.

Camping isn't allowed at the hot springs, but there's a campsite at Bugle Basin on a bench above the creek, just a 5-minute walk upstream. A rock outcrop there is a good spot to observe wildlife in the early mornings.

The hot springs: The bluff is shrouded by billowing clouds of steam. Tendrils of 180-degree F/82-degree C water issue from a multitude of fractures in the travertine and drop over the rocky bank into a small pool at the base. Meanwhile, ice cold creek water enters between the rocks that dam the outer edge. As a consequence, one side of you will be roasting while the other side freezes, and the hot and cold currents don't stay blended without constant stirring. There's no siesta time in this pool—staying comfortable is a full-time job!

In the winter, thermal heating around the springs creates a hole in the surrounding blanket of deep snow, and special plants and lichen keep the area green all year. Deer and elk are attracted to the tender shoots, and an occasional mountain goat scrambles by to sample the mineral licks.

The springs are spectacular any time of year, but the prime time for a soak is around the middle of August. Before then the streamside soaking

Dewar Creek Hot Springs

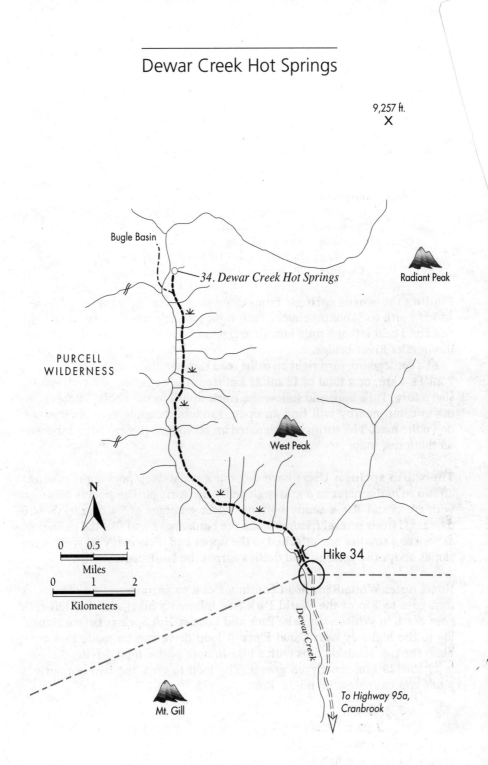

9,257 ft.
X

Bugle Basin

34. Dewar Creek Hot Springs

Radiant Peak

PURCELL
WILDERNESS

West Peak

N

0	0.5	1

Miles

0	1	2

Kilometers

Hike 34

Dewar Creek

Mt. Gill

To Highway 95a,
Cranbrook

pool might still be partly submerged, and by September it could be high and dry. With an icy torrent on one side and a waterfall of scalding water on the other, there's not much room for error.

35 Ram Creek Warm Springs

General description:	Warm pools on a hillside above a dirt road. Swimwear advised, especially on weekends.
Elevation:	4,800 ft/1,463 m.
General location:	The East Kootenays.
Map:	Invermere or Cranbrook Forest District.
Contact:	BC Forests, Invermere Forest District.

Finding the warm springs: From Cranbrook, take Highway 93/95 30 mi/ 48 km north to Skookumchuck. Turn right just past town on Premier Lake Road and bear left at 5 mi/8 km. Turn right at another mile/1.6 km and cross the Lussier River bridge.

At a cattleguard, turn right on a dirt road signed "White-Ram" and follow it 7 mi/11.4 km, or a total of 13 mi/21 km from the highway, to a pullout at a sharp turn. Park here and follow the track uphill to the pools. Those wishing to camp nearby will find an open, random camping area about a km down the road. The springs, designated an ecological reserve, aren't marked on the forest map.

The warm springs: Users have dug out a waist-deep pool approximately 20 ft/6 m in diameter in a grassy slope by the springs. The pool is dammed with rocks and has a sandy bottom. Water emerges at 94 degrees F/34.6 degrees C from several fissures along the bank above and fills the main pool as well as a smaller one attached to the upper end. Poison ivy thrives on the slopes above the springs, and daisies carpet the landscape.

Road note: White-Ram Road continues east to an intersection. The right fork goes to Top of the World Park (see following hike), and the left fork goes north to Whiteswan Lake Park and Lussier Hot Springs before returning to the highway near Canal Flats. A loop drive can be made that combines the two roadside dips with a hike in both parks; total driving distance is 77 mi/123 km, mostly on gravel. The loop to only the two hot springs totals approximately 58 mi/93 km.

Ram Creek Warm Springs • Lussier (Whiteswan) Hot Springs • Whiteswan Lake

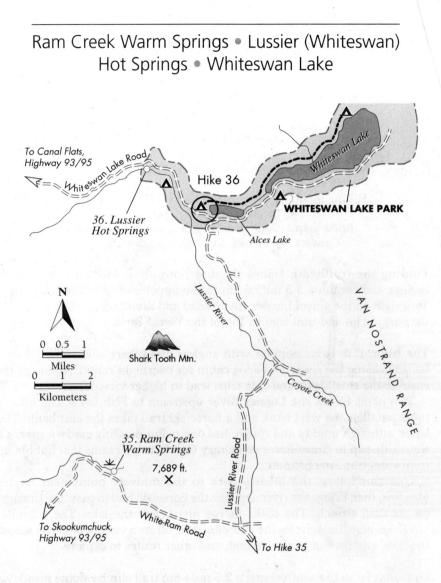

To Canal Flats, Highway 93/95

Whiteswan Lake Road

Hike 36

36. Lussier Hot Springs

WHITESWAN LAKE PARK

Whiteswan Lake

Alces Lake

N

0   0.5   1
Miles

0   1   2
Kilometers

Shark Tooth Mtn.

Lussier River

VAN NOSTRAND RANGE

Coyote Creek

35. Ram Creek Warm Springs

7,689 ft.
X

Lussier River Road

To Skookumchuck, Highway 93/95

White-Ram Road

To Hike 35

HIKE 35 *Fish Lake*

General description:	A day hike or backpack to a popular lake in the Rocky Mountains, near Ram Creek Warm Springs.
Difficulty:	Easy.
Distance:	7.5 mi/12 km round trip.
General location:	The East Kootenays.
Elevation gain:	+700 ft/212 m, -250 ft/76 m.
High point:	5,800 ft/1,768 m at Fish Lake.
Hiking quad:	Queen Creek 82G/14 NTS or Top of the World Park brochure.
Road map:	Cranbrook Forest District or park brochure.
Contact:	BC Parks, East Kootenay District.

Finding the trailhead: Follow the directions above to Ram Creek Warm Springs and continue 3.5 mi/5.6 km to the upper end of White-Ram Road. Turn right on the gravel Lussier River Road and drive 9.3 mi/15 km south to the parking lot and trail sign in Top of the World Park.

The hike: Fish Lake, popular with anglers and hikers alike, offers scenic tentsites along the shore and a log cabin for overnight rental. Alpine peaks encircle the small lake, and side trips lead to higher viewpoints.

Two paths follow the Lussier River upstream to Fish Lake. The hiker's route parallels the west bank and a horse/ski trail takes the east bank. The latter, although muddy and rough, has one major drawing card—it makes a short side trip to Crazy River and Crazy Creek, two streams that bubble up from subterranean channels.

One can follow the hiker's path to the midway point near Sayles Meadow, then bridge the river and take the horse/ski trail to pass "the Crazies" on the final stretch. The paths merge just below the lake. The 1.2-mi/2-km Lakeshore Trail circles the shoreline and offers a variety of views across the lake, glimpses of peaks beyond, and other routes to explore.

Options: From the south shore, a 2.5-mi/4-km trail climbs alpine meadows to Summer Pass with a gain of 1,410 ft/430 m. Nearby, a 2-mi/3.2-km scramble on scree slopes gains nearly 2,000 ft/600 m to Alpine Viewpoint and offers panoramic views of the Lussier Valley as well as of Mount Morro. Morro, at 9,554 ft/2,912 m the highest point in the park, dominates the Van Nostrand Range to the east. From the west shore, a 1.7-mi/2.8-km path climbs to Sparkle Lake with a gain of 1,148 ft/350 m, while an offshoot zigzags 2 mi/3.2 km up to Wildhorse Ridge. The stiff 3,000-ft/640-m gain is offset by views of nearby Dolomite Lake backed by Mount Doolan to the north plus jagged peaks of the Hughes Range to the west.

Fish Lake

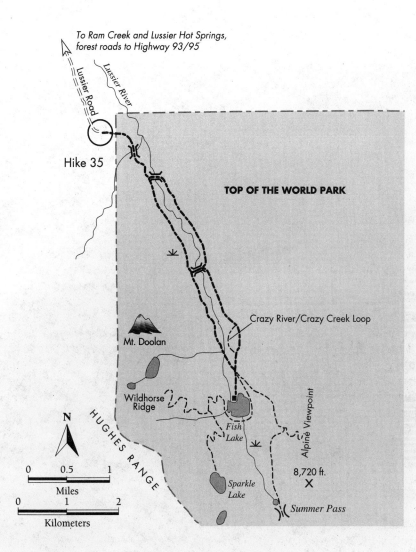

To Ram Creek and Lussier Hot Springs,
forest roads to Highway 93/95

Lussier River

Lussier Road

Hike 35

TOP OF THE WORLD PARK

Mt. Doolan

Crazy River/Crazy Creek Loop

Wildhorse
Ridge

Alpine Viewpoint

Fish
Lake

N

HUGHES RANGE

Sparkle
Lake

8,720 ft.
X

Summer Pass

0   0.5   1
Miles

0   1   2
Kilometers

The shoreline at Fish Lake offers glimpses across the silvered surface.

36 Lussier (Whiteswan) Hot Springs

General description:	Easy access riverside soaks in Whiteswan Lake Park. Swimwear required.
Elevation:	4,000 ft/1,219 m.
General location:	The East Kootenays.
Map:	Cranbrook Forest District.
Contact:	BC Parks, East Kootenay District.

Finding the hot springs: The most direct route to Lussier is to take Highway 93/95 north from Cranbrook to Whiteswan Lake Road, which is located 19 mi/30 km past Skookumchuck and 3 mi/4.8 km south of Canal Flats. Drive 10.5 dusty mi/17 km east into tiny Whiteswan Lake Park. The signed turnout is just inside the park boundary, and a covered stairway drops down the steep bank to the riverside pools.

The alternate route, a loop drive combining Ram Creek and Lussier Springs, can be located by following the directions and road note in 35 above past Ram Creek to the Lussier River Road. Turn left and follow the gravel logging road 9.5 mi/15.2 km north to Whiteswan Lake Road. Go left for 2 mi/3.2 km to Lussier. The springs aren't marked on the forest map.

The hot springs: Visitors will find a chain of rock-lined soaking pools along a gravel beach on the scenic Lussier River. All have comfortable sandy bottoms and are kept clean by the ample flow of the springs. The popular pools are accessible all year thanks to the logging trucks, and the uppermost pool should be above water even during spring runoff.

The springs bubble first into a small wooden tub that registers 110 degrees F/43.3 degrees C, then flow beneath a deck into a large and very toasty soaking pool. The outflow, tempered by a trickle from a cold spring, fills another large soaker just below. Succeeding pools, each slightly cooler than the one above, emerge as the river recedes through the summer.

HIKE 36 *Whiteswan Lake*

General description:	A day hike in a tiny park in the Rocky Mountains, near Lussier Hot Springs.
Difficulty:	Easy.
Distance:	Up to 7 mi/11.2 km round trip.
General location:	The East Kootenays.
Elevation gain:	Minimal.
High point:	4,000 ft/1,219 m.
Map:	Cranbrook Forest District.
Contact:	BC Parks, East Kootenay District.

Moose can often be seen browsing at Whiteswan Lake.

Finding the trailhead: Follow the directions above to Lussier and drive 2 mi/3.2 km east to the junction of Whiteswan Lake and Lussier River Road. The trailhead is located in nearby Alces Lake Campground.

The hike: Whiteswan Lake is nestled in a small but popular park that offers pleasant mountain scenery and excellent fishing. The 2.5-mile/4-km long Whiteswan Lake, along with tiny Alces Lake, are both stocked annually with 30,000 rainbow trout. Several family campgrounds accommodate the weekend crowds, and a fisherman's path·skirts the north shores of both lakes.

The lakeshore route begins at the west end of Alces Lake and hugs the rocky shore to a picnic site at the far end, then follows the meadowed inlet stream to the larger lake. One can look back past Alces to rugged Shark Tooth Mountain and other peaks across the Lussier Valley.

Whiteswan Lake sits just below White Knight Peak, but the upper slopes can't be seen from the trail. Looking south, the route offers increasing glimpses of the Van Nostrand Range. Pass a boater's camp about midway along; the path ends at Home Basin Campground at the northeast tip of the lake.

37 Fording Mountain (Sulphur) Warm Springs

HIKE 37 *To Fording Mountain Warm Springs*

General description:	A day hike to a thermal pond in the Elk River Valley. Swimwear advised if others present.
Difficulty:	Easy.
Distance:	2 mi/3.2 km round trip.
General location:	The East Kootenays.
Elevation gain:	Minimal.
Warm springs:	4,100 ft/1,250 m.
Map:	Cranbrook Forest District.
Contact:	BC Forests, Cranbrook Forest District.

Finding the trailhead: From Cranbrook, take Highway 3 about 78 miles/ 125 km to Sparwood and continue north on Highway 43. Make a right turn midway between Sparwood and Elkford and bridge the confluence of the Elk and Fording rivers. The final approach up the Elk River Valley is via a series of active and inactive logging roads. Contact the Forest Service in Cranbrook or the logging camp in Sparwood regarding the current route. The maps can't keep pace with the changing roads, and the springs aren't marked.

The hike: The last mile/1.6 km is over an old road that's now closed to motor vehicles. It leads through an evergreen forest to meadowed slopes above the Elk River. The route emerges near the springs at the upper end of a clearing. There is a small campground just beyond the springs and a view across the river valley to mountain ranges farther west.

The warm springs: One spring emerges from at least two outlets at the bottom of a large oval-shaped pond. Unfortunately, the temperature hovers around 76 degrees F/24.4 degrees C, but the pond looks like a classic swimming hole and even sports a diving board. The outflow snakes across the meadow, and a second spring bubbles to the surface at 78 degrees F/25.5 degrees C a couple of bends downstream.

Fording Mountain Warm Springs has a very high sulphur content and the associated smell of rotten eggs. The highly mineralized water attracts a variety of wildlife, and one can sometimes see moose, deer, and elk grazing nearby. The poplar-lined meadow, a pleasant spot to pitch a tent, doesn't see many visitors.

Fording Mountain Warm Springs

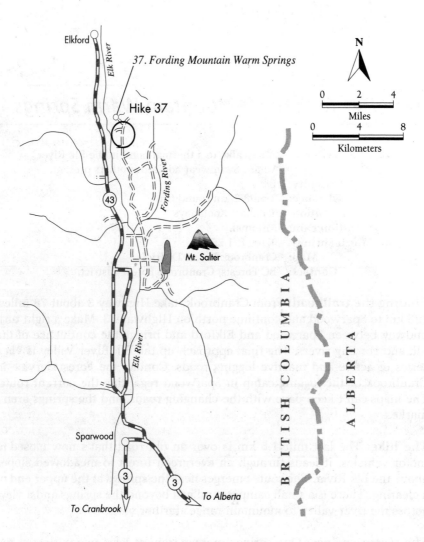

Elkford

Elk River

37. Fording Mountain Warm Springs

Hike 37

N

| 0 | 2 | 4 |
Miles

| 0 | 4 | 8 |
Kilometers

Fording River

43

Mt. Salter

Elk River

BRITISH COLUMBIA

ALBERTA

Sparwood

3

3

To Alberta

To Cranbrook

Idaho

AN OVERVIEW

The state of Idaho contains more than twice the number of geothermal gems than the thirty-eight described in Oregon, Washington, and British Columbia combined! This is truly an amazing fact. The eighty shown on the Idaho Locator Map are all located in prime hiking areas in national forests. Nearly a third lie either near the edge or well within the boundaries of protected wilderness areas. Still, surprisingly few backcountry buffs visit the "Potato State." Even the spectacular Sawtooths, congested by Idaho's standards, seem deserted to hikers accustomed to fighting the summer crowds in the Cascades or Olympics.

Compared to Oregon and Washington, the backcountry of Idaho is far less developed. Few forest roads are paved, many involve the time-consuming process of skirting rocks and potholes, and most cover vast distances in an endless cloud of dust.

Free campgrounds are a thing of the past, but persistent purists will have no trouble finding dispersed campsites. The hikes often involve wading, log balancing, or rock hopping. But Idaho's hot springs make up for any minor inconvenience. Most get relatively little use or abuse, and those reached by the longer access roads or located a few miles up a trail see few visitors at all.

Access areas A through K: Idaho's best hot springs are located in the central mountain ranges. They're grouped here by similar road access into the eleven areas shown on the Locator Map. These areas are grouped according to approach routes instead of political or wilderness boundaries so that the greedy gourmet with limited time may sample several on the same trip.

A tiny north-central area, covered in the first section of text (A), is located between Lewiston and Missoula, MT, via U.S. Highway 12. It lies along the Lochsa River in Clearwater National Forest. One of the springs here is tucked away in the Selway-Bitterroot Wilderness.

A west-central region, described in the next six areas (B through G), is accessed north and northeast of Boise via State Routes 55 and 21, and northeast of Mountain Home by US 20. It includes the backcountry west of the Sawtooth crest and extends north to the Salmon River and into the southwestern quarter of the River of No Return Wilderness. Outside of the two wildlands, the hot soaks and hikes are located in the rolling mountains of Payette, Boise, and Sawtooth national forests.

An east-central region, covered in the final four areas (H through K), is accessible north of Twin Falls via SR 75 and northwest of Pocatello and

Idaho Locator Map

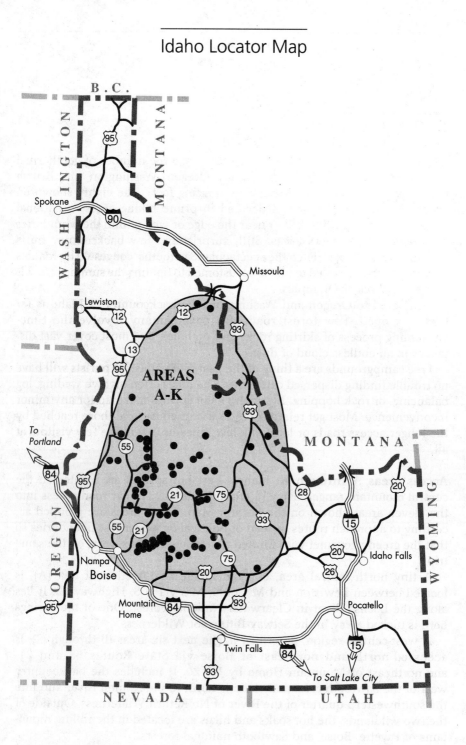

Idaho A–K Area Map

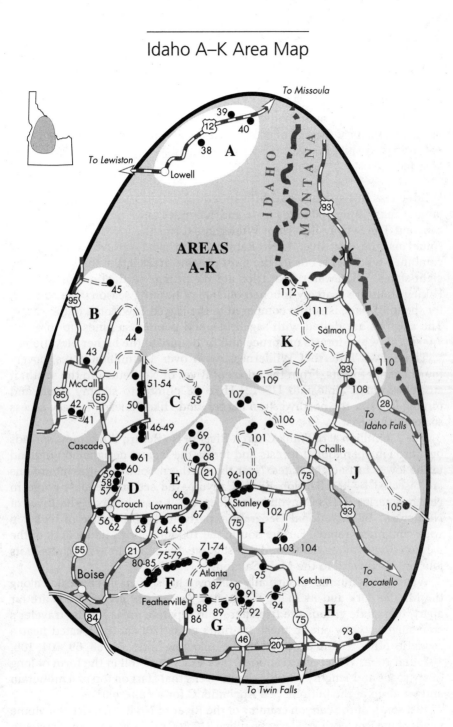

To Missoula

39
12
40
38
A

To Lewiston

Lowell

IDAHO
MONTANA
93

AREAS
A-K

45
95
B
44
43
McCall
95 55
51-54
50
C
55
42
41
Cascade
46-49
69
70
68
61
59 60
58
57 D
Crouch Lowman
66
56 62 63 64 65
67
21
E
96-100
101
106
107
109
112
111
Salmon
K
110
93
108
To
Idaho Falls
28
Challis
75
J
102
105
75
I
103, 104
Stanley
95
71-74
75-79
80-85
F
Atlanta
95
87 90
91
94
Ketchum
To
Pocatello
Featherville
88 89 92
86
G
75
H
93
55
Boise
21
84
46
20

To Twin Falls

Idaho Falls by U.S. highways 26 and 93. It consists mainly of the eastern side of the Sawtooths and the Sawtooth National Recreation Area plus the eastern half of the River of No Return Wilderness and adjacent mountains. This rugged country is administered by Sawtooth and Salmon/Challis national forests, and the Bureau of Land Management.

At the beginning of each area, you'll find a summary of the hot springs, hikes, and the best season for soaking. You'll also find an area map marking hot springs and hikes as well as back roads, campgrounds, ranger stations, and land features.

Wilderness hot springs and hikes: Central Idaho is composed of a mountainous mass, fully 100 miles wide and 300 miles long, etched by deep river canyons. The Selway-Bitterroot Wilderness forms the northern third of this spine, and the vast River of No Return fills in most of the remainder. The combined wildland is one of the most pristine areas left in the lower forty-eight states. Whitewater float trips are the primary attraction for tourists. Hiking trails are scarcely touched outside of hunting season. The scenery, for the most part, is subtle compared to the jagged Sawtooths to the south. The canyons are dotted with sagebrush and ponderosa pines up to about 7,000 feet, while forests of spruce and fir dominate the higher elevations.

The Selway-Bitterroot Wilderness, with over 1.3 million acres, covers four national forests. From the adjacent River of No Return to the south, it stretches north almost to US 12. Hike 38 climbs to steamy pools and remote lakes in the northwestern corner, and Hike 40 leads to easy-access soaks farther east.

The 2.3-million acre Frank Church-River of No Return Wilderness spreads out through six national forests and forms the largest designated wildland in the lower forty-eight states. Near the northern boundary, the mountains are bisected by the Salmon River Canyon—the second deepest gorge in North America (Hells Canyon is the deepest). It was dubbed "The River of No Return" by a National Geographic party in 1935 because of its steep walls and many rapids. Farther south, the 100-mile-long Middle Fork of the Salmon River carves the third deepest gorge, bisecting the wilderness in its journey northward to the Main Salmon.

A surprising number of virtually unknown hot springs lie concealed along the Middle Fork and its many tributaries. As the few access roads are far apart, this guide groups the trips here into separate areas for the traveler's convenience. Only one of these far-flung gems (70) can be located near a road; the other ten are accessed by the following hikes: 55, 68, 69, 101, 106, 107, and 109a. With few exceptions, they exact their toll in the form of long dusty roads and lengthy "upside-down" treks that start on top of a mountain and wind up at the bottom. See Appendix C for an alternative.

Just south of the canyon country of the River of No Return rise the alpine peaks of the Sawtooth Wilderness, filling 217,000 prime acres of the Sawtooth NRA. The Sawtooths draw hikers along 300 miles of well-tended paths through an intricate landscape of colorful granite shaped into countless needle-edged spires, peaks, and ridges. Small lakes and streams are fringed with postage stamp meadows lush with wildflowers and forests of spruce, fir, and pine. The area boasts more than forty-two peaks reaching over 10,000 feet.

The Sawtooths contain only one known hike-in hot spring (74). But they also offer several roadside springs not far from major trailheads. On the east side of the range, hot dips located in the Sawtooth NRA (96–100) may be alternated with popular hikes into the high country (96a–c). On the west side, trailhead soaks and less congested paths out of Grandjean (67a,b) and Atlanta (73a–c) do much to make up for the extra mileage on both tires and boots.

A. OUT OF KAMIAH

AN OVERVIEW

Hot springs and hikes: U.S. Highway 12 bisects north-central Idaho between Lewiston and Missoula, Montana, following the Lochsa River through lush Clearwater National Forest to an area spanning the 65 miles

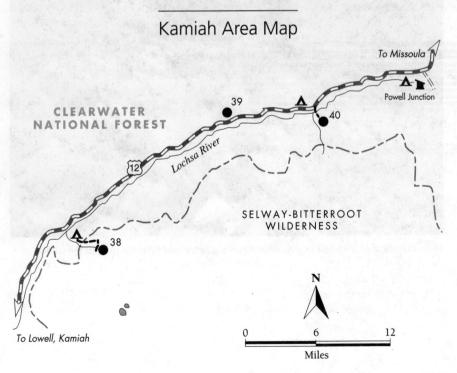

Kamiah Area Map

between Lowell and Powell Junction. A quiet trail in the Selway-Bitterroot Wilderness leads to hot soaks at Stanley (38). Twenty miles up the highway comes a toasty soak at Weir Creek (39). And 10 miles east up the road, comes a stroll to the ever-popular Jerry Johnson (40).

Season: Hot soaks at Stanley are best on cooler days from late spring through fall. The streamside path to Weir Creek limits access during spring runoff. Jerry Johnson, however, has easy access on packed snow through the winter, and the uppermost pools are usable year-round. Summer weather tends to be hot, and thunderstorms are fairly common.

38 Stanley Hot Springs

Soaking pools at Stanley Hot Springs offer hikers a quiet retreat from the cares of the world.

HIKE 38 *To Stanley Hot Springs*

General description:	A rugged day hike or overnighter to soaks in an age old forest, in the Selway-Bitterroot Wilderness. Swimwear optional.
Difficulty:	Moderate.
Distance:	11 miles round trip.
General location:	54 miles east of Kamiah.
Elevation gain:	+1,620 feet, -120 feet.
High point:	Hot springs, 3,600 feet.
Hiking quad:	Huckleberry Butte USGS.
Road map:	Clearwater National Forest.
Contact:	Lochsa Ranger District, Clearwater National Forest.

Finding the trailhead: From Kamiah, take U.S. Highway 12 about 28 miles east to Lowell and continue 26 miles to Wilderness Gateway Campground. Go past Loops A and B, and the amphitheater, to Trail 211 parking area. The springs are marked only on the USGS quad.

The hike: Trail 211 climbs a few switchbacks and then traverses a hillside well above Boulder Creek to enter the Selway-Bitterroot Wilderness at 2 miles. The elevated route lacks shade but provides a number of pleasant views up and down the wide valley. Bracken fern and thimbleberries line the path and cover the surrounding slopes between islands of Douglas-fir and pines.

At a signed trail junction at 5 miles, take the right fork (221) marked "to Huckleberry Flat." The path drops downhill to cross Boulder Creek on a rustic log footbridge and enters a dark forest with a plush green carpet. Continue south along the edge of Huckleberry Creek and you'll find the soaking pools in a large clearing above the trail just beyond some tentsites which are currently closed for restoration.

Note: The Forest Service says the footbridge over Boulder Creek is becoming hazardous and has posted signs accordingly. If it should fail, there are no plans to replace it in the near future.

The hot springs: Water steams out of a canyon bank at 120 degrees, tumbles through a chain of delectable hot pools, then continues past the trail to the creek below. Each pool is lined with logs that form a triangular enclosure, and the temperature can be fine tuned by shifting rocks to admit as much cold water as desired. Enjoy your stay, but please treat the fragile ecosystem around the springs with the respect it deserves. Remember to practice low-impact camping techniques.

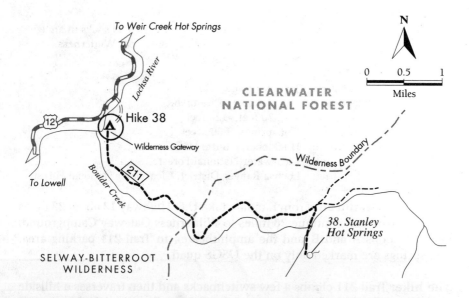

N

CLEARWATER
NATIONAL FOREST

0   0.5   1

Miles

To Weir Creek Hot Springs

Lochsa River

12

Hike 38

Wilderness Gateway

211

To Lowell

Boulder Creek

Wilderness Boundary

38. Stanley
Hot Springs

SELWAY-BITTERROOT
WILDERNESS

39 Weir Creek Hot Springs

General description:	A popular pool cloaked in greenery at the end of a primitive 0.5-mile creekside path. Swimwear optional.
Elevation:	2,900 feet.
General location:	73 miles from either Kamiah or Missoula, MT.
Map:	Clearwater National Forest.
Contact:	Powell Ranger District, Clearwater National Forest.

Finding the hot springs: From Kamiah, take U.S. Highway 12, 28 miles east to Lowell and continue 45 miles. Park in a pullout along the Lochsa River just east of Milepost 142. Parking can be a problem on summer weekends. Follow a slippery path up the west bank of the creek to reach the pool. The springs are named on the forest map.

The hot springs: A delightful pool sits under a canopy of evergreens above a lively creek. It's bordered by split logs and features a slab rock/sand bottom. The water is constantly cleaned by the ample flow from the 117-degree springs; the temperature can be lowered with the aid of a removable wooden gutter. If the gutter's gone, you're in for a very toasty soak.

Key-note: *I returned to my locked car after a dip to discover the key still hanging in the ignition. I was 80 miles from the nearest town, the sun was sinking fast, and my camping gear was in plain view but out of reach. Just when I'd absorbed these cold facts, a passing motorist came to the rescue. With a piece of fence wire bent into a loop, he fished for the doorlock pull through a slit in the window while I pulled down on the glass. He managed to ring it after several misses, but the loop slid off the slick-sided pull as soon as he tugged, thanks to modern burglar-proof engineering. By this time I'd lost all hope, but my determined new friend had not. He eventually succeeded in hooking the key ring itself, maneuvered it out of the ignition, and inched it out through the slit in the window! We immediately drank a toast to success with the cold beer liberated from my cooler.*

40 Jerry Johnson Hot Springs

HIKE 40 *To Jerry Johnson Hot Springs*

General description:	A day hike to popular soaks in a scenic valley. A skinnydipper's delight.
Difficulty:	Easy.
Distance:	2 miles round trip.
General location:	83 miles northeast of Kamiah or 62 miles southwest of Missoula, MT.
Elevation gain:	150 feet.
High point:	Hot springs, 3,200 feet.
Hiking quad:	Selway-Bitterroot Wilderness.
Road map:	Same or Clearwater National Forest.
Contact:	Powell Ranger District, Clearwater National Forest.

Finding the trailhead: Take U.S. Highway 12, 55 miles northeast of Lowell (or 10.5 miles southwest of Powell Junction) to Warm Springs Pack Bridge, which spans the Lochsa River 0.5 mile west of Milepost 152. There's ample parking nearby, but make sure to get your gear out of sight and lock up. "Car clouting" has long been a problem here. The springs are named on the forest map but omitted on the wilderness quad.

The hike: Three separate hot springs, each with two or more soaking pools, lie near a creek in a broad valley forested with stately old-growth cedar and grand fir. Cross the pack bridge to the sign for Warm Springs Creek Trail (49). A second sign sometimes posted on a nearby tree states a warning that unclothed bathers or hikers may be found beyond this point.

This is indeed the case at "J.J." Follow the sneaker-worn path a short mile upvalley to the springs.

The hot springs: The first batch of rock-lined soaking pools, known to many as "the waterfall pools," are down the bank from the trail, right at waterline by midsummer. These late-season pools are easy to miss if unoccupied. They need a creek water mix to drop into the comfort zone, as 115-degree water gushing from holes in the steep bank pours directly into one pool after the other.

You can't miss the next user-friendly group of pools. The broad outflow from the second spring crosses right over the trail en route to the creek. The hottest pool sits just above the path, and steamy rivulets lead over the rocks to more dips by the creek. These rocky pools vary in size and temperature; it isn't hard to find one that's just right.

The third spring, a short way beyond the others in a grassy meadow above the trail, has two rock-and-mud soaking pools. One is over knee-deep and large enough to float several cozy bodies; it maintains a steady 106 degrees without a mix from the creek. However, the silty bottom is easily stirred up. If you plan on climbing out clean, you'll have to find some means of doing it without standing up. Lots of luck!

Nighttime closure: Due to a variety of overuse and abuse problems arising from the year-round popularity of the springs, the Forest Service has been forced to turn Jerry Johnson into a day use area, 6 A.M. to 8 P.M. Nocturnal visits and overnight camping are no longer permitted. The new rules, posted at the trailhead, are strictly enforced.

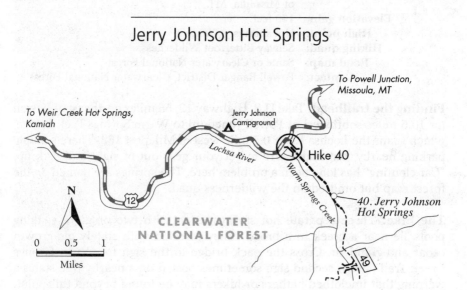

Jerry Johnson Hot Springs

To Powell Junction,
Missoula, MT

To Weir Creek Hot Springs,
Kamiah

Jerry Johnson
Campground

Lochsa River

Hike 40

40. Jerry Johnson
Hot Springs

N

Warm Springs Creek

12

49

CLEARWATER
NATIONAL FOREST

0   0.5   1

Miles

B. Out Of McCall

Hot springs and hikes: State Route 55, the Payette River Scenic Biway, runs south from McCall to Donnelly. To the west, a seasonal road along the Weiser River passes roadside baths at White Licks (41) and accesses a hike-in soak at Council Mountain (42). Next, a dirt road located between McCall and New Meadows hits a soak at popular Krigbaum (43). And northeast of town, back roads past Burgdorf lead the more adventurous hiker trekking to Secesh (44) and Cable Car Hot Springs (45). This area is in Payette National Forest.

Season: Winter road closures are the limiting factor on these springs. Soaks at Council Mountain and Cable Car are best in cooler weather. Krigbaum's pool escapes spring runoff and can be accessed in winter on cross-country skis. Wait until late summer to ford the river to Secesh. The hiking season varies with elevation; summer weather is generally warm to hot with scattered thundershowers.

The source at White Licks Hot Springs flows across a meadow and into two separate bathing shacks.

McCall Area Map

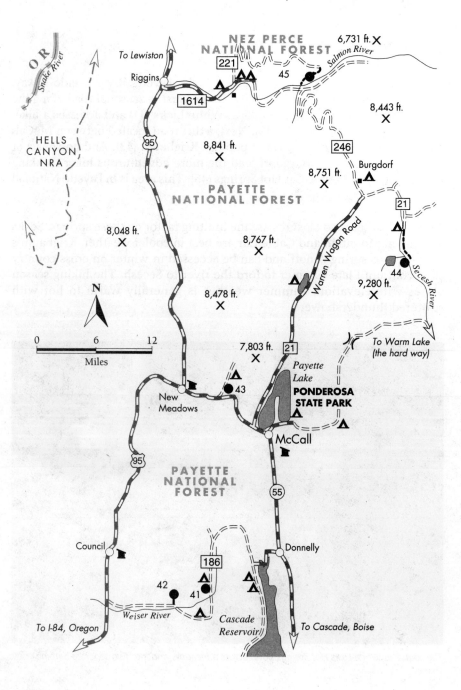

O R

Snake River

HELLS
CANYON
NRA

To Lewiston

Riggins

NEZ PERCE
NATIONAL FOREST

221

1614

95

6,731 ft. X

Salmon River

45

8,443 ft.
X

8,841 ft.
X

246

8,751 ft.
X

Burgdorf

21

PAYETTE
NATIONAL FOREST

8,048 ft.
X

8,767 ft.
X

44

Secesh River

9,280 ft.
X

8,478 ft.
X

Warren Wagon Road

N

0   6   12

Miles

7,803 ft.
X

21

Payette
Lake

PONDEROSA
STATE PARK

To Warm Lake
(the hard way)

New
Meadows

43

McCall

95

PAYETTE
NATIONAL
FOREST

55

Council

Donnelly

186

42

41

Weiser River

Cascade
Reservoir

To I-84, Oregon

To Cascade, Boise

41 White Licks Hot Springs

General description:	Roadside bathhouses in a camp on the Middle Fork Weiser River. Wear what you normally bathe in.
Elevation:	4,900 feet.
General location:	27 miles southwest of McCall.
Map:	Payette National Forest.
Contact:	Council Ranger District, Payette National Forest.

Finding the hot springs: From McCall, take State Route 55 south to Donnelly, where seasonal roads cross the mountains to U.S. Highway 95. Head west on Roseberry Road, signed to Rainbow Point Campgrounds, then left on Norwood and right on Tamarack Falls Road. Cross a bridge at Cascade Reservoir at 4 miles, where the pavement ends. Turn right on West Mountain Road, then left at a mile on No Business Road. Bear left after another 6 miles on the Middle Fork Weiser River Road (186), and reach White Licks 4 miles later. The springs, named on the forest map, are 15 miles west of Donnelly or 18 miles east of US 95.

The hot springs: Two small shacks, each housing a concrete bathing tub, sit in a grassy flat bordered by riverside woods. Each tub has two inlet pipes fed by the springs. One pipe runs up to 20 degrees hotter than the other; the temperatures are also said to vary depending on the outside air. Adjust the heat by plugging either pipe, and drain and clean the tubs each after use. The rustic bathhouses and primitive camp, on a parcel owned by Boise Cascade, are free of charge and maintained by users.

42 Council Mountain (Laurel) Hot Springs

HIKE 42 *To Council Mountain Hot Springs*

General description:	A day hike climbing to hidden hot pools in a wooded ravine. Swimwear superfluous.
Difficulty:	Moderate.
Distance:	4 miles round trip.
General location:	36 miles southwest of McCall.
Elevation gain:	720 feet.
High point:	Hot springs, 4,480 feet.
Hiking quad:	Council Mountain USGS.
Road map:	Payette National Forest, West half.
Contact:	Council Ranger District, Payette National Forest.

Council Mountain Hot Springs

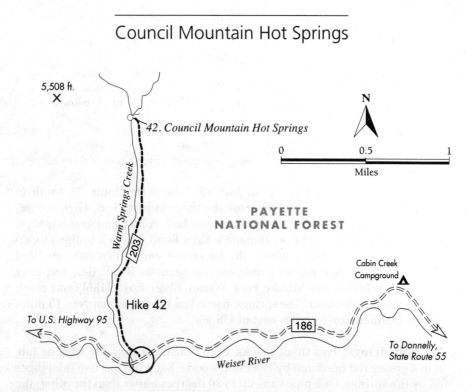

5,508 ft.
X

42. *Council Mountain Hot Springs*

N

0   0.5   1

Miles

PAYETTE
NATIONAL FOREST

Warm Springs Creek

203

Cabin Creek
Campground

Hike 42

To U.S. Highway 95

186

To Donnelly,
State Route 55

Weiser River

Finding the trailhead: Follow the directions above to White Licks and continue 9 miles. At Milepost 9, you'll reach the trailhead by a small pull-out. The springs, marked only on the USGS quad, are 24 miles west of Donnelly or 9 miles east of US 95.

The hike: Warm Springs Trail (203) is a steep and steady climb above the east bank of Warm Springs Creek, but a canopy of ponderosa and Douglas-fir shades the way. Keep an eye out for rattlesnakes in the summertime. The creek forks 2 miles upstream where the path drops to cross the water and continues up the other side. The hot springs, with a telltale border of orange algae, cascade down the rocky bank at the crossing.

The hot springs: There are two or more small and very hot pools in the bed of the creek just upstream. A shallow steamer at the base of the cascade checks in at 106 degrees and the springs above it are so hot that my digital thermometer stopped registering. A few yards downstream, the combined flow of hot and cold currents swirls down a slick waterslide into a bubbly Jacuzzi, and from there down yet another slide into the largest pool. This one registers approximately 92 degrees—just the ticket on a hot summer day.

43 Krigbaum (Last Chance) Hot Spring

General description:	A well-known soak above a forest road near McCall. Skinnydippable with discretion.
Elevation:	4,100 feet.
General location:	7 miles northwest of McCall.
Map:	Payette National Forest, either half.
Contact:	New Meadows Ranger District, Payette National Forest.

Finding the hot spring: From McCall, take State Route 55 west, 7 miles to Forest Road 453, signed to Last Chance Campground, at Milepost 152. The turnoff is 4 miles east of New Meadows. Follow the dirt road 0.3 mile up Goose Creek. Park by the bridge and take a short path up the east bank to the pool. Krigbaum is faintly marked on the forest map.

The hot spring: A curtain of trees hides Krigbaum's soaking pool from the road. Water from the 109-degree spring gushes from an overhead pipe into the rocky pool, and ample flow keeps it clean. Enclosed between boulders on the bank above Goose Creek, it's a pool big enough to pack maybe half a dozen human sardines side by side. The temperature runs 95 to 100 degrees.

This idyllic retreat gets heavily used through the summer and sometimes shows signs of abuse. It's on a private plot surrounded by national forest. The pool can be accessed and enjoyed year-round, but chances for a quiet soak are better in the off-season months. Please respect the landowner's rights and pack out what you pack in.

Note to hikers: For a pleasant half-day outing, drive 2 miles up to Last Chance Campground and take the Goose Creek Trail upstream to The Falls. It's a round trip of 5 miles that's easygoing except for a few stream fords, so it's best walked in late summer.

Krigbaum Hot Spring offers a quiet soak early in the day.

44 Secesh (Delta Mist, Whangdoodle) Hot Springs

HIKE 44 *To Secesh Hot Springs*

General description:	A late-season day hike or mountain bike ride to a lonesome hot spring on the wrong side of the Secesh River. Swimwear superfluous.
Difficulty:	Easy except for a major stream ford.
Distance:	8 miles round trip.
General location:	36 miles northeast of McCall.
Elevation gain:	140 feet.
High point:	Trailhead, 5,700 feet.
Hiking quad:	Loon Lake USGS.
Road map:	Payette National Forest, East half.
Contact:	McCall Ranger District, Payette National Forest.

Finding the trailhead: From the west side of McCall, take the Warren Wagon Road 28 miles northeast to a junction where the pavement ends. The left fork reaches Burgdorf Hot Springs Resort, a worthwhile stop, at 2 miles and continues on to Cable Car Hot Spring (see below). To reach Secesh, don't turn left here but continue straight for 6.7 miles, then right for 1.3 miles to Chinook Campground and the road-end trailhead. Secesh can't be found on any map but the state geothermal.

The hike: The Secesh River Trail (80) is a gentle descent through a deep canyon. The first 3.5-mile stretch reaches a bridge where most hikers cross to Loon Lake (a popular 10-mile round-trip hike or mountain bike ride). Don't cross the bridge but continue half a mile south to the Whangdoodle Trail sign. Then walk back up 50 yards and look across the river. That's your goal, but don't attempt a ford until late summer when the water is lower and slower.

The hot springs: Two small streams of scalding water tumble down to the river from source springs located high up the mountainside. Each channel cuts a broad swath through the forest, and each twists through a steep landslide of boulders. Rumor has it there's a hot pool buried somewhere in that jumble, maybe the one you've been looking for.

Note on names: The term *Secesh* was Civil War slang for "secessionist," or someone who sympathized with the South. During Gold Rush days, newcomers would be asked, "Are ye a Secesh?" Depending on the inquirer's

Secesh Hot Springs

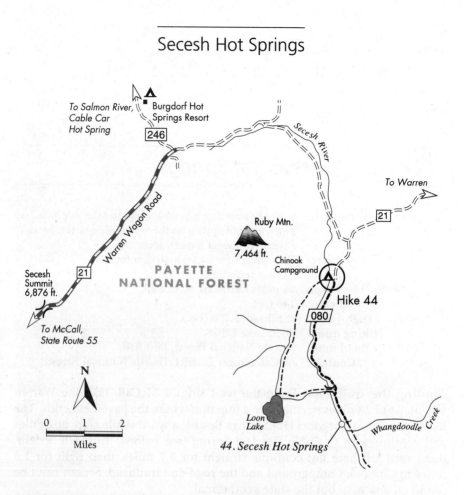

politics, the answer could bring a handshake or a fist. The name "Delta Mist" is used only by the most local of locals; it comes from a guy with a daughter named Delta. And the name "Whangdoodle" comes from the nearby creek.

Delta Drizzle: *When I was there in mid-July, the river was still too fast and deep to cross, so I tried a different approach. I retraced my steps to the bridge, started up the trail to Loon Lake until I could ford the creek, then tried bushwhacking the west riverbank. Impossible. The bank was too steep, the woods too thick, and the footing too slippery from pouring rain. After an hour of intense struggle, and beginning to look like something the cat dragged in, I called it quits and backtracked down the road for a "bird-in-the-hand" soak at Burgdorf.*

45 Cable Car (French Creek) Hot Spring

Cable Car Hot Spring features a giant log hollowed out into a long tub.

HIKE 45 *To Cable Car Hot Spring*

General description:	A major crossing plus a short climb to a one-of-a-kind hot spring, above the wrong side of the Salmon River. No need for a swimsuit.
Difficulty:	Problematic and strenuous.
Distance:	2 miles round trip.
General location:	58 miles north of McCall.
Elevation gain:	600 feet.
High point:	Hot springs, 2,520 feet.
Map:	Payette National Forest, East half or Nez Perce National Forest.
Contact:	Canyon Cats.

The choices: The first choice is the road. From McCall via Riggins it's 63 miles with all but the last 6 miles on pavement. Via Burgdorf, it's 58 miles but only 30 miles are paved. If you're already soaking at Burgdorf the choice is simple—it's just 26 dusty miles farther. And Burgdorf Hot Springs, though commercial, is so delightfully funky that it makes a perfect stopover between Secesh and Cable Car Hot Springs.

The second choice is access to the hot spring, which sits on the wrong side of the river. And this is the mighty "River of No Return." Don't mess with this one. The map shows a bridge 5 miles downstream with a trail back on the far side, but it crosses a parcel with no public access. There is also a lengthy drive above the far side that accesses a steep trek to the spring via Scott Saddle.

There happens to be a far easier approach. During the float season, which usually runs from Memorial Day to Labor Day, the main Salmon River becomes a busy highway with dozens of boats out every day. All you need to do is hitch a ride across. Simple as pie if you don't mind waiting for a lift. Or you could bring your own raft or canoe or kayak. There's a boat ramp 4 miles upstream at Carey Creek and one downstream at Spring Bar. When the river is just right, you can even paddle across on an inner tube (with a life jacket).

Finding the trailhead: From McCall, take the Warren Wagon Road 28 miles northeast to a junction where pavement ends. The continuing road leads to Secesh (see above). Turn left on Forest Road 246 at the sign "Burgdorf Hot Springs 2 miles." After the obligatory soak, proceed 26 miles on a surface that deteriorates as the scenery improves; the final switchbacks are awesome. At the bottom is a junction where the Salmon River Road bridges French Creek. There's a log house here that belongs to the friendly owners of "Canyon Cats," who run river trips on state of the art Catarafts, which make frequent stops at the hot spring.

Park a quarter mile upstream near the old tram shack. You can scramble down the rocks here to thumb your way across, or drive a tad farther to a "Leaving Payette Forest" sign where an even cruder path plunges down the bank to a gravel bar. A raft could beach at either spot. The hot spring isn't marked on any map but the state geothermal. Even there it's misnamed Cow Flats and shown as an area 1,200 feet higher up the hill where nobody has ever seen a hot spring.

The crossing: The rocky cove below the shack is directly across from a tiny beach, so a straight shot for any able-bodied rafter. However, the spot upstream can be spotted sooner, doesn't need such adroit paddling skills, and lands you at a beach favored for lunch breaks, thereby letting you out before the stop. Potential rides taper off by around 4 P.M., so be sure you don't dally too long in the tub or you might find yourself stranded at The Hot Spring of No Return.

Cable Car Hot Spring

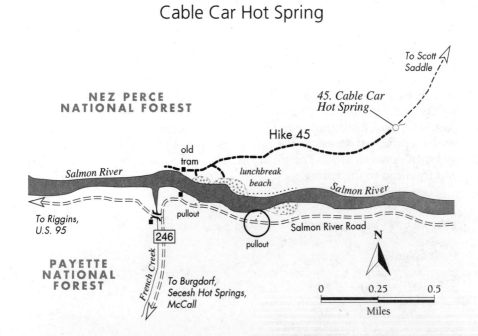

The hike: From both landing sites, paths zigzag up to join the main trail not far from the old tram. The trail makes a beeline up the grassy hill, then curves in through a stretch of midsummer blackberries and bouncing grasshoppers. Keep an eye peeled for poison ivy and rattlesnakes. One more long shadeless stretch takes you around a bend and into a small ravine, where you'll find what you've come this far to discover.

The hot spring: First, find a rocky tunnel filled with 95-degree water on the floor and a bevy of bats on the ceiling. If you're quiet you won't disturb them, and vice versa. It's a weird experience to climb in and walk back a few feet, knee deep in warm water, if you can stand the heady aroma.

Around the bend is a log bathhouse straddling the spring. A wide entrance and windows let in light while the roof keeps out the hot sun. Inside, you'll find a giant ponderosa log hollowed out into a tub. Steamy 100-degree water enters through a pipe; it can be drained like a whirlpool through a large hole in the bottom. The slick surface makes for a most comfortable soak.

Rumor has it that the spring sprung into being when a miner digging in the nearby shaft struck hot water instead of gold. Could that explain the missing Cow Flats Hot Spring up the hill listed on the state geothermal? Maybe the mine shaft broke into an underground reservoir for that spring and has been draining it dry ever since.

A bit of history: Both back roads into the canyon have historical interest. During the Gold Rush, they formed a vital link between the pioneer towns of Florence and Warren. These wagon roads also became part of a longer route between Grangeville and McCall. The middle link, a bridge that spanned the river, became a *missing* link when it collapsed in 1901.

Then, in the mid-1930s, a tramway was constructed at the mouth of French Creek. A cable spanned the river and a bucket hung by pulleys. Riders would climb in, let it rip, and glide to the midway point, then quickly pull hand over hand up the other side before losing steam. This cable car was the principal access to the hot spring until it was finally condemmed and torn down in 1995. The pillar on the far bank remains as a landmark and trailhead to the spring.

C. OUT OF CASCADE

AN OVERVIEW

Hot springs and hikes: The Warm Lake Highway leads northeast from Cascade to a variety of easy access soaks (46–50) on the South Fork Salmon River and a hike to Rice Peak, all in the Warm Lake area of Boise National Forest. To the north are roadside hot pools (51–54) together with quiet trails in Payette National Forest. And northeast of this area, a mad expedition into the River of No Return Wilderness plunges down a canyon to Kwiskwis Hot Spring (55).

Season: The dips in the Warm Lake area can be accessed by cross-country skiers and should escape the river's grasp at high water, making them usable year-round. Penny is best before the river's too low. Darling's Cabin requires a late-season ford. Enjoy the rest whenever road access allows. The hiking season stretches from mid-July through mid-October. Summer weather is generally hot with occasional thunderstorms.

Hot Springs near Warm Lake

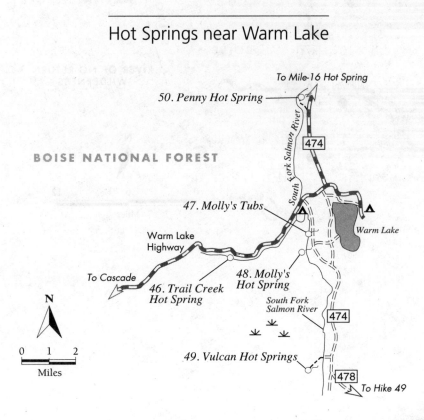

Cascade Area Map

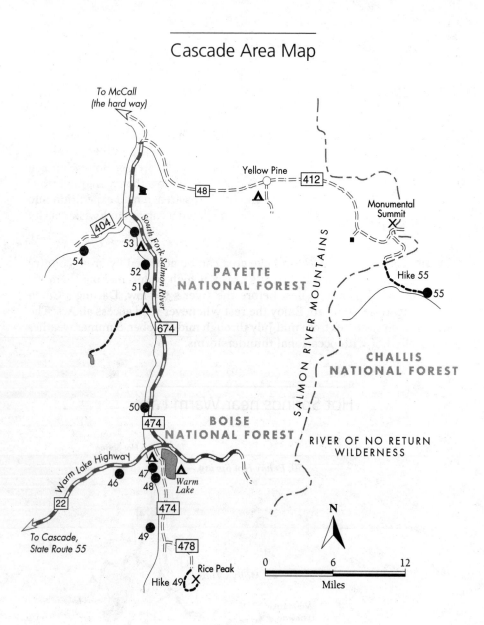

46 Trail Creek Hot Spring

General description:	Peekaboo pools in a wooded canyon below a highway. Keep cutoffs handy.
Elevation:	5,900 feet.
General location:	19 miles northeast of Cascade.
Map:	Boise National Forest.
Contact:	Cascade Ranger District, Boise National Forest.

Finding the hot spring: From State Route 55 at Cascade, take the Warm Lake Highway 19 miles northeast. Watch for a large pullout on your right 0.4 mile east of Milepost 61. Slide down a slippery 60-yard path from the west end to the canyon floor and up Trail Creek to the soaking pools. The spring isn't marked on the forest map.

The hot spring: A 122-degree spring spreads rivulets down the bank into a few pools. Between them you may or may not find a bathtub filled with steaming water, gravity fed by a pipe. Lower the temperature by adding creek water; a handy bucket sometimes sits nearby. The spot is visible from the west side of the pullout but just out of sight from passing motorists.

47 Molly's Tubs

General description:	A bevy of bathtubs on the South Fork Salmon River below a dirt road. A swimsuit/birthday suit mix.
Elevation:	5,200 feet.
General location:	24 miles northeast of Cascade.
Map:	Boise National Forest.
Contact:	Cascade Ranger District, Boise National Forest.

Finding the hot spring: From State Route 55 at Cascade, take the Warm Lake Highway 23 miles northeast (3.7 miles past Trail Creek Hot Spring) to graded Forest Road 474. Drive south for 1.3 miles to a pullout on your right and follow a short path down to the tubs. The spring isn't shown on the forest map.

The hot spring: Three bathtubs lined up side by side, plus five or six more sitting just below, collect the flow from this 138-degree spring with the aid of hoses that the soaker can move from one to another. Add river water with a bucket for a cooler soak. The tubs sit on raised platforms that span the muddy channel running from the spring to the nearby river. How civilized can a primitive hot spring get?

Molly's Tubs, at last count, had three bathtubs off to the side in addition to the six you see in the foreground.

48 Molly's Hot Spring

General description:	A sadly neglected pool above the South Fork Salmon River a quarter mile from a dirt road. Bathing suits optional.
Elevation:	5,300 feet.
General location:	25 miles northeast of Cascade.
Map:	Boise National Forest.
Contact:	Cascade Ranger District, Boise National Forest.

Finding the hot spring: Follow the directions above to Forest Road 474 and go south 1.9 miles (0.6 mile past Molly's Tubs) to a junction. Park here and walk west on a road closed to motor vehicles that leads to the river and soon bridges it. Immediately past the bridge, hang a right on an overgrown path that meanders back downstream and up a slippery slope to the pool. Molly's isn't marked on the forest map.

The hot spring: Molly hides out behind a wall of evergreens far enough above the river to escape the runoff. Her 129-degree spring streams down the hillside past a log-lined soaker built directly over the flow. Lower the temperature by diverting incoming hoses.

The shallow pool is lined with plastic but, at last report, the liner sadly needed replacing and the log dam needed some TLC. There's a plywood platform on which to dry off and a pleasant river view through the trees. Molly has great potential, she just needs a helping hand.

Molly's short cut: *I was trying to improve the pool when I was joined by a friendly young couple. In the course of conversation, it turned out that the woman was a professional barber who just happened to have all the tools of her trade in their camper. An hour later, wrapped in a plastic apron with a towel around my neck, shears clicking and hair flying to the winds, I sat on a handy stump at their camp in a nearby meadow while she treated me to an expert trim.*

49 Vulcan Hot Springs

General description:	A popular creek-wide soaker in the South Fork Salmon River Valley on a 0.75-mile path. Swimwear optional.
Elevation:	5,600 feet.
General location:	30 miles northeast of Cascade.
Map:	Boise National Forest.
Contact:	Cascade Ranger District, Boise National Forest.

Vulcan Hot Springs • Rice Peak

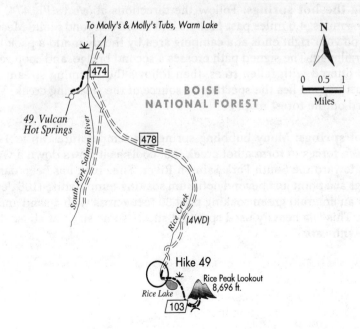

The steamy pool at Vulcan Hot Springs prompts a quick trip in and out.

Finding the hot springs: Follow the directions above to FR 474. Drive south 6.5 miles, 4.6 miles past Molly's and shortly beyond Stolle Meadows. A spur on your right ends at a camping area by the river and a pack bridge at the trailhead. The signed path crosses a second bridge and soon reaches a creek littered with fallen trees, then follows the warming stream to the pool. Just beyond lies the spectacular source of the steaming creek. Vulcan is named on the forest map.

The hot springs: Many bubbling springs, at temperatures up to 190 degrees, join forces to form a hot creek that cools as it flows down a wooded hillside toward the South Fork Salmon River. The creek has been dammed with logs at a point just beyond optimum soaking temperature (106 degrees) to form an emerald green soaking pool 30 feet across with a sand and mud bottom. This is a heavily used spot that shows some signs of abuse. Please treat it with care.

HIKE 49 *Rice Peak*

General description:	A short day hike to a peak with distant views, near Vulcan Hot Springs.
Difficulty:	Strenuous.
Distance:	3 miles round trip.
General location:	30 miles northeast of Cascade.
Elevation gain:	1,300 feet.
High point:	Lookout, 8,700 feet.
Hiking quad:	Rice Peak USGS.
Road map:	Boise National Forest.
Contact:	Cascade Ranger District, Boise National Forest.

Finding the trailhead: Follow the road access above to Vulcan. Continue south for just under a mile and bear left on Rice Peak Road (478). The 6-mile road gradually deteriorates, and you may be better off walking the final 2-mile stretch unless you have a 4WD. Check with the Forest Service in Cascade for current conditions; mud often makes access impossible before July. If you hike the last 2 miles up Rice Creek to the trailhead, you can tack on an extra 1,000-foot gain.

The hike: Warm Lake is a better area for geothermal gems than for interesting hikes, but the climb to Rice Peak is one exception. The 360-degree view from the lookout reveals an expanse of distant peaks ranging from the Salmon River Mountains to the double silhouette of the Sawtooths backed by the White Clouds, around to the wooded mountains above Cascade and McCall.

Rice Peak Trail (103) continues up Rice Creek where the road leaves off and soon reaches tiny Rice Lake. Cross the outlet on a bridge and circle the north shore past some grassy campsites. Now the path climbs a steep mile to a saddle just south of the peak, takes a short break, then zigzags up the last 0.5 mile to the summit.

50 Penny Hot Spring

General description:	A secluded spring in the South Fork Salmon River Canyon on a quarter-mile path. Naked bodies welcome.
Elevation:	4,800 feet.
General location:	28 miles northeast of Cascade.
Map:	Boise National Forest.
Contact:	Cascade Ranger District, Boise National Forest.

At Penny Hot Spring, river water at your elbow can be channeled into the pools to produce whatever temperature you prefer.

Finding the hot spring: From Cascade, take the Warm Lake Highway 24 miles northeast (a mile past FR 474 south) and turn left on the paved South Fork Road (474/674). Drive 3.6 miles north, then turn left just past the Nickel Creek sign, near what used to be Penny Spring Campground. This overgrown road soon transforms into a path that shows more deerprints than footprints. The route curves north around a hill above the river, then drops sharply beside a cliff to the pools at the bottom. The spring isn't marked on the forest map or even on the state geothermal.

The hot spring: Steaming 144-degree spring water flows down the side of a cliff into a few rock and sand pools along a scenic bend in the river. You can spot several other hot springs both upstream and on the opposite bank by the telltale orange slime. The fragile pools swamp during high water but get landlocked and far too hot once the river is low. There's plenty of hot water just waiting for some energetic soul to rebuild a proper soaking pool, so if you're intent on a bath, bring a shovel and plenty of elbow grease.

For what it's worth: The road from Warm Lake to Penny Hot Spring passes Two-bit and Six-bit creeks on one side, then Dime and Nickel creeks on the other. Dollar Creek lies just beyond. To sum it up: A penny's just a penny, but this one's got potential.

51 Mile-16 (Sugah) Hot Spring

General description:	A sylvan soak in the South Fork Salmon River Canyon hidden below a paved road. Highly skinnydippable.
Elevation:	4,150 feet.
General location:	40 miles northeast of Cascade.
Maps:	Boise and Payette National Forests.
Contact:	Krassel Ranger District, Payette National Forest.

Finding the hot spring: Follow the directions above to Forest Road 474. Drive north past Penny into Payette National Forest, where the road number changes to 674, to Poverty Flat Campground, a total of 15 miles. Continue 1.25 miles north to a pullout and walk the final 0.25 mile up the road. For southbound travelers, the spring is 1.2 miles beyond Fourmile Camp. Hunt for a path that drops over the steep bank to the riverside pool. Mile-16 isn't marked on the forest map.

The hot spring: A crystal-clear soaking pool, well concealed from the nearby road, sits at the base of a steep bank on the river's edge. It's enclosed by attractive chunks of stream rock mortared tightly in place. A large slab at one end makes a backrest for enjoying the view up the tree-studded canyon. Spring water, cooling from 115 degrees as it trickles down the bank, can be diverted by means of a long pipe coupled to a hose.

Locals refer to this spot as Mile-16 because of its strategic location on the road. It's also known as Sugah, Fire Crew, and Holdover. Whatever it's called, this is a tastefully designed pool in a great setting. Please don't abuse the privilege of using it—remember, no soap or shampoo.

Mile-16 Hot Spring is a prime example of how to design and build a proper soaking pool.

Mile-16 Hot Spring • Blackmare Lake

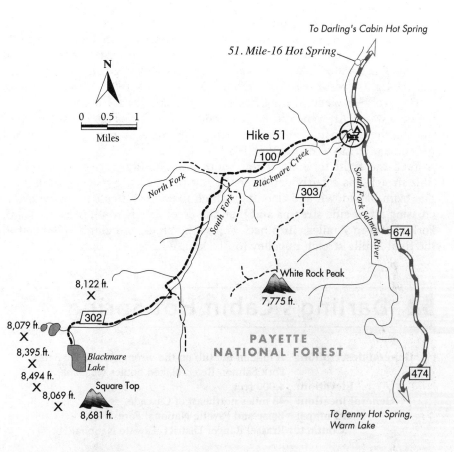

To Darling's Cabin Hot Spring

51. Mile-16 Hot Spring

N

0   0.5   1
Miles

Hike 51

100

Blackmare Creek

North Fork

South Fork

303

South Fork Salmon River

674

8,122 ft.
X

White Rock Peak
7,775 ft.

8,079 ft.
X

302

8,395 ft.
X

Blackmare
Lake

PAYETTE
NATIONAL FOREST

8,494 ft.
X
8,069 ft.
X

Square Top

474

8,681 ft.

To Penny Hot Spring,
Warm Lake

HIKE 51 *Blackmare Lake*

General description:	An overnight trek to a remote lake, near Mile-16 Hot Spring.
Difficulty:	Moderate.
Distance:	18 miles round trip.
General location:	40 miles northeast of Cascade.
Elevation gain:	+3,100 feet, -500 feet.
High point:	7,040 feet.
Hiking quads:	Blackmare and White Rock Peak USGS.
Road maps:	Boise and Payette National Forests.
Contact:	Krassel Ranger District, Payette National Forest.

Finding the trailhead: Follow the directions above to Poverty Flat Campground and walk from there to the pack bridge.

The hike: Sapphire blue Blackmare Lake, which lies in a basin flanked by granite walls, makes a pleasant overnight trip. Half a dozen 8,000-foot peaks rim the basin, and narrow bands of trees mark the ridges with diagonal stripes. The isolated lake nestles at the head of a glacial valley.

Turn right across the bridge onto Blackmare Trail (100). You can count on getting wet feet when fording Blackmare Creek, which is treacherous during high water. After the creek the wooded route climbs the north bank and follows the creek up the steep-walled valley. At a branch at just under 4 miles, bear left to a second junction.

Take the right fork along the South Fork of Blackmare Creek (302). This stretch has a fairly gentle grade, but the trail has taken some severe hits from blowdown and flooding, which make it difficult to follow. After crossing a few side streams and then the creek itself, you'll pass the South Fork Cutoff in 7 miles. Turn back across the creek and climb 1,360 feet in the final 2-mile stretch upvalley to Blackmare Lake.

52 Darling's Cabin Hot Spring

General description:	A hidden hot tub on the wrong side of the South Fork Salmon River. Naked bodies welcome.
Elevation:	4,000 feet.
General location:	43 miles northeast of Cascade.
Road maps:	Boise and Payette National Forests.
Contact:	Krassel Ranger District, Payette National Forest.

Finding the hot spring: Follow the directions to Forest Road 474 given in 50. Drive north 19 paved miles (2.5 miles past Mile-16 Hot Spring or 2.2 miles south of Camp Creek Campground). Watch for some old cabins on a flat by the river and park in the closest turnout. In late season, you can ford near the cabins and follow a faint path up the bank to the tub. The spring is unmarked on the forest map and omitted on the state geothermal.

The hot spring: Spring water is piped into a stock tank hidden in the woods above the river. The soaking temperature runs around 92 degrees. It's located on an unpatented mining claim and appears to be rarely visited.

53 Teapot Hot Spring

General description:	A hot spring sandwich spread between a forest road and the South Fork Salmon River. Swimwear vital while standing up.
Elevation:	3,840 feet.
General location:	47 miles northeast of Cascade.
Road maps:	Boise and Payette National Forests.
Contact:	Krassel Ranger District, Payette National Forest.

Finding the hot spring: Follow the directions to Forest Road 474 given in 50. Drive north 23 paved miles (2 miles north of Camp Creek Campground or a mile south of Buckhorn Creek Road) and squeeze into a narrow pullout at the south end of a long straight stretch. The spring, marked only on the state geothermal, is located just below the road.

The hot spring: Water issues from the riverbank at 140 degrees and flows or seeps into a string of small pools at the river's edge. These shallow soakers get submerged during runoff, but when the river is down they can be cooled by shifting the rocks enclosing them. There are three strikes against Teapot that keep it in the minor leagues: lack of privacy, lack of shade, and lack of a decent soaking pool.

54 Buckhorn Hot Spring

HIKE 54 *To Buckhorn Hot Spring*

General description:	A day hike or mountain bike ride up a closed road to a former easy access soak. A skinnydipper's fantasy.
Difficulty:	Strenuous.
Distance:	8 miles round trip.
General location:	49 miles northeast of Cascade.
Elevation gain:	1,000 feet.
High point:	4,900 feet.
Hiking quad:	Fitsum Peak USGS (optional).
Road maps:	Boise and Payette National Forests.
Contact:	Krassel Ranger District, Payette National Forest.

Teapot Hot Spring • Buckhorn Hot Spring

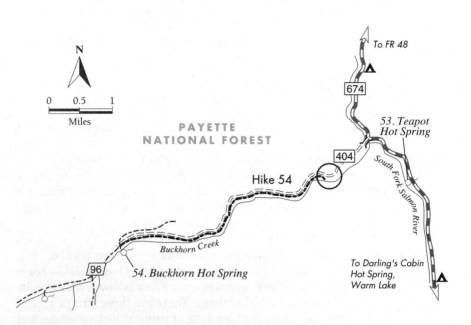

Finding the trailhead: Follow the directions to Forest Road 474 given in 50. Drive north 24 paved miles to Buckhorn Creek Road (404) (a mile past Teapot). If you're coming from McCall, take the Lick Creek Road 36 miles east, then FR 674 8.5 miles south.

Bad news! Buckhorn Creek Road was severely trashed by flooding and slides in early 1997, and the Forest Service has no plans at present on rebuilding it. Cross the river bridge and drive a mile to the roadblock and new trailhead at Little Buckhorn bridge. Buckhorn is marked correctly on the newer forest map, but misplaced on the USGS quad and omitted on the state geothermal.

The hike: Visitors must now hike or bike the remaining 4 miles up the old road, following a series of switchbacks that climb the bank above Buckhorn Creek to a trail sign at the road end. Next, back up 0.1 mile and find the path in the woods going down to the creek. Cross on a nearby log and head 30 yards upstream over a gravel bar to the spring.

The hot spring: A steamy channel flows down a wooden gutter and splashes into a shallow rock-lined pool just above Buckhorn Creek. The source checks in at a toasty 106 to 112 degrees. There's no way to lower the setting except to divert the gutter and wait for the pool to cool.

The *real* Buckhorn is nestled in a mountain meadow bordered by forest. It's out of sight from the road and offers total privacy. All in all, it's not bad for a hot spring that doesn't belong where it ended up.

55 Kwiskwis Hot Spring

Kwiskwis Hot Spring spreads out a feast of hot water and Indian Creek supplies the cold. The rare guest must furnish the only thing missing, a proper soaking pool.

HIKE 55 *To Kwiskwis Hot Spring*

General description:	A wild and woolly overnight trek to a hot spring buried in the River of No Return Wilderness. Swimwear nonfunctional except for sun protection factor.
Difficulty:	Strenuous.
Distance:	13 miles round trip.
General location:	97 miles northeast of Cascade.
Elevation gain:	+340 feet, -2,780 feet.
High point:	Trailhead, 8,120 feet.
Hiking quad:	River of No Return Wilderness, southern half.
Road map:	Same.
Contact:	Middle Fork Ranger District, Salmon and Challis National Forest.

Warning: This rugged expedition is for wilderness buffs and hot springs fanatics only. The trailhead at Mule Hill, on the brink of the vast River of No Return Wilderness, is over 70 miles from Warm Lake. The final 23 teeth-jarring miles of corrugated and rocky dirt from the closest town, Yellow Pine, are enough to test the mettle of the most determined adventurer, not to mention his or her vehicle. The primitive trail plunges downhill to a creek valley that reaches a hot spring few folks have ever heard of and fewer still have ever visited.

If you decide to brave the trip in, you'll be rewarded with views of undulating mountains and gentle valleys, acres of solitude in a lovely creekside meadow with idyllic camping, and a guarantee that you won't have to wait in line for a soak at Kwiskwis Hot Spring.

Finding the trailhead: Follow the directions to Forest Road 474 given for Spring 50. Drive north 35 paved miles to the upper end. Turn right on the East Fork Road (48) and proceed 15 dusty miles to Yellow Pine. This is your last chance to buy gas or anything else you might need. Check with the sheriff on the status of Meadow Creek Lookout Road. Continue the grind east for 14 miles on FR 412, an active mining road, to an eye-catching four-way stop sign at Stibnite.

A tiny gold mining settlement during the 1930s, Stibnite mushroomed to a population of over a thousand during World War II when it became the country's biggest producer of tungsten. When the war boom ended, it dwindled into a ghost town. But Stibnite has sprung back to life once again as the home of an ambitious gold mining venture.

Climb 5 rocky and serpentine miles on FR 375 to Monumental Summit, which is open from July 1 to November 15, and watch for a primitive road (FR 641) signed "to Meadow Creek Lookout" dropping off to your right. The ridge road winds out to the trailhead on Mule Hill. Drivers of low-clearance vehicles will have to skirt a few rocks, if the width of the road allows, or stop to toss them over the edge, but the road is usually passable.

Keep your eyes peeled at 4 miles for signs of a horse camp in a clearing on the ridgetop. This is the certified trailhead at 8,120 feet. Park here and walk back to the woods. Search for Trail 219 on your right (south), and you'll find an overgrown path by a wilderness area sign. This is it—last chance to change your mind! Kwiskwis is named on the map.

The hike: The crude track drops down the flank of Mule Hill, passes the crumbling remains of an old log cabin, then plunges in earnest down a twisting ridge. In one or two places it snakes down sloping meadows with wall-to-wall views, but for most of the 2.5-mile, 2,000-foot drop, the route is engulfed in virgin forest. The path finally comes to rest in a peaceful valley at the junction of Indian Creek Trail (225). The creek flows southeast to join the Middle Fork Salmon River in 15 miles, and Kwiskwis, at 5,680 feet, lies 4 miles downstream.

You'll soon reach broad Kiwah Meadow, a delightful spot to settle down for a lunch break or a week's retreat from the cares of the world. The path is hard to see through the knee-high grass but picks up more clearly beyond the meadow.

After crossing the first side creek, the route climbs the north bank to traverse a precipitous talus slope. It's hard to be sure of the official trail since there are a maze of game paths crisscrossing at varying heights. Most are badly eroded and hard to cling to but all lead in the same direction—downstream. You'll know you're on the right track at the third stream crossing (Kwiskwis Creek) if you see a faded sign that labels it "Quis Quis." A short distance beyond, you should intersect the upper springs.

Just for the record: Upstream on Big Chief Creek lurks another hot spring marked on the wilderness map but not on the state geothermal. And several miles downstream, on the Middle Fork of Indian Creek, are two springs reported by the state geothermal to have the highest surface temperature range (161-190 degrees) of any in the wilderness!

The hot spring: Scalding water emerges from the ground at up to 156 degrees but drops into the comfort zone by the time it reaches Indian Creek below. More springs appear as you follow the broad flow downhill. The shallow pool(s) at the bottom fill in with creek gravel and will need some excavation work, but that's the price you pay for "the wilderness experience" and a steamy soak at the end of the trail. There's a small campsite across the creek, but the best camping is back at Kiwah Meadow.

Footnote: An element that adds even more spice to the adventure is the fact that the Forest Service has little firsthand information to help the hiker. This remote area is a slice of the Frank Church-River of No Return "wilderness pie" held by Boise National Forest but administered by Salmon and Challis National Forest. However, the district office sits roughly 70 air miles across the state map from Mule Hill.

Kwiskwis Hot Spring

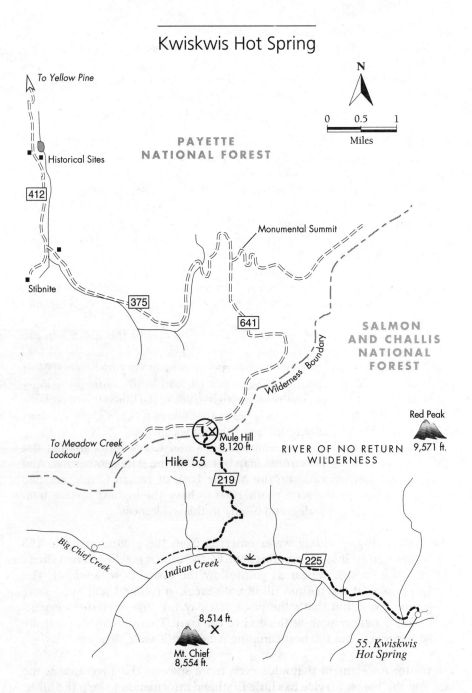

By a series of roundabout roads, a trail crew based in Challis would have to drive a staggering 180 miles to reach the trailhead, and only 115 of them would be on pavement. The final 40 miles of dirt get progressively worse as they travel over potholes and rock. As a result, this is one piece of wilderness that seems more than likely to remain just that!

D. OUT OF CROUCH

AN OVERVIEW

Hot springs and hikes: Midway between Boise and Cascade on State Route 55, the Banks-Lowman Highway shoots 8 miles east from Banks past Bronco Billy (56) to the tiny town of Crouch. A back road follows the Middle Fork Payette River northeast of town to more roadside hot dips (57–59) followed by a batch on a river trail upstream, notably, Moondipper, Pine Burl, and Bull Creek (60, 61). East of town are Campground Hot Springs (62) en route to Lowman. This area is in Boise National Forest.

Crouch Area Map

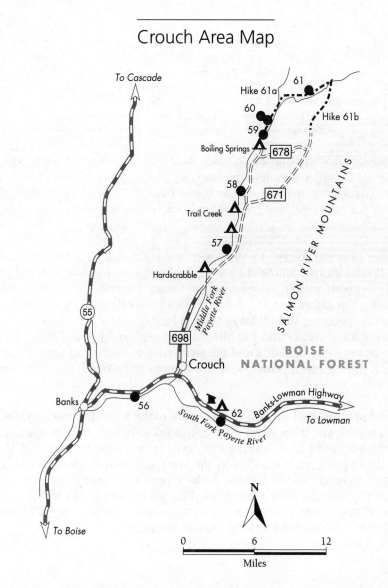

Season: Low elevation promotes a long soaking season limited only by winter road closures and spring runoff in the riverside pools. Fire Crew and Moondipper are best in early summer while Rocky Canyon, Boiling Springs, and Pine Burl are usable well into the fall. The pool at Campground Hot Springs can be enjoyed all year. The hiking season for the trek to Bull Creek has a narrow window, while the river is low and before the pool is left stranded. Summer weather runs hot and dry, but thunderstorms are not uncommon.

56 Bronco Billy (Deer Creek) Hot Spring

General description:	A back-burner hot pot on the South Fork Payette River. Swimwear is essential.
Elevation:	2,950 feet.
General location:	4 miles west of Crouch.
Map:	Boise National Forest.
Contact:	Emmett Ranger District, Boise National Forest.

Finding the hot spring: From State Route 55 at Banks, take the Banks-Lowman Highway to a pullout midway between Banks and Crouch at Milepost 4. The spring, marked on the forest map, flows down a bank to the highway 0.2 mile east, and from there it still pours through a culvert onto the riverside rocks.

The one that got away? In 1996, a minor hot spring had its moment of fame. Winter storms followed by a week of warm rains left much of Boise County without power, telephones, or roads. The rains caused massive mudslides. On December 31, slides on both banks dammed up the river at the spring, covering the highway with 2 feet of water. The highway was closed for three weeks and the hillsides were altered beyond recognition. The source pool up the bank and the steep road to it, the riverside soaker— all were gone in an instant. Even the Bronco Billy rapids were virtually wiped out.

The hot spring: Will Bronco Billy, once a rocky little hot pool hidden on the steep bank and frequented by river rats (usually with the aid of a tarp to keep the hot water from leaking out), ever spring back to life? Will Deer Creek Hot Spring, as it's called on the state geothermal (even though the real Deer Creek is on the far side of the river a mile upstream) ever again register 176 degrees, with a source pool up the hill you could boil eggs and unwary soakers alike in? Will our little saga yet have a happy ending? Chances are, by the time you read this the answer is already yes.

At Bronco Billy Hot Spring, travelers should still be prepared to stop.

57 Rocky Canyon Hot Spring

General description:	Highly visible hot pools on the wrong side of the Middle Fork Payette River. Swimwear essential.
Elevation:	3,440 feet.
General location:	12.5 miles northeast of Crouch.
Map:	Boise National Forest.
Contact:	Emmett Ranger District, Boise National Forest.

Finding the hot spring: From State Route 55 at Banks, take the Banks-Lowman Highway 8 miles east to Crouch. Follow Forest Road 698 northeast of town. The first 8 miles are paved, but the remainder makes up for it. Go 12.5 miles (1.5 miles past Hardscrabble Campground) and park in a pullout on your left. You'll have to wade the wide river, which could be dangerous during high water. The spring is marked on the forest map.

The hot spring: Near the mouth of Rocky Canyon, a spring emerges at 120 degrees from the steep hillside and flows down to the river. Bathers have chiseled out a family-sized soaking pool well up the bank and a few smaller pools dropping step-by-step down the rocky ledges even higher up. Each pool is slightly cooler than the one above. Take your pick!

58 Fire Crew Hot Spring

General description:	Roadside hot dips screened by woods on the Middle Fork Payette River. Keep cutoffs handy. Elevation: 3,600 feet.
General location:	15 miles northeast of Crouch.
Map:	Boise National Forest.
Contact:	Emmett Ranger District, Boise National Forest.

Finding the hot spring: Follow the directions above to Forest Road 698. Drive 15 miles (2.5 miles past Rocky Canyon Hot Spring) to a junction at Trail Creek Campground. Take the left fork (still FR 698) for 0.3 mile, then bear left on a rough spur ending at the river. A loop encircles an unofficial camping area; the pools are out on a gravel bar to your right. Fire Crew isn't shown on any map, not even the state geothermal.

The hot spring: A few pools framed by sun-warmed rocks are concealed from the road just upstream from Rocky Canyon. Also at the river's edge, but luckily on the near side, these little-known dips are frequented chiefly by the local fire crew.

The water-level pools at Fire Crew Hot Spring are swamped in the spring runoff and left high and dry by midsummer.

Early in the season, the 128-degree flow through the pools can be fine-tuned by adjusting a rock or two around the edges, but later on the pools become landlocked and get too hot for soaking. It's an attractive spot and sometimes a pleasant surprise.

59 Boiling Springs

General description:	Major springs and minor soaks on the Middle Fork Payette River. Nudity is a no-no if you're over five years old.
Elevation:	4,000 feet.
General location:	23 miles northeast of Crouch.
Map:	Boise National Forest.
Contact:	Emmett Ranger District, Boise National Forest.

Finding the hot springs: Follow the directions to Forest Road 698 given in 57. Drive 23 lengthy miles, past Rocky Canyon and Fire Crew Hot Springs, to the road-end campground and trailhead. Stroll 0.25 mile north to find the

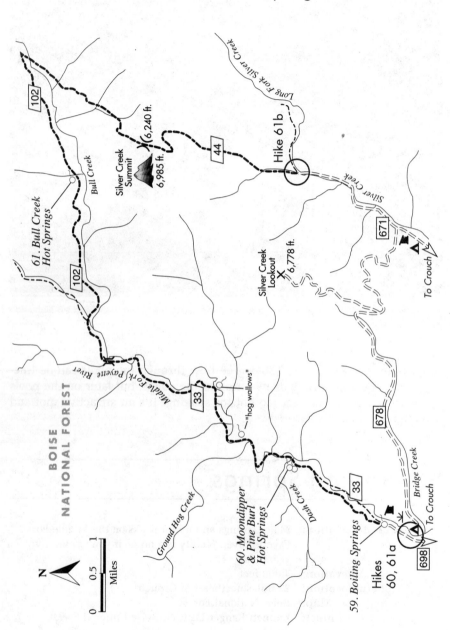

Long Fork Silver Creek

102

X 6,240 ft.

Silver Creek Summit

6,985 ft.

44

Hike 61b

Silver Creek

671

To Crouch

Bull Creek

61. Bull Creek Hot Springs

102

Silver Creek Lookout
X 6,778 ft.

BOISE NATIONAL FOREST

Middle Fork Payette River

33

"hog wallows"

678

Bridge Creek

To Crouch

Ground Hog Creek

Drop Creek

60. Moondipper & Pine Burl Hot Springs

33

59. Boiling Springs

Hikes 60, 61a

698

To Crouch

N

1

0.5

0

Miles

From the steamy source at Boiling Springs, visitors look across a lovely meadow to the rustic rental cabins that were formerly a guard station. BOB WESTERBERG PHOTO

springs flowing down a bank beside a couple of cabins. The cabins, formerly a Forest Service guard station, are now rented to the public for recreational use. Please ask permission before entering and try to avoid the cabin area as much as possible. Boiling Springs is named on the forest map.

The hot springs: Steaming water emerges at over 185 degrees from many fissures in a cliff just beyond the cabins, and a broad cascade streams down the hillside. One spring flows through a shallow soaking pool at the base. The water gradually cools as it runs through a ditch across a wide meadow. A few rock-lined pools at the river's edge are usually filled on weekends with kids from the nearby campground. River water can be added for a cooler soak.

60 Moondipper and Pine Burl Hot Springs

Pine Burl Hot Spring offers a soothing soak to a tired hiker. BOB WESTERBERG PHOTO

HIKE 60 *To Both Hot Springs*

See Map on Page 200

General description:	A double feature playing near the Middle Fork Payette River. A bathing suit/birthday suit mix.
Difficulty:	Easy.
Distance:	4 miles round trip.
General location:	23 miles northeast of Crouch.
Elevation gain:	80 feet.
High point:	4,080 feet.
Hiking quads:	Boiling Springs and Bull Creek Hot Springs USGS (optional).
Road map:	Boise National Forest.
Contact:	Emmett Ranger District, Boise National Forest.

Finding the trailhead: Follow the directions above to Boiling Springs and take your pick of two routes upstream. The springs are marked on the forest map but not on the USGS quad.

The soaking pool at Moondipper Hot Spring requires some remodeling every year, but th͏ͤtting makes up for the effort.

The hike: Moondipper and Pine Burl enjoy a setting worthy of their captivating names. Two separate springs at 120 degrees flow down the banks of a creek just above the river into a pair of scenic soakers spaced 200 yards apart along the tree-studded canyon. Both get swamped during high water, but are well worth a bit of annual maintenance.

One trail, steep and slippery in spots, hugs the west side of the river all the way; this is the safer route when the water level is high, usually until August. The Middle Fork Trail (33) is more direct, but you'll have to ford twice in the 2-mile hike upstream. If in doubt, check at the ranger station in Garden Valley.

The hot springs: When you reach Dash Creek, the first side stream on the west side, you'll find Moondipper against a rocky bank. The large, sandy-bottomed pool can hold several happy soakers and offers a lovely view up the canyon. It's usually landlocked by midsummer and can get too hot for comfort by then without some means of transporting cold water from the creek.

Pine Burl, a tiny gem tucked out of sight a few bends up the creek, is a hot springer's fantasy of the perfect spot for a quiet party for two. The name is proudly inscribed, along with those of its four volunteer builders, on a small masonry dam at the downstream end. The spring perks up through the sandy bottom, and if the water gets too hot you can shift the rocks at the other end to let creek water trickle in.

61 Bull Creek Hot Springs

HIKE 61a *To Bull Creek Hot Springs via the Middle Fork*

See Map on Page 200

General description:	A very wet backpack, best suited for spawning salmon, to a far-flung dip up the Middle Fork Payette River. No need to pack a swimsuit.
Difficulty:	Moderate.
Distance:	22 miles round trip.
General location:	23 miles northeast of Crouch.
Elevation gain:	1,200 feet.
High point:	Hot springs 5,200 feet.
Maps:	Same as above.
Contact:	Emmett Ranger District, Boise National Forest.

Finding the trailhead: Follow the directions above to Boiling Springs. The springs are named on both maps.

The hike: This trip combines the 2-mile stroll to Moondipper and Pine Burl with a 9-mile extension upstream to access Bull Creek Hot Springs in a total of 11 miles. The path snakes back and forth across the swift-moving river an exhausting total of twelve times en route to Bull Creek. See above for a choice of routes from the trailhead to Dash Creek.

Immediately after passing Moondipper, the Middle Fork Trail (33) begins crossing the wide stream at almost every bend in its convoluted course. In the next few miles, you'll pass several minor hot springs and seeps marked on the maps. The condition of whatever pools they may have depends on how many flocks of sheep have plodded through them en route to or from their summer pastures. One local ranger calls them all "hog wallows," but he's obviously not a true fanatic dedicated to the cause of investigating every hot puddle no matter how remote. Unlike some of us, he's a man of common sense.

The route climbs briefly away from the river, then continues up the west bank for a mile or so. Two more fords and you'll reach a welcome camping area near the mouth of Bull Creek at 7.5 miles, 4,400 feet. It's best to camp here since there aren't any good campsites at the hot springs.

Cross the Middle Fork one last time, this time on a bridge, to pick up the Bull Creek Trail (102) on the north bank of the creek. Follow the path 3.5 miles east to find the hot springs on a bluff near a small stream. See below for a much less difficult route from a different direction.

The hot springs: The remote springs overlooking Bull Creek may or may not have a bather-friendly pool to greet you just when you really need a hot soak. Too late in the season, when a nearby side creek dries up, the stranded pools grow hot enough to boil eggs and hikers alike; too early, you'll freeze more than your toes in the cold river en route. This venture would be sheer madness when the water level is high; be sure to check at the ranger station in Garden Valley before setting off.

HIKE 61b *Bull Creek Hot Springs via Silver Creek Trail*

See Map on Page 200

General description:	A backpack (with dry feet) to the hot springs above from an alternate trailhead.
Difficulty:	Comparatively easy.
Distance:	18 miles round trip.
General location:	26 miles northeast of Crouch.
Elevation gain:	+1,540 feet, -1,280 feet.
High point:	Silver Creek Summit, 6,240 feet.
Hiking quads:	Bull Creek Hot Springs and Wild Buck Peak USGS.
Road map:	Boise National Forest.
Contact:	Emmett Ranger District, Boise National Forest.

Finding the trailhead: Follow the directions to Trail Creek Campground given in (58). Bear right on Silver Creek Road (671) and drive to the road-end trail sign, 2 miles beyond the guard station.

The hike: Silver Creek Trail offers a far drier, more scenic, and slightly shorter approach to Bull Creek than the wet trek up the Middle Fork described above but minus the hot springs en route. You'll gain an extra 1,300 feet climbing over Silver Creek Summit, but the views along the trail make up for it.

Two trails begin here. Be sure to take Silver Creek Trail (44) and not the one branching off to your right. Follow the route over Silver Creek Summit at 6,240 feet, enjoy the broad views and maybe a nice dry lunch, then drop down the far side to reach Bull Creek at 6 miles, a pleasant spot to spend the night. Cross the creek and watch for the Bull Creek Trail (102) at 0.25 mile. Turn left and follow it 3 miles downstream above the north bank of Bull Creek to reach the hot springs (at 5,200 feet) on a bluff overlooking the canyon.

62 Campground Hot Springs

General description:	A popular soak between a highway campground and the South Fork Payette River. Swimwear highly recommended.
Elevation:	3,100 feet.
General location:	6 miles east of Crouch.
Map:	Boise National Forest.
Contact:	Emmett Ranger District, Boise National Forest.

Finding the hot springs: From State Route 55 at Banks, take the Banks-Lowman Highway east to Hot Springs Campground, a mile inside the forest boundary. There's a pullout on the bank, and steps lead down to the pool. The campground is named on the forest map.

The hot springs: A comfortable soaker big enough for a family group has been dug out of the bank well above the river. The shallow pool, dammed with rocks, offers a toasty soak year-round courtesy of a showerpipe that transports the flow from the 113-degree springs. At the river's edge, you may find one or more seasonal dips not far from a concrete slab that once supported a public bathhouse.

Hot springers springing between Crouch and Lowman can make a convenient stopover at Campground Hot Springs.

E. Out Of Lowman

AN OVERVIEW

Hot springs and hikes: State Route 21, the Ponderosa Pine Scenic Biway, runs northeast of Boise to easy-access soaks on the South Fork Payette River at Pine Flats and Kirkham (63, 64) near Lowman, and on to Tenmile and Bonneville (65, 66); these soaks mix well with treks to Red Mountain and beyond. Next, Sacajawea (67) leads hikers into the western Sawtooths. In the wilderness to the north is the hike to Bear Valley (68) and a backpack to Trail Flat and Sheepeater (69) on the Middle Fork Salmon River, with a bonus dip at Dagger Creek (70) near the trailhead.

Season: Although early summer through fall is the prime time, the uppermost pools at Pine Flats, Kirkham, and Bonneville are usable all year. Spring runoff buries Tenmile and Sacajawea, and prevents access to Bear Valley before late summer. The rest can be enjoyed whenever the roads are open, but the trek down the Middle Fork is best after July. The hiking season in

Lowman Area Map

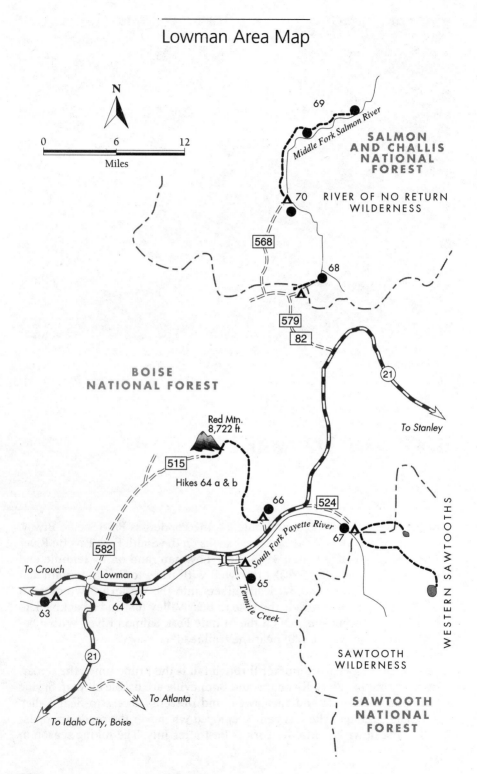

N

0   6   12

Miles

SALMON AND CHALLIS NATIONAL FOREST

69

Middle Fork Salmon River

RIVER OF NO RETURN WILDERNESS

70

568

68

579

82

21

BOISE NATIONAL FOREST

To Stanley

Red Mtn. 8,722 ft.

515

Hikes 64 a & b

66

524

67

582

South Fork Payette River

WESTERN SAWTOOTHS

To Crouch

Lowman

65

63

64

Tenmile Creek

21

SAWTOOTH WILDERNESS

To Atlanta

To Idaho City, Boise

SAWTOOTH NATIONAL FOREST

the high Sawtooths generally runs from late July through mid-September. Summer weather tends to be hot with occasional thunderstorms and with cold nights at higher elevations.

Note: The only services at Lowman are the district ranger station and a few highway pit stops.

63 Pine Flats Hot Spring

General description:	Hot dips and cliffside showers (too) near a family campground, on the South Fork Payette River. Bathing suits required.
Elevation:	3,700 feet.
General location:	5 miles west of Lowman.
Map:	Boise National Forest.
Contact:	Lowman Ranger District, Boise National Forest.

Finding the hot spring: From Boise, take State Route 21 about 70 miles northeast to Lowman. Turn left on the paved road to Garden Valley and drive 5 miles to Pine Flats Campground, where they now collect a day-use fee. From the west end, follow the signed path 0.3-mile downstream to a wide gravel bar. Look for the hottest pools on paths that wind up the back side of the rocky cliff, and slightly cooler soaks at the bottom. The 138-degree spring isn't marked on the forest map.

The hot spring: A cascade pouring over a cliff decorates one side of a pool hidden 20 feet above the river. This one is big enough to pack maybe half a dozen human sardines side by side and hot enough to turn them into lobsters. Cooler pools at the bottom collect the runoff, and a large swimming hole at the river's edge adds the final touch. Those who prefer more privacy can wade along the base of the cliff in late summer to find yet another hot pool with a shower hidden in the rocks just around the bend.

This user-friendly pool at Pine Flats Hot Spring features a steamy hot shower. Bob Westerberg photo

64 Kirkham Hot Springs

General description: Hot waterfalls and pools below a highway campground on the South Fork Payette River. Swimwear a must.

Elevation: 3,900 feet.

General location: 4 miles east of Lowman.

Map: Boise National Forest.

Contact: Lowman Ranger District, Boise National Forest.

Finding the hot springs: Drive 4 miles east of Lowman on State Route 21. Cross the bridge to Kirkham Campground and park at the west end. The Forest Service now collects a day-use fee, but penny pinchers can just park outside and walk in. Follow a short path down to the river. The springs are not marked on the forest map.

The hot springs: In plain view below the highway, these popular pools are frequently filled with boisterous teenagers and large family groups. The rock-and-sand pools, interspersed with steaming showers from the 149-degree springs, come in all sizes, shapes, and temperatures. Kids of all ages love to leap off the rocks into deep holes in the river, and older folks lie scattered about on boulders dozing in the sun. The adjacent campground adds to the congestion here; it's usually Winnebago City on summer weekends. It's worth it to try early mornings or the off-season months.

Note: The once-wooded hills around Kirkham were devastated by a severe windstorm in addition to the 1989 Lowman fire; but it's not clear what hit this area hardest—wind, fire, or the recent boom in tourism. The Forest Service now enforces strict rules on everything from swimwear and user fees at the hot springs to primitive camping, allowed only in designated sites, along the crowded river corridor between Lowman and Sacajawea.

Kirkham Hot Springs has it all, and early enough in the day you may even have it all to yourself.
Bob Westerberg photo

HIKE 64a *Red Mountain Loop*

General description:	A day hike to a viewpoint and off-trail lakes below, not too far from Kirkham Hot Springs.
Difficulty:	Strenuous.
Distance:	10 miles round trip (including a 4.5-mile part cross-country loop).
General location:	17 miles northeast of Lowman.
Elevation gain:	2,560 feet (1,180 feet to start of loop; loop, 1,380 feet).
High point:	Lookout, 8,722 feet.
Hiking quads:	Cache Creek and Miller Mountain East USGS.
Road map:	Boise National Forest.
Contact:	Lowman Ranger District, Boise National Forest.

Finding the trailhead: Take State Route 21 to Lowman and turn north on Forest Road 582. Drive 12 dusty miles toward Bear Valley, then turn right on FR 515 and go 5 bumpy miles to a roadblock with grassy space nearby for horses and a few cars. The trailhead is a mile past the barrier.

The hike: A brisk climb up a mountainside carpeted with wildflowers leads to a lookout crowning the rocky summit of Red Mountain. Look straight down on three lakes and out across a sea of green ridges and valleys to the Salmon River Mountains and the Sawtooths. The bird's-eye view is worth the climb. A cross-country scramble down past the Red Mountain Lakes loops back to a connecting trail. With time to spare, you could continue from this point along a scenic ridge route ending at Bonneville Hot Springs in 20 miles (see below).

Walk the last road mile to the register box and Clear Creek Trail (145). The route soon bridges Rough Creek and follows a second creekbed up a wooded slope, then veers away to climb through chaparral followed by open meadows. Turn left onto the lookout spur and switchback north toward the summit. In early summer, you'll pass patches of flaming Indian paintbrush, lavender shooting star, Red Mountain heath, and Mariposa lilies along the way. Take a break to enjoy the broad view from the lookout at 8,722 feet, 4 miles from the trailhead.

To reach the nearest lake, just east of the summit, pick your route carefully down the precipitous slope past a small pond on your left. Circle the blue green lake, rimmed by tall trees, on a faint path along the north shore and hop across its outlet. Next, scramble east down a wooded gully to reach the largest of the Red Mountain Lakes at 7,850 feet. The deep green surface mirrors a wall of pines and firs.

Angle due south through a rocky cleft and pass a long pond on your right. Next, turn southeast to pass one more lake on your left, the last chance to fill your water bottle. Pick the easiest route south down a grassy slope to

Red Mountain Loop
• Red Mountain to Bonneville Hot Springs

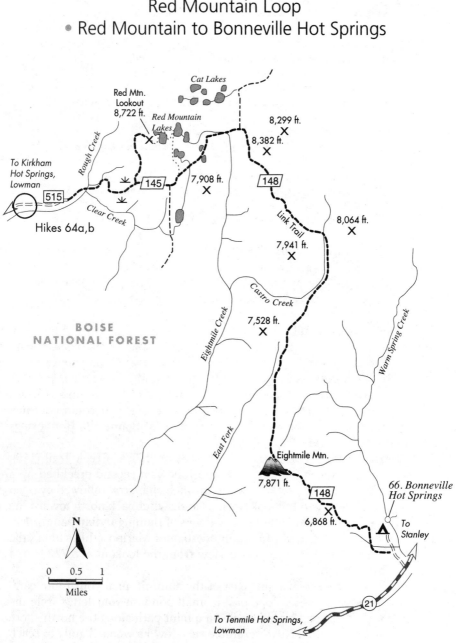

Cat Lakes

Red Mtn. Lookout
8,722 ft.

Red Mountain Lakes

Rough Creek

8,299 ft.
X

8,382 ft.
X

To Kirkham
Hot Springs,
Lowman

515

145

7,908 ft.
X

148

Clear Creek

Hikes 64a,b

Link Trail

8,064 ft.
X

7,941 ft.
X

Castro Creek

BOISE
NATIONAL FOREST

7,528 ft.
X

Eightmile Creek

Warm Spring Creek

East Fork

Eightmile Mtn.

7,871 ft.

148

66. Bonneville
Hot Springs

X
6,868 ft.

To
Stanley

N

0   0.5   1
Miles

21

To Tenmile Hot Springs,
Lowman

intersect Kirkham Ridge Trail 2 miles below the summit. Unless you plan to continue the 14 scenic miles from here to Bonneville, turn right for 0.5 mile on Kirkham Ridge Trail and right again on Clear Creek Trail. Follow it west past the lookout spur, then back out the way you came in.

HIKE 64b *Red Mountain to Bonneville Hot Springs*

General description:	A point-to-point overnight trip linking the Red Mountain climb to hot dips farther up the highway.
Difficulty:	Strenuous.
Distance:	20 miles one way.
General location:	17 miles northeast of Lowman.
Elevation gain:	+4,480 feet, -6,080 feet.
High point:	Lookout, 8,722 feet.
Maps:	Same as above plus Bull Trout Point and Eightmile Mountain USGS.
Contact:	Lowman Ranger District, Boise National Forest.

Finding both trailheads: Drive 19 miles northeast of Lowman on State Route 21 and leave a car at Bonneville Campground. Shuttle a second car 37 miles from here to the trailhead on Clear Creek Road described above.

The hike: The Link Trail may well provide not only the most spectacular views of any hike in Boise Forest but also the best vantage point for seeing the entire length of the Sawtooth Range. The route parallels these jagged peaks from just enough distance for the hiker to absorb their full impact. Mile after mile along the sharp crest, the trail offers breathtaking views as it winds south toward State Route 21.

This hike combines the climb over Red Mountain with a trek along the Link Trail ending after a total of 20 miles at Bonneville Campground and Hot Springs. It's recommended as a one-way trip because the gain is much more gradual in this direction. (There is a grueling gain of 2,920 feet in the first 4 miles when hiked from the lower end.) The only drawback is the car shuttle involved. See above for the route over Red Mountain from Clear Creek Trailhead.

When you drop south from the Red Mountain lakes, you'll intersect Kirkham Ridge Trail at 6 miles, 7,680 feet. Turn left for another 2 miles to access the Link Trail. There's a campsite with a broad view but no water by the junction of Clear Creek and Kirkham Ridge Trails, at 7,600 feet, and a few more grassy spots in the area where Eightmile Creek crosses Kirkham Ridge Trail.

Turn south onto the upper end of the Link Trail (148) at 8 miles, 7,480 feet. Climb the ridge above Eightmile Creek and enjoy the views over your shoulder of the many small lakes fanning out beneath the rugged east face of Red Mountain. The high point on the trail, at 8,120 feet, traverses the side of an unnamed peak. Soon, you'll reach a narrow saddle with the first view to the Sawtooths.

The next stretch crosses the shady side of another peak that may still have snow patches in late July. The path then drops 760 feet down a canyon to reach Castro Creek at 11 miles, 7,360 feet. Cross on logs to a large camping area in a clearing, the best on the Link Trail and the only year-round water source.

The trail continues south along Castro Creek and then climbs to a knoll with another vista. For the next few miles, it dips and rises along the crest at 7,300 feet. Near a sign marked "East Fork," you'll pass a few campsites with access to early-season creek water.

This prime stretch offers magnificent panoramas as it slowly winds south to pass beneath the 7,871-foot summit of Eightmile Mountain at 15.5 miles. You'll get a close-up look up Grandjean Canyon before plunging a nonstop 2,920 feet in 4 miles to the base of the mountain.

When you reach the register box at the lower end of the Link Trail, you'll be just 0.5 mile from your car. Cut left through the woods on a faint path that leads down a gully and intersects the dirt road to reach Bonneville Campground and Hot Springs at 20 miles, 4,680 feet.

Rain-check: *The first time I was here, it started spitting rain as I arrived at the Link Trail. By the time I reached the top, there was almost zero visibility. A cold wind seemed to be gusting from all directions at once, and the drizzle increased to a driving downpour. The trail turned into a creek that flowed past me as I sloshed up every hill. It reversed direction on the downhill stretches, and ponds formed on the level spaces between grades. I could barely make out my wet running shoes, much less the sweeping vistas I'd been anticipating.*

When I reached the campsite on Castro Creek, I found to my horror that everything in my pack was soaked, even my sleeping bag. Left with no choice, I hiked out, splashing uphill, downhill, and across a pond only to repeat this dreary sequence mile after mile as the cold rain turned to sleet and hail. I reached the dry refuge of my car just after dark and the warm haven of Bonneville shortly thereafter, determined to try again for the gold next season!

65 Tenmile Hot Springs

General description:	A creekside soak on an abandoned road near the South Fork Payette River. Highly skinnydippable.
Elevation:	4,500 feet.
General location:	15 miles east of Lowman.
Map:	Boise National Forest.
Contact:	Lowman Ranger District, Boise National Forest.

Finding the hot springs: Take State Route 21, 13 miles east of Lowman or 8.5 miles past Kirkham to a sign for Tenmile trailhead between Mileposts 85 and 86. Bridge the river onto Tenmile Road (531). The dirt road follows the river upstream past a road branching right, then a spur on the left in a mile signed to Tenmile Trail and Camp, followed by a road forking right. It then turns south and tracks Tenmile Creek a mile upstream to a bridge washout.

Cross the creek on a log bridge and continue on foot or mountain bike. You'll pass a spot where the creek takes a huge bite out of the old road, but this can be skirted with care. When you reach a grassy strip, you'll notice a thermal stream alongside the creek. Follow the flow upstream to its source. Tenmile, 0.3 mile from your car, is not marked on any map.

The hot springs: Some years back, I found a steamy pool 10 feet in diameter dug out right on top of the 118-degree source. Last summer I found instead a shallow, plastic-lined pool a few yards downstream. It was half the size of the former pool, but it did have a soakable temperature. By late summer, a few more pools may show up along the creek bank as well. The soaker brings a shovel or takes potluck in this poor man's alternative to Bonneville.

66 Bonneville Hot Springs

General description:	Private bathing and communal soaking in a scenic canyon, very near a popular family campground. Nude bathing in bathhouse only.
Elevation:	4,700 feet.
General location:	19 miles northeast of Lowman.
Map:	Boise National Forest.
Contact:	Lowman Ranger District, Boise National Forest.

Finding the hot springs: Follow State Route 21 about 19 miles northeast of Lowman or 6 miles past Tenmile to Bonneville Campground, where you now pay a day-use fee. Park at the far end and follow a creekside path 0.25 mile north to the springs. The springs are named on the forest map.

The hot springs: There is no time a hot soak is more welcome than right after a cold hike (see "Rain check" above). The relief is immediate and the contrast between hike and soak unforgettable. Bonneville is a haven, especially if you are just off the trail. An aging bathhouse straddles the outflow, and hoses channel hot water into a knee-deep wooden tub, which you can drain and refill after each use. Your clothes stay dry while your tired body gets wet.

This creek-wide soaking pool at Bonneville Hot Springs can be cooled down by adjusting the rocks upstream. BOB WESTERBERG PHOTO

The springs check in at temperatures up to 185 degrees. They flow past the bathhouse and tumble directly over a rocky cliff into a giant soaking pool that spans one arm of Warm Spring Creek. This is a sandy-bottomed gem that measures a good 25 by 30 feet. More hot water flows down the bank into a chain of smaller pools downstream as well as a secluded waterfall pool or two upstream. Bonneville is said to be usable year-round and accessible in winter by cross-country skiers. The off-season months are indeed the only time for a quiet soak at this all too popular retreat.

67 Sacajawea Hot Springs

General description:	Roadside hot dips on the South Fork Payette River, near the Grandjean Trailhead into the Sawtooths. Nudity is a no-no.
Elevation:	5,000 feet.
General location:	26 miles northeast of Lowman.
Map:	Boise National Forest.
Contact:	Lowman Ranger District, Boise National Forest.

Finding the hot springs: Drive 21 miles northeast of Lowman or 2 miles past Bonneville on State Route 21 and turn right on graded Forest Road 524 to Grandjean Campground. Drive 4.8 miles to Waipiti Creek junction and

The riverside pools at Sacajawea Hot Springs take on a new look every summer.

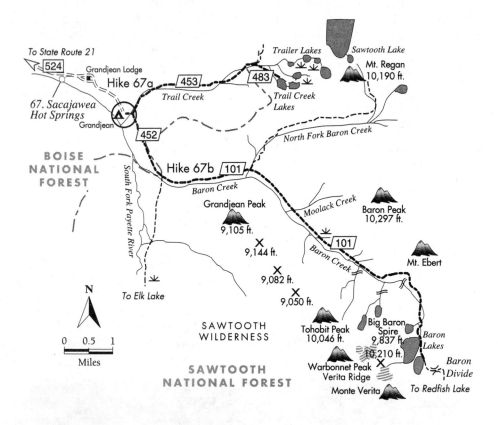

continue 0.6 mile. Park wherever you can find space and climb down the rocks to the pools. Sacajawea is not shown on the forest map.

The hot springs: A number of soaker-friendly pools line a beach along the scenic river. The outflow from several springs, at temperatures up to 153 degrees, cools as it fans out down the bank. Fine-tune the pool temperatures by adding river water. Another welcome refuge for weary hikers, Sacajawea is found just a mile from one of the principal gateways into the Sawtooths. You couldn't ask for a nicer finish to any hike.

HIKE 67a *Trail Creek Lakes*

General description:	A day hike or overnight that climbs to timberline meadows and lakes in the Sawtooth Wilderness, near Sacajawea Hot Springs.
Difficulty:	Strenuous.
Distance:	12 miles round trip.
General location:	27 miles northeast of Lowman.
Elevation gain:	3,085 feet.
High point:	8,245 feet.
Hiking quads:	Grandjean and Stanley Lake USGS.
Road map:	Boise National Forest.
Restrictions:	Recreational user pass required.
Contact:	Sawtooth NRA.

Finding the trailhead: Follow the directions above to Sacajawea and continue another mile southeast to the end of the road. The trailhead for both Trail Creek and Baron Lakes is at the east end of Grandjean Campground.

The hike: Each of these small glacial lakes has a character all its own. As the route rises closer to timberline, rocky knolls and basins of pink Sawtooth granite gradually replace tree-studded lower slopes, and tight clusters of subalpine fir reluctantly give way to a land of stark rock.

Walk east through woods for the first 0.25 mile and bridge Trail Creek to a junction. The right fork heads south to Baron Lakes (see below), and the left fork (453) climbs Trail Creek. You'll have to cross five times on logs or rocks on the way up the narrow V-shaped canyon. This can be dangerous during high water. The route enters the wilderness just before the fourth ford, then snakes up a steep slope to the Trail Creek junction with a 2,400-foot gain at 4 miles.

Turn right on Trail 483, cross the creek one last time in a boggy patch, then climb a ridge to a viewpoint looking down the precipitous canyon. The final piece of eroded track zigzags over a rocky bench, passes some creekside campsites in a grove of tall trees, then tops a last short pitch and comes to rest by the first of the lakes at 4.75 miles, 8,000 feet.

Lower Trail Creek Lake has a waterfall at its far end. Level campsites at the outlet look out across the blue green water to granite walls rimming the thickly wooded basin. A conical peak juts up from the southeast shore, and brook trout ripple the surface late in the day. Circle the northern shore on a fisherman's path to a flat with a few more campsites in the woods.

The path climbs a slope just beyond the clearing to reach the second lake at 8,225 feet. The wide basin here has fewer tall trees. The small meadows are interspersed with outcrops of rock. Mount Regan stands out at 10,190 feet a mile to the east. Follow the north shore and, as you near the end of the lake, pick a cross-country route heading north. Scramble up a talus slope and work your way through a maze of granite knolls and small ponds to reach the third lake at 6 miles, 8,245 feet.

A moonscape of boulders and granite slabs rims the shoreline of Upper Trail Creek Lake, and tiny wildflowers dot the subalpine meadows. A scree slope tails out across the shallow center of the lake; from the last stone you can see every detail on the rocky bottom.

Slip-sliding away: *When I reached the uppermost lake, I slithered down the talus to fill my canteen at the deep end. Just as I leaned forward with bottle in hand, all the rocks around me suddenly started to move. Before I had time to react, the rocks and I were sliding together into the lake! I didn't really object to the unexpected swim, although I would rather have had time to leave my clothes, boots, and lunchbag behind. The thought foremost in my mind as the cold water engulfed me was of my poor camera. This trusty old Olympus, which had survived untold watery adventures in our travels together, had finally met its Waterloo.*

HIKE 67b *Baron Lakes*

General description:	An overnight featuring alpine lakes and panoramic views in the Sawtooth Wilderness, near Sacajawea Hot Springs.
Difficulty:	Moderate.
Distance:	21.5 miles round trip.
General location:	27 miles northeast of Lowman.
Elevation gain:	+3,440 feet, -100 feet.
High point:	8,505 feet.
Maps:	Same as above plus Warbonnet Peak USGS.
Restrictions:	Recreational user pass required.
Contact:	Sawtooth NRA.

Finding the trailhead: Follow the road access above.

The hike: The name "Sawtooths" conjures up images of sharp craggy peaks rising above serrated ridges. The Baron Lakes country shows the Sawtooths at their best. The two deep blue upper lakes lie in glacial bowls hemmed in by peach and rose-hued walls of Sawtooth granite. Stands of fir thin out as you climb from one lake to the next and as colorful rock becomes ever more dominant. The view back across the lakes from Baron Divide highlights countless rocky spires and peaks.

This is the quieter of two equally scenic routes to the popular Baron Lakes. It travels up the U-shaped glacial canyon of Baron Creek to reach Upper Baron Lake in 10.75 miles. The east-side trailhead at Redfish Lake is 3 miles shorter. You could see the best of both routes by entering at Grandjean, crossing over Baron Divide, and exiting at Redfish Lake in 18.5 miles.

Stroll east for the first 0.25 mile to a junction. The left fork climbs to Trail Creek Lakes (see above), and the right turns south to Baron Lakes. Follow the level South Fork Payette River (Trail 452) 1.5 miles southeast, then turn east onto Baron Creek Trail (101) and climb 2 miles along the grassy slope above the wide canyon. Just beyond a creek ford that can be difficult in early summer, North Baron Trail branches off to the left, climbing to Sawtooth Lake in 6 miles. The main canyon veers southeast for several miles as the rocky walls slowly converge.

Ford Moolack Creek at 5 miles, 6,200 feet. This major stream, set in a grove of cottonwoods, is followed by several tiny creeks lined with wildflowers and quaking aspen. The grassy slopes between fords are brushed with stands of spruce and fir. As the walls finally close in, you'll have a good view of Tohobit Falls and Peak on the opposite bank at 7 miles and then Warbonnet Falls and Peak. The trail hairpins 800 feet up the headwall alongside the roaring Baron Creek Falls. Above the hairpin, the trail crosses the first bridge after the one at Trail Creek 9 miles back.

Little Baron Lake lies in a shallow basin off the trail a short hop west of the third stream crossing. It has several uncrowded campsites in the trees near the outlet. Subalpine firs ring the small lake and give it acres of privacy but limited views.

Baron Lake is the next stop, at 10.25 miles, 8,312 feet. A jagged wall of granite across the lake is mirrored in the sapphire blue water. The most level campsites lie on the west side of the outlet facing the view. If these are full, try the west shore across from the trail.

The two lower lakes are bordered to the west by 9,837-foot Big Baron Spire. Just south of this flat-faced peak, the sawtoothed silhouette of Verita Ridge parallels Baron Lake to the west and eclipses 10,210-foot Warbonnet Peak. Southwest of the half-mile-long lake rise the two towering crests of Monte Verita.

The short trail to Upper Baron climbs the ridge that separates them. The only semi-level campsite is right beside the path where you first drop into the rocky basin at 10.75 miles, 8,505 feet. The continuing trail over the divide climbs sharply above the east shore, with a broader view at every switchback, and Baron Lake becomes more visible just below the upper lake. From Baron Divide, at a skyscraping 9,120 feet, the Sawtooths appear to stretch out forever.

68 Bear Valley Hot Springs

Soakers enjoy comparing notes at Bear Valley Hot Springs.

HIKE 68 *To Bear Valley Hot Springs*

General description:	A day hike or overnighter to a chain of pearls locked up in the River of No Return Wilderness. Swimwear superfluous baggage.
Difficulty:	Easy except for a major stream ford.
Distance:	7 miles round trip.
General location:	45 miles northeast of Lowman or 29 miles northwest of Stanley.
Elevation gain:	+160 feet, -320 feet.
High point:	Trailhead, 6,360 feet.
Hiking quad:	River of No Return Wilderness, South half.
Road map:	Same or Boise or Challis National Forest.
Contact:	Middle Fork Ranger District, Salmon and Challis National Forest.

Bear Valley Hot Springs

Finding the trailhead: On State Route 21, drive 37 miles northeast of Lowman or 21 miles northwest of Stanley. Turn west on Forest Road 82/579 signed to Bruce Meadows and Boundary Creek. At 8 miles, a sign marks the turnoff to Fir Creek Campground. Park at Fir Creek Pack Bridge. The springs aren't marked on any map.

The hike: Bear Valley Creek has a claim to fame apart from its hot springs. It joins Marsh Creek downstream to become the headwaters of the Middle Fork Salmon River.

Cross the bridge onto Bear Valley Creek Trail (12). Follow the creek east for the first 1.5 miles, then watch for a spot in the second large meadow where the trail seems to disappear. What happens is that it reappears across the creek. This ford would be suicidal during high water—the stream is fast, a good 20 yards wide and the footing is treacherous. It's also knee-deep through mid-August.

After the ford, the path winds through a tangle of lodgepole pines strewn about on the ground like an oversized child's game of pick-up sticks. Cross

3 streams, then watch for a tree on your left at about 3.5 miles that once bore the hand-carved message "HS." Take your choice of faint paths winding down the steep slope. (Sorry, no better landmark!)

Don't be discouraged when you reach the bottom and find only one murky, ankle-deep pool filled with algae. Stroll a ways downstream to a larger flow and track it past a grassy campsite to a chain of pools dropping step by step to the creek's edge.

There is an alternate route that saves fording the creek as well as 0.5 mile of walking. It's a primitive path that follows the south bank from Fir Creek Campground to the point where the Forest Service trail crosses over. The catch is that it is eroded as it traverses a slippery stretch well up the steep bank. It's not a route for small children or anyone afraid of heights. The prudent choice would be to hold off until late August and take the official trail.

The hot springs: Imagine a string of clear pools drawing you down to the edge of a lively creek. The uppermost and largest is the 130-degree source pool, sheltered under a canopy of evergreenery. The creekside dips, lined with sun-warmed rocks, give a feeling of openness and contact with the stream. You can adjust the temperature in the lower pools by shifting the rocks around.

69 Trail Flat and Sheepeater Hot Springs

HIKE 69 *To Both Hot Springs*

General description:	A backpack to a double bubble in the Middle Fork Salmon River Canyon. Public nudity prohibited within river corridor.
Difficulty:	Strenuous.
Distance:	26 miles round-trip.
General location:	62 miles northeast of Lowman or 38 miles northwest of Stanley.
Elevation gain:	+500 feet, -1,100 feet.
High point:	Trailhead, 5,800 feet.
Maps:	Same as above.
Contact:	Middle Fork Ranger District, Salmon and Challis National Forest.

Finding the trailhead: Follow the road access above but continue past the landing strip. Turn north on Forest Road 568 and drive approximately 15 miles to a junction near the end. The right fork goes to Dagger Creek Hot Spring (see below), and the left fork goes to Boundary Creek Campground and Trailhead, 23 dusty miles from State Route 21. The Forest Service has someone on duty there all summer. Only Sheepeater is shown on the map.

The hike: Two remote hot springs lie 6 miles apart near the upper end of the Middle Fork Salmon River. The streamside soaks at Trail Flat are submerged at high water but should be fine by midsummer, while Sheepeater's secluded dips lie on a rocky terrace well above the river's grasp. The 100-mile-long river, the only navigable stream of such length in the northwest where powerboats are banned, lies within the National Wild and Scenic Rivers system of the River of No Return Wilderness.

The route to both springs follows the west side of the river downstream from Boundary Creek, a launch site where rafts splash down over a 100-foot-high ramp. By early August, the rafts are flown to a lower put-in at Indian Creek. From this time on, the hot pools and nearby campsites should be deserted and the trail high and dry above the river. The access road is open until mid-October.

The Middle Fork Trail (1) follows an abandoned road for the first mile or so over wooded hills, passing a private airstrip and side trails at Sulphur and Prospect creeks; it reaches the river at 4 miles, near a point overlooking a turquoise pool by the bridge over Ramshorn Creek.

The path briefly hugs the river, then climbs well up the bank. As it traverses this slope, it seems to drape loosely from the base of one anchoring tree to the next like a Christmas tree chain drooping from bough to bough. There are no views until you reach an open hill above Trail Flat. Once you spot the gravel bar, you can usually make out the steam rising from the pools. Drop down a rocky slope to reach the campsites at 7 miles, 5,400 feet. The pools lie along the beach just below.

The 12-mile round trip from Trail Flat to Sheepeater is the most scenic stretch of the hike; you can complete it in one long day with ample time to enjoy the soaking pools at both ends. The route stays close to the river much of the way, and when it climbs it keeps the river in sight. Hills wooded with tall ponderosas alternate with boulder-strewn slopes, and there are many pleasant views up and down the canyon.

About a mile below Trail Flat, the path drops to bridge Elkhorn Creek. It climbs and then dips again to cross Deer Horn Creek at 10 miles. When you pass Joe Bump's log cabin, followed by a grave marked "Elmer Set Trigger Purcell, prospector/trapper, 1936," you'll be in the home stretch. Watch for steam from Sheepeater's springs in a clearing off to your left at 13 miles, 5,200 feet. There's a large camp by the river and another in a clearing just above.

Trail Flat and Sheepeater Hot Springs
• Dagger Creek Hot Spring

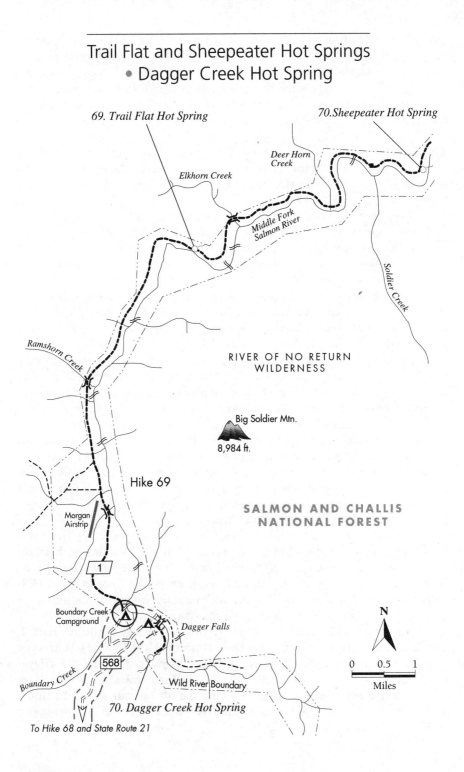

69. Trail Flat Hot Spring

70. Sheepeater Hot Spring

Deer Horn Creek

Elkhorn Creek

Middle Fork Salmon River

Soldier Creek

Ramshorn Creek

RIVER OF NO RETURN WILDERNESS

Big Soldier Mtn.
8,984 ft.

Hike 69

SALMON AND CHALLIS NATIONAL FOREST

Morgan Airstrip

1

Boundary Creek Campground

Dagger Falls

568

Boundary Creek

Wild River Boundary

70. Dagger Creek Hot Spring

To Hike 68 and State Route 21

N

| 0 | 0.5 | 1 |
Miles

Late summer is the perfect time for backpackers to visit Trail Flat Hot Springs.

The hot springs: Trail Flat has one large, very hot source pool midway along the gravel beach. The steamy outflow runs through several increasingly cooler soaking pools fanning out to the river's edge. The sizes and shapes vary, as users have to scoop out new pools each year after the spring runoff.

At Sheepeater, you'll find a square soaking box lined with split logs. Big enough to house a small army, the pool makes a cozy though a bit cloudy cocoon, landlocked by late summer. Shortly beyond it are three tiny pools tucked up against the bank. These hotter dips have an ample flow to keep them clean but no handy means of lowering the temperature. You can track the broad outflow down the hill to two cooler pools hidden in the woods.

Note: These hot springs receive high use during the early float season. Please treat them with TLC and use low-impact camping techniques.

70 Dagger Creek Hot Spring

See Map on Page 228

General description:	A peaceful soak near the trailhead above. Swimwear optional.
Elevation:	5,800 feet.
General location:	62 miles northeast of Lowman or 38 miles northwest of Stanley.
Map:	Same as above.
Contact:	Middle Fork Ranger District, Salmon and Challis National Forest.

Finding the hot spring: Follow the road access above to the junction near the end of Forest Road 568. The right fork will take you to Dagger Falls. Park at the tiny campground and follow a fisherman's path along the Middle Fork Salmon River. Go past the falls 0.5 mile upstream to the mouth of Dagger Creek and then follow the creek a short way upstream to the pool. The spring isn't marked on the forest map.

The hot spring: This little dip has a double distinction. It's the only hot spring in the River of No Return Wilderness that doesn't require a rugged hike to reach. It's also the only one you can plop your tired body into right after a lengthy hike to other geothermal delights. It lies just within both the wilderness and the Wild and Scenic River boundaries and less than a mile from a quiet backwoods campground.

Dagger Creek Hot Spring perks up through the silty bottom of a rock-lined pool in the grass along the creek bank. The pool is shallow and barely big enough for a cozy couple to stretch out in, but the temperature at a toasty 103 degrees is hard to beat. It offers a handy remedy for stiff muscles after the trek to Trail Flat and Sheepeater.

F. OUT OF ATLANTA

AN OVERVIEW

Hot springs and hikes: The Atlanta Trailhead into the western Sawtooths, 90 miles northeast of Boise, is accessed by 45 miles of dirt roads from State Route 21. Trailhead soaks add much to the appeal of the area as does the tiny backwoods town of Atlanta, established in 1864. From the hot springs (71–73), wilderness buffs can trek to Spangle Lakes and beyond or to Lynx Creek (74), the uppermost soak on the Middle Fork. West of town, collectors can drive downstream to no less than eleven more soaks (75–85). Hikers will enjoy exploring the nearby Trinity Alps. Except for the Sawtooth hikes, this area is all in Boise National Forest.

Season: All of the hot springs, except Atlanta, Phifer, and Loftus, are submerged during spring runoff. Many require a major river ford; the fording window is usually mid-August through early October. The hiking season in the high Sawtooths and Trinity Alps doesn't get underway until late July and usually runs through mid-September, while the foothills and the hot springs downstream enjoy a longer season. Summer weather can be hot with cold nights at higher elevations. Hikers should be equipped for foul weather.

Getting to Atlanta: The best route from Boise leaves State Route 21, 19 miles above Idaho City or 15 miles south of Lowman. The next 30 miles of dirt are graded and signed, on Forest Roads 384 and 327, with a final 15-mile grind up the Middle Fork Road (268). The slow route is the latter road all the way up since the lower stretch is a tedious crawl past Arrowrock Reservoir. Thus the "11-soaks tour" along the middle stretch is recommended as a side trip from Atlanta.

Visitors can also reach Atlanta from Featherville (Area G) via 23 miles of seasonal roads with a steep climb over James Creek Road (126), a shortcut from FR 156. The latter connects Featherville with the Middle Fork Road 15 miles west of Atlanta. This is a longer but easier route that also accesses the Trinty Alps.

Note: Atlanta offers no services except the Whistle Stop cafe, a small lodge or two, post office, and public phone. The nearest gas station is back in Idaho City.

Atlanta Area Map

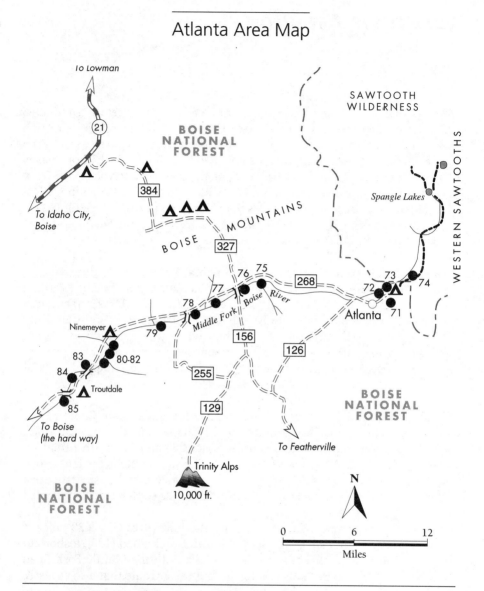

71 Atlanta Hot Springs

General description:	A roadside pool near the Atlanta Trailhead into the Sawtooths. Skinnydippable after dark.
Elevation:	5,400 feet.
General location:	Just east of Atlanta.
Map:	Boise National Forest.
Contact:	Mountain Home Ranger District, Boise National Forest.

The present pool at Atlanta Hot Springs was tastefully designed and solidly built.

Finding the hot springs: Follow the directions above to Atlanta. Continue a little over a mile northeast on the road to Power Plant Recreation Area, which is just past the turnoff to Chattanooga, then watch for a large pond on your right. A spur just beyond it has room for a car or two to park, and a short path leads to the pool. The springs aren't marked on the forest map.

The hot springs: A rock-and-masonry soaking pool sits in a grassy clearing in the woods a scant quarter mile from the Atlanta Trailhead. It's usable by late spring since it's well above the river. Steamy water is piped in from the 140-degree spring, and the soak averages 105 degrees. The user-built pool measures a good 6 x 12 feet and has a hand-hewn bench at one end. An outlet pipe allows for easy draining. The runoff flows into the "frog pond," which doubles in hot weather as a fine swimming hole. You may have a few hungry chiggers for company, but the soak is worth the risk.

Over and out: *After a soak some years back, I remembered a call I'd promised a friend. I sped into town to find that the only contact Atlanta had with the outside world was a radiotelephone on the counter of the cafe.*

I was briefed by the short-order cook on the art of conducting a one-way conversation. It required precision timing. I pushed a button to transmit and released to receive. Release too soon and my sentence was cut off; release too late and I lost the reply. I had to end every remark with a loud "OVER," or the other party wouldn't know it was time to speak. As I stood there fumbling with the button and shouting birthday greetings into the microphone, I must have provided the townsfolk of Atlanta with the best live entertainment they'd had in some time!

Shortly thereafter, probably around 1989, Atlanta joined the rest of modern civilization and had standard service brought in via a microwave link. The old radiotelephone and its live entertainment are now history.

72 Chattanooga Hot Springs

General description:	A five-star soak on the Middle Fork Boise River, near the Atlanta trailhead into the Sawtooths. Swimwear optional.
Elevation:	5,360 feet.
General location:	Just east of Atlanta.
Map:	Boise National Forest.
Contact:	Mountain Home Ranger District, Boise National Forest.

Finding the hot springs: Follow the directions above to Atlanta and continue a mile northeast on the road to Power Plant Recreation Area. Just west of the pond by Atlanta Hot Springs, look for a side road to the left marked by a tree that bisects it. Follow it north to a grassy flat by the cliff. The flat

Chattanooga Hot Springs offers wayfarers a scenic soak and showerbath.

234

is on private land; no camping is allowed. Park here and choose between two extremely steep and slippery paths dropping down to the pool. Chattanooga isn't shown on the forest map.

The hot springs: Bubbly springs at 122 degrees cascade over a cliff into a large, knee-deep pool lined with rocks and logs. It has a sandy bottom, and the temperature seems to stay a steady perfect. There's also a little hot pot with a shower hidden on a ledge approximately 50 feet west of the main pool.

This topnotch retreat, near the trailhead for the following hikes, is tucked between the base of the 100-foot cliff and the nearby river. The jagged Sawtooths across the canyon form a dramatic backdrop. It's a great place to pause and unwind between the rigors of a long, dusty trail and those of an even longer, bumpy road!

73 Greylock Hot Spring

General description:	Another hot dip on the Middle Fork Boise River, at the Atlanta Trailhead into the Sawtooths. Keep swimwear within reach.
Elevation:	5,460 feet.
General location:	Just east of Atlanta.
Map:	Boise National Forest.
Contact:	Mountain Home Ranger District, Boise National Forest.

Finding the hot spring: Follow the directions above to Atlanta and continue 1.3 miles northeast to Power Plant Recreation Area, just past Atlanta and Chattanooga Hot Springs. You'll see a meadow at the campground entrance. On the right is the Atlanta trailhead and on the left is a campsite on the bank. Park here and follow a track down to the riverside pool. This spring isn't marked on any map, not even the state geothermal.

The hot spring: Travelers can discover one more hot soak near Atlanta, and it couldn't be closer to either the trailhead or a fine campsite. The spring flows out across a gravel bar into one or more of the rocky soaking pools. The biggest has a sandy bottom that four to six bodies can shoehorn into. The temperature runs at approximately 104 degrees; adjust it by adding river water.

Greylock would be submerged during spring runoff, but since the following hikes are best done in mid- to late summer, the timing would coincide. The site is visible only to people camping on the bank above, and the view across the rushing water to jagged Greylock Mountain, the spring's unofficial namesake, is nothing short of spectacular.

Spangle Lakes • Tenlake Basin and Ardeth Lake • Ingeborg, Rock Slide, and Benedict Lakes

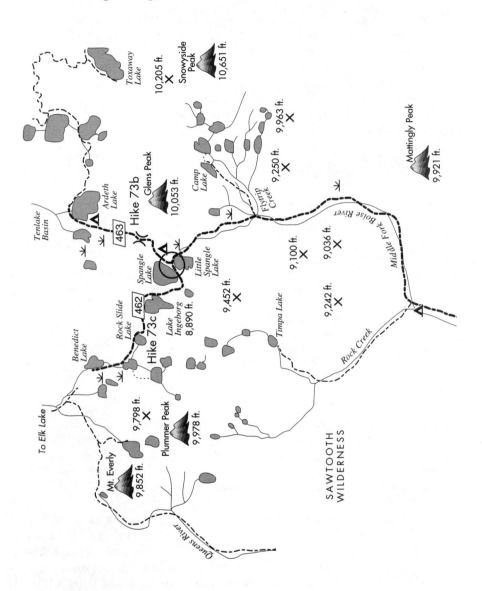

Atlanta, Chattanooga and Greylock Hot Springs
• Lynx Creek Hot Spring

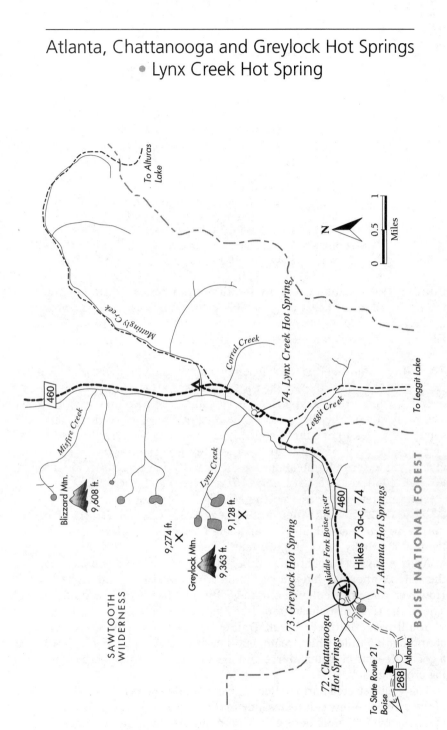

HIKE 73a *Spangle Lakes*

See Map on Page 236

General description:	A multi-day backpack featuring meadows and lakes in the heart of the Sawtooths, near Atlanta, Chattanooga, and Greylock Hot Springs.
Difficulty:	Strenuous.
Distance:	31 miles round trip.
General location:	Just east of Atlanta.
Elevation gain:	+3,480 feet, -320 feet.
High point:	Upper Spangle Lake, 8,600 feet.
Hiking quads:	Atlanta East and Mount Everly USGS.
Road map:	Boise National Forest.
Restrictions:	Recreational user pass required.
Contact:	Sawtooth NRA.

Finding the trailhead: Follow the directions above to Atlanta and continue 1.3 miles northeast to Power Plant Recreation Area. The trail sign is located on the right side of a large meadow at the campground entrance. Give the car a well-earned rest and put your boots to work.

The hike: A bonsai effect of delicate meadows, rock gardens, and dwarfed, twisted trees defines the setting for Little Spangle Lake. Upper Spangle is a deep blue circle rimmed by thick woods and cream colored granite walls. The basin sits on the threshold of the magnificent high country, and lonesome campsites tempt the visitor to linger and explore farther (see hikes below). The price of admission is a lengthy access on a trail that doesn't give much to write home about for the first 12 miles; it is a gradual ascent through a uniform forest of Douglas-fir relieved only by occasional meadows.

The first few miles east on the Middle Fork Boise River Trail (460) are an easy stroll. The route then crosses Leggit Creek, which is difficult to ford during high water, and hairpins up a hill. Leggit Lake Trail forks south from the top of a rocky knoll at 6,050 feet.

Note: A mystery hot spring on Leggit Creek, unmarked on any map but the state geothermal, hides away about a mile upstream and undiscovered. However, one unlisted even on the geothermal has been found on the trail side of the river just ahead (see Hike 74a).

You'll pass Mattingly Creek Trail at 5 miles and cross the creek itself at another 0.5 mile. This stream, another difficult ford during high water, is a good late-season water source and has fine campsites on both sides of the log crossing.

The 4-mile stretch north to Rock Creek is a moderate climb up the east side of the canyon. A few campsites hide in the woods west of the trail at the end of a meadow 0.25 mile before the first river crossing. The route crosses two wide channels here in a rocky outwash that could be dangerous too early in the summer. Just beyond the second ford, at 6,400 feet, the trail splits. The left branch climbs Rock Creek to Timpa Lake, and the main trail turns east.

The trail crosses the river four times in the 3.5 miles to Flytrip Creek. Scout for footlogs hidden up or downstream. Next, wade a meadow with chin-high wildflowers and a view of Mattingly Peak over your shoulder. Later, the path reaches a few campsites in a flat where the river, just a small stream by this point, splits into several channels and the trail disappears. Wade the stream and aim for a grove of tall trees ahead, where you'll find more campsites. The Flytrip Creek Trail junction, at 7,500 feet, branches off to your right.

A scenic side trip can be made up the steep 1.5-mile trail to Camp Lake at 8,500 feet. Follow a faint path southeast from its inlet to reach Heart Lake in another 0.25 mile. Low ridges separate the many tiny lakes just south and east. Beyond them rises the jagged crest of the Sawtooths topped by 10,651-foot Snowyside Peak. To explore these lakes, you'll need the Snowyside Peak quad.

The final 3-mile stretch offers broad views as the trail switches back up the headwall. Continue over the crest past a meadow to Little Spangle Lake. Peninsulas and inlets around the shallow basin offer a variety of photogenic scenes; rocky islands breaking the surface adopt a new shape from each viewpoint. An idyllic campsite lies across a small meadow at the northeast corner.

Cross a low ridge 200 yards north to reach Upper Spangle Lake at 8,600 feet. The large, circular lake is hemmed in by a steep basin crowded with subalpine fir, lodgepole, and whitebark pine. The only decent campsites lie up a small valley on the northeast side. The Middle Fork Trail ends at Spangle Junction near the south shore. Two new trails begin here, both easy day trips from Spangle Lakes.

HIKE 73b *Spangle Lakes to Tenlake Basin and Ardeth Lake*

See Map on Page 236

General description:	A day hike from Spangle Lakes to more high views and lakes in the Sawtooths.
Difficulty:	Moderate.
Distance:	5 miles round trip.
General location:	15 trail miles northeast of Atlanta.
Elevation gain:	+352 feet, -712 feet.
High point:	8,952 feet.
Maps:	Same as above.
Restrictions:	Recreational user pass required.
Contact:	Sawtooth NRA.

Finding the trailhead: Follow the route above to Spangle Lakes.

The hike: Look south from Spangle Summit to jagged peaks rising above the river canyon far below. To the west, above Spangle Lake Basin, is the snow-capped escarpment by Lake Ingeborg. Look straight up at 10,053-foot Glens Peak to the east. To the north lies the rocky Tenlake Basin. Count at least six of the many small lakes from here.

Turn right (northeast) at Spangle Junction and climb the ridge above the east side of the lake on a well-maintained trail (463). Enjoy the panoramic views from the 8,952-foot summit, the high point on the hike, just a mile up the trail.

Drop down the steep talus slope on the north side of the ridge. You may still find snow patches here in midsummer. The route passes just west of a marshy pond and continues north through a forest of subalpine fir and lodgepoles leading down to Ardeth Lake at 2.5 miles, 8,240 feet.

The path emerges from the woods to overlook beach campsites on the southwest shore. Follow the trail down the west side of the lake to more campsites and viewpoints near the outlet on the northwest side. There's a marvelous outlook from here of permanent snowfields and the jagged silhouette of Glens Peak mirrored in the clear water.

HIKE 73c *Spangle Lakes to Ingeborg, Rock Slide, and Benedict Lakes*

See Map on Page 236

General description:	A day hike from Spangle Lakes to the highest lake reached by trail in the Sawtooth Wilderness.
Difficulty:	Moderate.
Distance:	6 miles round trip.
General location:	15 trail miles northeast of Atlanta.
Elevation gain:	+320 feet, -640 feet.
High point:	8,920 feet.
Maps:	Same as above.
Restrictions:	Recreational user pass required.
Contact:	Sawtooth NRA.

Finding the trailhead: Follow the route above to Spangle Lakes.

The hike: No trek to Spangle Lakes is complete without a side trip to these beautiful lakes. The lightly traveled route offers unlimited opportunities to explore and enjoy the magnificent alpine scenery on all sides. Don't miss it!

The trail (462) begins at Spangle Junction and zigzags up the steep basin on the southwest side. The grade tapers off near a small gem of a lake rimmed with granite walls. Bear northwest a mile across the 8,920-foot plateau to

Rock Slide Lake earned its new name from the slide falling derectly into the small triangular lake from a nearby peak.

reach sky-high Lake Ingeborg at 8,890 feet, the highest major lake accessible by trail in the Sawtooths, which sits on a bench between the Boise River and Benedict Creek drainages. Rosy granite juts above the western side. The shoreline is dotted with limber pine and subalpine fir between tiny campsites.

Circle the east side, then drop 200 feet to Rock Slide, a smaller lake in a similar setting, at another 0.75 mile. The trail descends through the maze of boulders that give the lake its present name. The label shown on the forest map, Robert Jackson Lake, came from a man who decided to name it after himself. When the USGS learned that Mr. Jackson was not only still alive but had no historical connection with the lake, they changed it to the present name.

The path follows the east side of Rock Slide Lake and descends a wooded hillside to a large pond. The meadow on the east shore is cut by serpentine channels that resemble dragons in an oriental rug pattern. Continue north across a marsh sprinkled with tiny wildflowers, then drop down a wooded ridge to reach Benedict Lake at 3 miles, 8,260 feet. Green meadows and a thick border of subalpine fir line the west wall, and two sharp peaks mark the south end of the valley.

74 Lynx Creek Hot Spring

HIKE 74 *To Lynx Creek Hot Spring*

See Map on Page 237

General description:	A day hike to the uppermost hot spring on the Middle Fork and the only one in the wilderness. Swimwear superfluous.
Difficulty:	Strenuous.
Distance:	9 miles round-trip.
General location:	Just east of Atlanta.
Elevation gain:	+780 feet, -620 feet.
High point:	6,050 feet.
Hiking quad:	Atlanta East USGS.
Road map:	Boise National Forest.
Restrictions:	Recreational user pass required.
Contact:	Sawtooth NRA.

Finding the trailhead: Follow the road access above.

The hike: Those not planning to backpack into the Spangle Lakes may be interested in this day's jaunt to a mini-soak hidden at the river's edge at the base of a steep bank below the trail. This spring isn't marked on any map at all.

Stroll the Middle Fork Boise River Trail (460) east through a forest of Douglas-fir and scattered meadows. Leggit Creek is a difficult ford during spring runoff, but on the far side the route hairpins up a hill to a high point of 6,050 feet at the Leggit Lake Junction. This is the 4-mile mark. The route continues well above the river. At another 0.25 mile a faint game path plunges down the bank to the spring.

The hot spring: Totally screened from the path far above, Lynx Creek Hot Spring trickles into a shallow pool at the river's edge a short distance downstream from the mouth of Lynx Creek on the opposite bank. Rebuilt by the few souls who frequent it each year after the river level drops, the pool offers a toasty footbath in a tranquil alpine setting. The temperature is adjustable by shifting a rock or two in the dam.

75 Weatherby (Hot Creek) Hot Springs

General Description:	Potluck dips up a creek on the wrong side of the Middle Fork Boise River. Naked bodies welcome.
Elevation:	4,500 feet.
General location:	13 miles west of Atlanta.
Map:	Boise National Forest.
Contact:	Mountain Home Ranger District, Boise National Forest.

Finding the hot springs: Refer to "Getting to Atlanta" above and take the Middle Fork Road (268) 13 miles downstream. Watch for a sign labeling Hot Creek between Mileposts 55 and 54. Turn left to an airstrip and park on the bank near the windsock end. By mid-August you should be able to wade safely across to the mouth of the creek. Weatherby isn't marked on the forest map, but the creek is.

The hot springs: Weatherby, one of the least known springs along the Middle Fork, has the advantage of invisibility from the road. The strike against it is the problem of crossing the river to investigate. Word has it that several 120-degree seeps and springs hide away about half a mile up the creek. It's a narrow and brushy V-shaped canyon, and the creekbed is said to be the easiest route up. With perseverance and a dash of luck, you may find a soaking pool worth developing.

76 Phifer (Weatherby Mill) Warm Spring

General description:	A shower shack supplied by an artesian well on the Middle Fork Boise River. Wear what you normally bathe in.
Elevation:	4,400 feet.
General location:	15 miles west of Atlanta.
Map:	Boise National Forest.
Contact:	Mountain Home Ranger District, Boise National Forest.

Finding the warm spring: Refer to "Getting to Atlanta" and take the Middle Fork Road (268) 15 miles downstream to the intersection of Forest Roads 327 north and 156 south. Cross the river bridge and turn left into a primitive camp. Park here and rock-hop across the creek. The shack

This shower shack at Phifer Warm Spring looks like it's on its last legs.

sits out in a clearing past a home-built outhouse. The site, once part of the old Weatherby Mill, is currently a mining claim on public land. The spring isn't marked on the forest map, but you can't miss the container.

The warm spring: Spring water gushing from an artesian well is piped into a very funky bathhouse to provide the passerby with a torrent of 86-degree bath water. The 5 x 7-foot shack is lined with plastic and floored with astroturf. A partition separates a changing room (it has stumps for clothes) from the shower cubicle. The old shack may not last another season, but hopefully it will be replaced with a newer model.

Note to hikers: Not too far away are the Trinity Alps, a tiny wonderland of lakes and panoramic views along a 5-mile trail between Big Trinity Lake Campground and the lookout capping 10,000-foot Trinity Mountain. It's definitely worth the trip with a day to spare. Reach this area by either Forest Road 156 or 255.

77 Granite Creek Hot Spring

General description: A roadside soak on the Middle Fork Boise River. Swimsuits essential when standing up.

Elevation: 4,200 feet.

General location: 18 miles southwest of Atlanta.

Map: Boise National Forest.

Contact: Mountain Home Ranger District, Boise National Forest.

Finding the hot spring: Refer to "Getting to Atlanta" and take the Middle Fork Road (268), 15 miles downstream to the junction of Forest Roads 327 north and 156 south. Continue 3.4 miles to a pullout 0.5 mile east of a sign for Granite Creek and hop down the rocks to the pool. The spring isn't marked on the forest map.

The hot spring: Sun-warmed boulders line a large soaking pool at the river's edge just below the road. The outflow from the nearby spring (130 degrees) keeps the sandy-bottomed pool clean. From early to mid-season, users lower the pool temperature by removing a rock or two in the up-stream dam. As the river level drops, dig deeper channels to keep cold water flowing in. The only drawback to this spring is the proximity of the dusty road.

78 Dutch Frank (Roaring River) Hot Springs

General description: Steamy springs and tiny pools on the Middle Fork Boise River. Swimwear advised.

Elevation: 4,100 feet.

General location: 21 miles southwest of Atlanta.

Map: Boise National Forest.

Contact: Mountain Home Ranger District, Boise National Forest.

Finding the hot springs: Refer to "Getting to Atlanta" and take the Middle Fork Road (268), 21 miles downstream to the junction with Forest Road 255 signed to Trinity Lakes, at the Roaring River bridge. *(Hikers:* See Note in 76 above.) Park across the river and follow a short path upstream. Dutch Frank isn't marked on the forest map.

The hot springs: A cluster of springs issues from the ground at temperatures up to 150 degrees, and steamy channels flow across a broad and highly visible flat on the south side of the river. A few small pools dug out of the rocks right at waterline allow a variable blend of temperatures. As the river level drops through the season, new dips must be dug lower down.

79 Brown's Creek Hot Spring

General description:	Hot showerfalls on the wrong side of the Middle Fork Boise River. Swimwear and a life preserver recommended.
Elevation:	3,900 feet.
General location:	25 miles southwest of Atlanta.
Map:	Boise National Forest.
Contact:	Mountain Home Ranger District, Boise National Forest.

Finding the hot spring: Refer to "Getting to Atlanta" and take the Middle Fork Road (268), 25 miles downstream (3.5 miles past the bridge at Forest Road 255). Watch for a sign labeling Brown's Creek Trail, just east of Brown's Creek. There's a pullout where you can look directly across at the plunge. The spring isn't marked on the forest map.

The hot spring: Hot water gushing from fissures in the rocks at 122 degrees cascades down a cliff in several graceful falls. One lands on a tiny beach exposed at low water. This lovely stand-up shower is a bit tricky to reach even when the river's at its lowest, which is usually in late August. It's swift and deep at this bend with rapids just downstream. An inner tube or raft might help.

80 Ninemeyer Hot Springs

General description:	Hot springs flowing down an open hillside, on the wrong side of the Middle Fork Boise River. Swimwear advised.
Elevation:	3,800 feet.
General location:	30 miles southwest of Atlanta.
Map:	Boise National Forest.
Contact:	Mountain Home Ranger District, Boise National Forest.

Travelers aiming for Ninemeyer Hot Springs must be prepared for a long, cold trip across.

Finding the hot springs: Refer to "Getting to Atlanta" and take the Middle Fork Road (268) nearly 30 miles downstream (5.4 miles past Brown's Creek) to Ninemeyer Forest Camp at Milepost 38. The springs, directly across from Ninemeyer Creek, are not marked on the forest map.

The hot springs: Early morning steam blankets the slopes above Ninemeyer as scalding 169-degree water forms rivulets that flow downhill. The geothermal area forms a broad mound above the riverbank, and water pours over the lip. Scalding water also forces it's way up from below and blasts out underwater into an alcove at the east end of the mound.

It's possible to ford the river here from around mid-August through early October. An island in the center greatly eases the crossing. Folks sometimes try to dig out a dip or two right at waterline, where the hot and cold stand a chance of mixing.

81 Round the Bend Hot Spring

General description:	A late-season soak around the bend from Ninemeyer, on the far side of the Middle Fork Boise River. Bathing suits recommended.
Elevation:	3,800 feet.
General location:	30 miles southwest of Atlanta.
Map:	Boise National Forest.
Contact:	Mountain Home Ranger District, Boise National Forest.

Finding the hot spring: Follow the directions above to Ninemeyer and ford the river to the island. Walk to the west end and wade or swim the second half, aiming for the final waterfall downstream. The hot spring is not marked on the forest map.

The hot spring: Many folks who manage to cross the river to Ninemeyer miss another geothermal display just around the downstream bend. Scalding water flows down a sheer cliff coated with streaks of orange algae and hits the river in a quiet eddy that can still be waist-deep by midsummer. The hot water fans out underwater, and within a 3-foot radius it's possible to find a perfect temperature without any pool at all!

The original Round the Bend gang basks in the sun while enjoying a well-earned soak.

82 Pete Creek Hot Spring

General description:	One last hot shower on the far side of the Middle Fork Boise River. Swimwear advised.
Elevation:	3,700 feet.
General location:	32 miles southwest of Atlanta.
Map:	Boise National Forest.
Contact:	Mountain Home Ranger District, Boise National Forest.

Finding the hot spring: Refer to "Getting to Atlanta" and take the Middle Fork Road (268), 32 miles downstream (2.3 miles past Ninemeyer Camp and shortly past the Pete Creek sign) to a very narrow pullout across from the falls. The spring isn't marked on the forest map, but the creek is.

The hot spring: A 30-foot, hot waterfall streams down the side of a cliff into the river on the far bank. By late August through early October it should be possible to ford directly across and build a rocky pool beneath the spray.

83 Loftus Hot Spring

General description:	Roadside grotto pools on a wooded bank above the Middle Fork Boise River. Swimwear recommended if standing up.
Elevation:	3,600 feet.
General location:	34 miles southwest of Atlanta.
Map:	Boise National Forest.
Contact:	Mountain Home Ranger District, Boise National Forest.

Finding the hot spring: Refer to "Getting to Atlanta" and take the Middle Fork Road (268) nearly 34 miles downstream (1.7 miles past Pete Creek) to a pullout at Milepost 34. Climb the short path up to the pools, but beware of poison ivy. Loftus is not marked on the forest map.

The hot spring: Users have dug out a pool beneath an overhanging rocky ledge, and the hot spring (129 degrees) trickles directly over the lip into the water below. The shallow pool, which runs a toasty 105 to 108 degrees, is 8 feet in diameter with sandy bottom. Once seated, if you can take the heat, you have a sense of total privacy. The outflow cools to 100 degrees en route to a second, smaller pool a few feet downhill. Loftus, a popular hideaway, can be enjoyed virtually year-round.

The grotto pool at Loftus Hot Spring sees a steady stream of summer visitors (the tree is no longer there).

84 Smith Cabin Hot Springs

General description:	Hot springs on both banks of the Middle Fork Boise River. Swimwear advised.
Elevation:	3,600 feet.
General location:	35 miles southwest of Atlanta.
Map:	Boise National Forest.
Contact:	Mountain Home Ranger District, Boise National Forest.

Finding the hot springs: Refer to "Getting to Atlanta" and take the Middle Fork Road (268), 34 miles downstream (0.2 mile past Loftus) to a bridge where the road crosses to the south bank. Continue 0.7 mile and park wherever you can find room. Several tracks drop down to converge at the springs. Smith Cabin isn't marked on the forest map.

The hot springs: Spring water emerges from the riverbank at 138 degrees; users sometimes dig a pool in the rocks right at waterline where the temperatures can blend. By mid-August, you should be able to safely ford the river upstream to a line of bushes that conceal more hot springs and a potential dip or two on the opposite bank.

Geothermal note: Locals report a number of springs and seeps in the stretch downstream to Sheep Creek Bridge. Not marked on any map, they can only be pinpointed by their early morning steam.

85 Sheep Creek Bridge Hot Spring

General description:	One last special, for the do-it-yourselfer, on the Middle Fork of the Boise River. Bare buns not recommended.
Elevation:	3,400 feet.
General location:	38 miles southwest of Atlanta.
Map:	Boise National Forest.
Contact:	Mountain Home Ranger District, Boise National Forest.

Finding the hot spring: Refer to "Getting to Atlanta" and take the Middle Fork Road (268) 38 dusty miles downstream (2.7 miles past Troutdale Forest Camp) to a bridge at Milepost 30 where the road recrosses the river. Park at the east end by a trail sign and follow a short path that forks to the right from the trail. The spring, on a rocky bench above the river, isn't marked on the forest map.

The hot spring: Last on the Middle Fork list, this 142-degree spring feeds into a scalding hot, algae-laden source pool 10 feet across. The outflow trickles down a boulder-strewn slope to the river. Dipping diehards sometimes dig a cooler pool out of the rocks lower down and use a tarp to keep it from draining dry, but you'll need a bucket for adding river water.

Note: If you happen to be heading farther down the road, check out the Twin Springs Resort 4 miles downstream. Hot springs on a cliff above the road are piped down to three riverside cabins, each with a hot tub on the deck. Luxury soaks with a view for anyone tiring of the do-it-yourself routine.

G. Out Of Featherville

AN OVERVIEW

Hot springs and hikes: The remote outpost of Featherville, faintly marked on the state map midway between Boise and Ketchum, is the gateway to hot springs along the South Fork Boise River and Smoky Creek. After a bridge-stop south of town (86), we take the Ketchum Road into the Smoky Mountains. Heading east through Sawtooth Forest, the scenic route accesses a variety of soaks as well as many fine campsites in exchange for 32 teeth-jarring miles of washboard road. The first stop is Willow Creek (87), then popular Baumgartner (88). Next is the elusive Lightfoot (89), followed by a hike-in soak at Skillern (90) and a roadside dip at Preis (91). Last but not least comes a geothermal delight at Worswick (92).

Season: The limit on these soaks is the seasonal road, open from mid-May through October, and spring runoff at the streamside pools. The hiking season ranges from May through October in the lower elevations to late June through late September in the higher country farther east. Summer weather is generally hot with scattered thunderstorms and cold nights at higher elevations.

Getting to Featherville: The most direct access from the outside world is via 60 miles of pavement leaving Interstate 84 at Mountain Home: U.S. Highway 20 leads to the South Fork Boise River Road (61), which takes you north past Anderson Ranch Reservoir and Pine. Featherville can also be reached from Atlanta (Area F).

If you are traveling from the Twin Falls area, follow State Route 46 north to Fairfield, home of the district ranger station, then continue north on Forest Road 94 to hit FR 227 near Worswick, midway between Featherville and Ketchum. The 85-mile route is paved to the turnoff to Soldier Mountain, but the last 10 miles are slow. From Ketchum, the route west on FR 227 is all on dirt with a tedious crawl over Dollarhide Summit.

Note: The only services you'll find in Featherville are a bar, a cafe, a tiny general store, and a public phone. The nearest gas station is 10 miles south in Pine.

Featherville Area Map

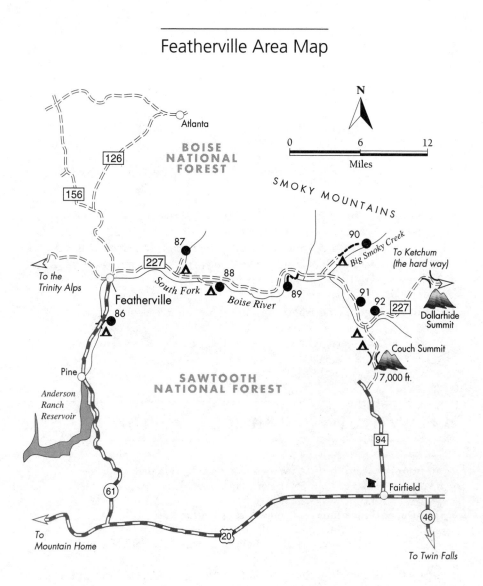

86 Bridge Hot Spring

General description:	Popular roadside soaks on the South Fork Boise River. Swimwear essential.
Elevation:	4,340 feet.
General location:	6 miles south of Featherville.
Map:	Boise National Forest.
Contact:	Mountain Home Ranger District, Boise National Forest.

Finding the hot spring: Refer to "Getting to Featherville" above and take the paved South Fork Road (61) a scant 6 miles south of the FR 227 junction (4.5 miles north of Pine) to the highway bridge that spans the river. You can park on the south bank at Elks Flat Camp. The springs, unmarked on the forest map, are beneath both ends of the bridge.

The hot spring: Spring water emerges from the riverbank at 138 degrees, and steamy channels trickle across the sand into a series of shallow pools. Bathers dig these seasonal dips right at waterline where the river water mixes into the hot pools.

87 Willow Creek Hot Spring

General description:	A toasty soak by a creekside path, near the South Fork Boise River. Swimwear optional.
Elevation:	5,100 feet.
General location:	8.6 miles east of Featherville.
Map:	Sawtooth National Forest.
Contact:	Fairfield Ranger District, Sawtooth National Forest.

Finding the hot spring: Refer to "Getting to Featherville" above and take the Ketchum Road (227) 7 miles east of town to Forest Road 008. Turn left, pass Willow Creek Campground, and go 1.6 miles to a horse camp at the road end. A wooded path follows the creek a good half mile upstream to the pools. The spring is marked on the forest map.

The hot spring: Bubbles rise to the surface of a source pool at 131 degrees through a jungle of algae, and several soakers have been dug in the thermal stream. The uppermost is usually 6 to 10 feet across and a foot or so deep, dammed with logs and sometimes a tarp; it registers a toasty 105 to 108 degrees. One or more cooler, rock-bordered pools can often be found in the bushes where the thermal stream joins the creek. The day I was there, the

The thermal stream at Willow Creek Hot Spring is interspersed with hot pools en route to the creek.

sandy path displayed one bike track, a few footprints, and mostly deer prints. A gathering of huge golden butterflies shared the sunny clearing around the springs.

88 Baumgartner Hot Springs

General description: A campground swimming pool near the South Fork Boise River. Public nudity prohibited.
Elevation: 5,100 feet.
General location: 11 miles east of Featherville.
Map: Sawtooth National Forest.
Contact: Fairfield Ranger District, Sawtooth National Forest.

Finding the hot springs: Refer to "Getting to Featherville" and take the Ketchum Road (227) 10 miles east (3.1 miles past Willow Creek Hot Spring) to the turnoff to Baumgartner Campground. This camp is a fully developed site, which is rare in these parts. You'll find the pool at the road end. Baumgartner is prominently marked on the forest map.

For a bit of civilized soaking, check out Baumgartner Hot Spring's popular swimming pool.

The hot springs: A 15- x 20-foot concrete pool houses the outflow from Baumgartner Hot Springs. The pool, furnished with decking and benches, is maintained by the Forest Service and kept at 104 degrees. There's a fee for camping, but passersby can use the pool free of charge, once they've paid the day-use parking fee. It's open daily from dawn to dusk, May 20 through September. Alcohol or glass containers prohibited.

John Baumgartner deeded the site to the Forest Service for public camping and bathing "in its natural state so far as that is practicable." It's about as far from its natural state as any you'll find in this guidebook, but it's equally far from the commercial resorts at the other end of the spectrum. All things are relative, and the Forest Service has done a tasteful job of developing it.

89 Lightfoot Hot Springs

HIKE 89 *To Lightfoot Hot Springs*

General description:	A day hike to thermal streams on the wrong side of the South Fork Boise River. Swimwear optional.
Difficulty:	Easy.
Distance:	3 miles round trip.
General location:	20 miles east of Featherville.
Elevation gain:	Minimal.
Hot springs:	5,400 feet.
Map:	Sawtooth National Forest
Contact:	Fairfield Ranger District, Sawtooth National Forest.

Finding the trailhead: Refer to "Getting to Featherville" and take the Ketchum Road (227) 20 miles east (1.6 miles past the Lightfoot Hot Springs sign) to a footbridge across the river to Boardman Creek Trail. The springs are named on the forest map.

The hike: There's more to Lightfoot than the algae-laden swamp in the ditch beside the road. The rest lies hidden across the river. Reach it by fording near the sign (not recommended during high water) or by driving upstream to the footbridge and following a user-built path back on the opposite bank. Start hunting for clues after you pass a cabin in the woods and enter a clearing.

The hot springs: Three adjacent springs issue from the ground at 133 degrees and form shallow streams. One boasts a 110-degree pool dammed with rocks and a log; it's clean except for a layer of algae on top and bottom. Another, closer to the river, contains a tiny seasonal pool dug out of a rocky wash. Both are usable in a pinch, and chances are you'll have them all to yourself. There's also a rumor that there is something worth checking out over against the hillside.

Lightfoot Hot Springs • Skillern Hot Springs
• Preis Hot Spring • Worswick Hot Springs

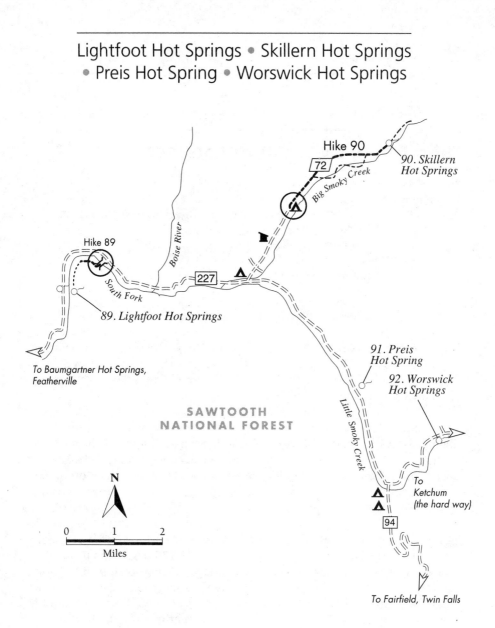

Hike 90

72

Big Smoky Creek

90. *Skillern Hot Springs*

Hike 89

Boise River

227

South Fork

89. *Lightfoot Hot Springs*

To Baumgartner Hot Springs,
Featherville

91. *Preis Hot Spring*

92. *Worswick Hot Springs*

SAWTOOTH
NATIONAL FOREST

Little Smoky Creek

To
Ketchum
(the hard way)

94

N

0   1   2

Miles

To Fairfield, Twin Falls

90 Skillern Hot Springs

HIKE 90 *To Skillern Hot Springs*

General description:	A day hike to secluded hot pools in the Smoky Mountains. Swimwear superfluous.
Difficulty:	Easy.
Distance:	5 miles round trip.
General location:	25 miles east of Featherville.
Elevation gain:	+300 feet, -100 feet.
High point:	5,900 feet.
Hiking quad:	Paradise Peak USGS.
Road map:	Sawtooth National Forest.
Contact:	Fairfield Ranger District, Sawtooth National Forest.

Finding the trailhead: Refer to "Getting to Featherville" and take the Ketchum Road (227,) 24 miles east (4 miles past the footbridge to Lightfoot) to a turnoff to Big Smoky. It's also the same distance from Fairfield, and it's 5.5 miles from Forest Road 94. The side road soon forks right, passes Big Smoky Guard Station, and ends in 1.3 miles at Canyon Campground. The trailhead is at the end of the loop. Skillern is named on the maps.

The hike: After the first easy mile, Big Smoky Creek Trail (72) hugs the stream a bit too closely, requiring four crossings, so an alternate route has been built up the bank. The high trail not only keeps your feet dry but offers views up and down the canyon. Grass and sagebrush speckle the southeast facing hills. The cooler slopes across the canyon are wooded with ponderosa. At 2 miles the trails converge by the creek, and you'll reach the springs in another 0.5 mile. *Note:* You'll pass several trails branching left including two signed to Skillern Creek. Don't be tempted—stay in the main canyon.

The hot springs: Water gushing from the rocks at 140 degrees cascades down a cliff, then flows across a grassy flat to the creek. Here you'll find one or more seasonal pools where you can blend the temperatures into a half-decent soak, but only if you keep stirring nonstop. Upstream, around the side of the cliff, there's a hidden pool partway up the side. This little gem, a depression in the rocky wall well above the high water mark, features a steamy shower spraying the surface and a rock and log dam to contain it.

Geothermal note: A second hot spring 6 miles upstream, marked on the forest map and named Big Smoky on the state geothermal, is reported by locals to be unusable for humans but very popular with the elk and deer population.

91 Preis Hot Spring

General description:	A roadside hot box in the Smoky Mountains. Swimwear essential.
Elevation:	5,500 feet.
General location:	27 miles east of Featherville.
Map:	Sawtooth National Forest.
Contact:	Fairfield Ranger District, Sawtooth National Forest.

Finding the hot spring: Refer to "Getting to Featherville" and take the Ketchum Road (227) 27 miles east (3.5 miles past the Skillern turnoff at Big Smoky Creek). It's 2.2 miles from Forest Road 94. There's no landmark but a rock pile near the road. Preis is named on the forest map.

The hot spring: Rocks form a border screen around a 3- x 4-foot box recessed into the ground. Spring water bubbles up into the cozy container at 106 degrees, and the temperature can be lowered by plugging the inflow. You can drain and refill the box after each soak, and a submerged bench makes a handy seat. The dubious function of the border, besides providing the only landmark, is to conceal the box itself. It's not high enough to screen any soaker over age five from full view by passing motorists.

92 Worswick Hot Springs

General description:	A hot springer's fantasy spread out on both sides of the road, in the Smoky Mountains. Swimwear advised.
Elevation:	5,600 feet.
General location:	32 miles east of Featherville.
Map:	Sawtooth National Forest.
Contact:	Fairfield Ranger District, Sawtooth National Forest.

Finding the hot springs: Refer to "Getting to Featherville" and follow the Ketchum Road (227) 2.1 miles east of the junction with Forest Road 94, a distance of nearly 32 miles from Featherville. There's ample space south of

The pools at Worswick Hot Springs appeal to a variety of happy soakers.

the road to park or pitch a tent. The springs are signed by the road and named on the forest map.

The hot springs: A complex of fifty springs issues from a grassy hillside at temperatures up to 180 degrees and branches into a thermal stream flowing at a staggering rate of 250 gallons/min. It runs through a series of pools, flows through pipes under the road, and then snakes across a flat into Little Smoky Creek. The temperature rises through the summer as the output of an incoming cold stream diminishes.

There's a toasty soaker dammed with a log partway up the hill, a rock-lined pool by the culvert, and one or more shallow pools near the creek. Smaller dips are scattered in between. When I was there in early June, the upper pool clocked in at 110 degrees, the "culvert pool" at 100, and the creekside one at 95 degrees. Take your choice!

The area around Worswick is home to a number of unique plants including a variety of tiny sunflower. Wildlife frequent the springs when human life has left. The number of visitors has increased over the years, and it's important to remember the basics: tread lightly and leave no trace.

H. OUT OF KETCHUM

AN OVERVIEW

Hot springs and hikes: From Ketchum, roadside hot springs fan out in three directions. To the southeast, we find an oasis at Milford Sweat (93) on the road to Craters of the Moon. Next come some scenic soakers west of town at Frenchman's Bend and Warfield (94). Then, State Route 75 runs northwest through the Sawtooth NRA, where a last roadside dip (95) on the way up to Stanley combines well with alpine hikes into the Smoky Mountains.

Season: While the pools at Milford Sweat and Russian John should be accessible and usable nearly year-round, the streamside dips west of Ketchum are limited mainly by spring runoff. The hikes in the high country of the Smoky Mountains are best done in July, after the runoff, through mid-September. The summer climate varies with changing elevations, and travelers should come prepared for the full gamut.

Ketchum Area Map

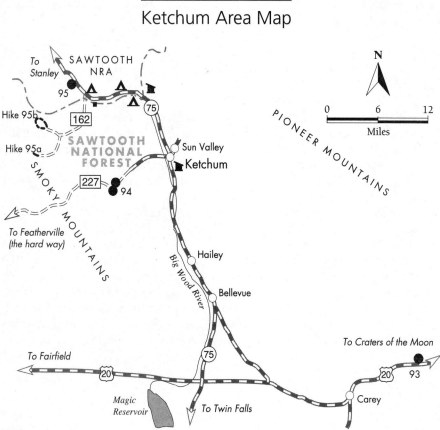

93 Milford Sweat (Wild Rose) Hot Springs

General description:	A lava hot pool on the road to Craters of the Moon. Swimwear recommended if standing up.
Elevation:	5,000 feet.
General location:	55 miles southeast of Ketchum.
Map:	Shoshone District, BLM.
Contact:	Shoshone District, BLM.

Fnding the hot springs: From State Route 75 in Ketchum, drive south 26 miles, then take U.S. Highway 20 east 19 miles to Carey. Continue 9.7 miles to a small pullout on the north side, midway between Mileposts 214 and 215 or 15 miles west of Craters of the Moon Visitor Center. Follow a path 50 yards north and east to the pool. The hot springs are marked on the map.

The hot springs: A desert oasis bordered by sunflowers lies barely concealed from the busy highway behind a low ridge. The pool, encased in chunky black lava rock with a gravel bottom, is 12 feet across and over 4 feet deep at the near end where plywood forms a crude deck. The

This lava rock pool at Milford Sweat Hot Springs has year-round access.

111-degree springs cool to a comfortable soak as the stream winds through a marsh to the pool.

The springs are on public land, but the pool itself is on a parcel owned by the Milford Sweat family. The owners don't mind people using the pool as long as they don't abuse the privilege. No soap or shampoo, no glass containers, and please pack out what you pack in.

Note to hikers: Craters of the Moon National Monument is well worth a visit. A variety of hiking trails access points of interest in the lava-strewn landscape, including several caves and tunnels. The Visitor Center has all the specs, and there's a campground at the start of the loop drive.

94 Frenchman's Bend and Warfield Hot Springs

General description:	Popular roadside soaks on a creek in the Smoky Mountains. Public nudity a no-no.
Elevation:	6,400 feet.
General location:	10.5 miles west of Ketchum.
Map:	Sawtooth National Forest.
Restrictions:	Recreational user pass required.
Contact:	Ketchum Ranger District, Sawtooth National Forest .

Fnding the hot springs: From State Route 75 in Ketchum, take the Warm Springs Road (227) west on a surface that deteriorates from pavement to gravel in 4 miles. Just beyond a bridge at 10.5 miles, a sign welcomes visitors to Frenchman's Bend. Park in the designated area and walk a short way upstream to the pools. It's labeled Warfield on the forest map, but there are actually two separate springs here. Find the latter by walking down the gated dirt road by the bridge.

The hot springs: Frenchman's Bend consists of two highly seasonal soaking pools roughly 4 feet across and 1 to 2 feet deep, nestled side by side in the creekside boulders right below the road. The springs bubble in at 124 degrees, but the pool temperature is easy to lower by shifting rocks in the dam. There should also be a pool or two on the opposite bank a few yards upstream that emerges from the spring runoff a bit sooner.

The site has rules posted that are strictly enforced: no public nudity, no alcohol or glass containers, no parking except in designated areas, and no soaks between 10 P.M. and 4 A.M. The list may be objectionable to some, but it's alleviated the overuse/abuse problems encountered in the past. The access road is plowed up to the homes a few miles back, and folks sometimes ski in for a quiet winter soak.

264

A dyed-in-the-wool skinnydipper takes his chances in the roadside pools at Frechman's Bend Hot Springs.

Warfield sits out on a grassy flat bordering a bend in the creek less than a quarter mile downstream. At one time, there was a "two-holer" soaking shack here, but now it just consists of several hot seeps that flow down and merge into the creek. The elevated banks allow users to dig shallow pools even during runoff.

95 Russian John Warm Spring

General description:	A roadside retreat with a mountain view. Semi-skinnydippable.
Elevation:	6,900 feet.
General location:	18 miles northwest of Ketchum.
Map:	Sawtooth National Forest.
Restrictions:	Recreational user pass required.
Contact:	Ketchum Ranger District, Sawtooth National Forest.

Finding the warm spring: From Ketchum, drive 18 miles northwest on State Route 75, the Sawtooth Scenic Biway. The turnoff is located 2.5 miles past Baker Creek Road (see following hikes). Turn west onto a dirt road just

A meadow with a backdrop of snow-capped peaks in the Boulder Mountains is the setting for Russian John Warm Spring.

south of Milepost 146, then south to the parking area by the pool. The spring is not marked on the forest map.

The warm spring: A short stack of logs barely shelters an old sheepherder's soaking pool from sight of the busy highway 200 yards away. Spring water perks up through the sand, at 100 degrees, into a user-friendly pool 6 feet across and a foot or so deep. There's a plug for draining, but it takes a good hour to refill. The pool runs 85 to 95 degrees; a pleasant soak in a semi-secluded spot.

HIKE 95a *Baker Lake*

General description:	A brisk stroll to a popular lake in the Smoky Mountains, near Russian John Warm Spring.
Difficulty:	Moderate.
Distance:	4 miles round-trip.
General location:	25 miles northwest of Ketchum.
Elevation gain:	880 feet.
High point:	8,800 feet.
Hiking quad:	Baker Peak USGS.
Road map:	Sawtooth National Forest.
Restrictions:	Recreational user pass required.
Contact:	Ketchum Ranger District, Sawtooth National Forest.

Finding the trailhead: From Ketchum, drive 16 miles northwest on State Route 75. Turn left on Baker Creek Road (FR 162) (2.5 miles south of Russian John) and drive 9 dusty miles to the road-end parking area and trail sign.

The hike: This pretty lake, a pleasant family outing, is well worth the short climb. Tall stands of fir rim the grassy shore, and pink granite cliffs cast their reflections in the clear water. Baker Lake Trail (138) starts off by crossing a branch or two of Baker Creek and then follows a track up a grassy hillside and through a forest. The rerouted path doubles the mileage, but the net result is an easier grade. The route then follows a wooded ridge westward to the lake.

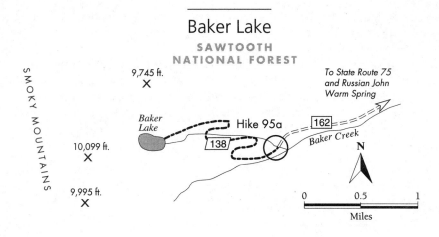

Baker Lake
SAWTOOTH NATIONAL FOREST

S M O K Y   M O U N T A I N S

9,745 ft.
X

To State Route 75
and Russian John
Warm Spring

Baker Lake

Hike 95a

162

Baker Creek

138

10,099 ft.
X

9,995 ft.
X

N

0   0.5   1
Miles

HIKE 95b *Norton Lakes Loop*

General description:	A day hike to secluded lakes in the Smoky Mountains, near Russian John Warm Spring.
Difficulty:	Strenuous.
Distance:	5.5 miles round trip (including a 3.5-mile, part cross-country loop).
General location:	23 miles northwest of Ketchum.
Elevation gain:	1,840 feet (520 feet to start of loop; loop, 1,180 feet; to Upper Norton Lake, 140 feet).
High point:	9,300 feet.
Maps:	Same as above.
Restrictions:	Recreational user pass required.
Contact:	Ketchum Ranger District, Sawtooth National Forest.

Finding the trailhead: Follow the road access above, taking Baker Creek Road (162), 6 miles southwest to Norton Creek. Turn right on Norton Creek Road (170) and drive a mile to the end. Park wherever you can find room and dig out your boots.

The hike: Most visitors take the steep trail to the Norton Lakes, pause for lunch, and head back the way they came in. The adventurous hiker can make a loop that circles from Lower Norton Lake through a maze of granite ridges and basins past Big Lost and Smoky Lakes before dropping down a canyon to rejoin the trail. In addition to excellent scenery, the off-trail route offers the fun of exploration and discovery.

Wade the deep gully of Norton Creek (treacherous during high water). Turn right at the register box and climb the wooded west bank on Norton Lake Trail (135). Cross a side creek and continue up a valley with a view of a serrated ridge. The 2-mile trail to the lakes has a gain of 1,300 feet. Lower

Norton Lakes Loop

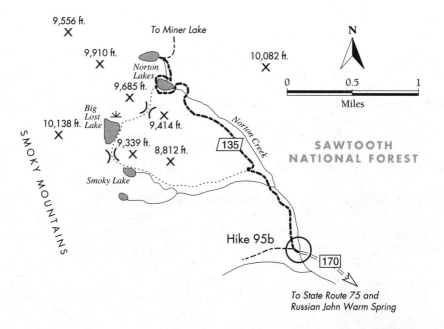

Norton Lake is fringed with wildflowers spaced between stands of tall trees; rocky slopes back the far shore. Upper Norton is reached by a short path that climbs the flower-choked inlet.

Leave the trail behind at Lower Norton Lake and walk around to the west end. Pick a route heading due south up a scree-filled gully. Cross over the lowest point on the ridge and the highest point on the hike at 9,300 feet. Bear right (southwest) as you descend the far side and head across a rocky valley to the next lake.

The moonscape setting for Big Lost Lake is a wide shoreline strewn with giant boulders; a jagged ridge tops the scree slope rising directly above the west side. Huge chunks of gnarled driftwood punctuate meadows and wide beaches along the eastern shore. This is a prime place to explore and take a break for lunch.

Cross a low saddle at the south end of the lake and wind down a rocky hill on a faint path curving east to Smoky Lake. This emerald green gem lies in a rocky bowl backed by wooded ridges. Skirt the northeast shore and follow an overgrown path down the north side of the outlet through clusters of shooting stars and monkeyflowers.

Contour eastward down the widening canyon, staying high to avoid the tangle of downed trees below. Continue 1.5 miles below Smoky Lake to intersect Norton Lake Trail in a forested area. You can't miss this junction. Follow the trail back down the hill for the last mile.

I. OUT OF STANLEY

AN OVERVIEW

Hot springs and hikes: The Salmon River near Stanley is home to a family of roadside hot dips (96–100) as well as a variety of alpine hikes in the eastern Sawtooths. A remote trail north of Sunbeam leads to wilderness hot springs on Upper Loon Creek (101). Following State Route 75 farther east, a back road leads to a bath at Slate Creek (102) with a nearby hike. And still farther east, a longer back road accesses a hike in the White Clouds and ends with soaks at West Pass and Bowery (103, 104). Everything in this area, except for Loon Creek, is within the Sawtooth NRA.

Season: Elkhorn's "boat box" is usable year-round, and the tubs at West Pass and Bowery would be except for the seasonal road. The riverside pools are mostly underwater during runoff. Access to Upper Loon depends on road closures; the prime time for soaks is July through October. The high Sawtooths are often obscured by snow until late July and snowed in again by mid-September. Summer weather brings warm days and cold nights at higher elevations, and hikers should travel prepared for rain or even snow.

Hot Springs near Stanley

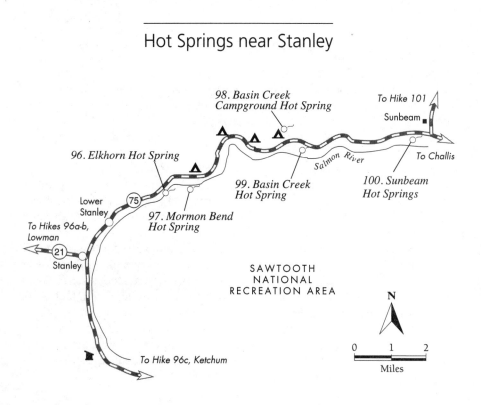

270

Stanley Area Map

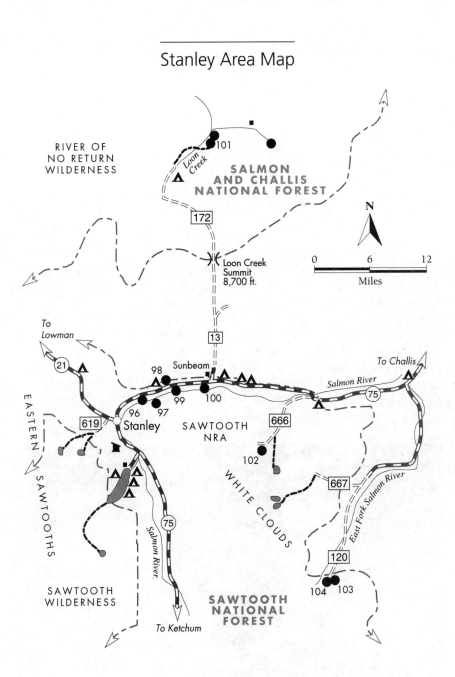

RIVER OF
NO RETURN
WILDERNESS

Loon Creek

101

SALMON
AND CHALLIS
NATIONAL FOREST

172

N

Loon Creek
Summit
8,700 ft.

0   6   12
Miles

13

To
Lowman

21

Sunbeam

To Challis

98

Salmon River

75

99   100

96   97

Stanley

SAWTOOTH
NRA

666

619

EASTERN

102

SAWTOOTHS

WHITE CLOUDS

667

East Fork Salmon River

75

Salmon River

120

SAWTOOTH
WILDERNESS

104   103

SAWTOOTH
NATIONAL
FOREST

To Ketchum

96 Elkhorn (Boat Box) Hot Spring

General description:	A riverside hot box below the highway, near the eastern Sawtooth trailheads. Swimwear essential.
Elevation:	6,100 feet.
General location:	2 miles east of Stanley.
Map:	Sawtooth National Forest.
Restrictions:	Recreational user pass required.
Contact:	Sawtooth NRA.

Finding the hot spring: Drive 2 miles east of Lower Stanley on State Route 75. Watch for a small pullout by the river in the middle of a left curve, 0.7 mile east of Milepost 192. Park here and climb down the rocks. Elkhorn isn't marked on the forest map.

The hot spring: This is the first of several hot dips along the Salmon River Scenic Biway that begins east of Stanley. One or two seasonal pools and a year-round soaking box tucked between boulders mark the highly visible spot. Scalding hot, 136-degree water is piped under the highway to the tub, and the only way to cool it is to scramble back and forth to the river with a bucket. If somebody has made off with the bucket, you're out of luck.

Locals call this tub at Elkhorn Hot Spring the "boat box" because of its popularity with kayakers and raft groups. It looks like some bicyclists have hit the jackpot as well.

HIKE 96a *Alpine, Sawtooth, and McGown Lakes*

General description:	A day hike or overnighter featuring alpine views and the largest lake in the Sawtooths, near Elkhorn Hot Spring.
Difficulty:	Moderate.
Distance:	12 miles round trip.
General location:	5.5 miles west of Stanley.
Elevation gain:	+2,090 feet, -280 feet.
High point:	8,800 feet.
Hiking quad:	Stanley Lake USGS.
Road map:	Sawtooth National Forest.
Restrictions:	Recreational user pass required.
Contact:	Sawtooth NRA.

Finding the trailhead: Drive 2.5 miles west of Stanley on State Route 21. Turn left onto gravel Iron Creek Road (619) and drive 3 miles to a campground loop at the road end. The trailhead for these lakes as well as for Goat Lake is located near the far end of the loop.

The hike: The star attraction of this highly popular trip is the giant sapphire oval of Sawtooth Lake. Craggy Mount Regan dominates the skyline directly across the granite bowl, and trails around both sides offer a variety of unobstructed views. This may well be the most photographed scene in the Sawtooths. **Note:** Campfires are prohibited within 200 yards of both Alpine and Sawtooth lakes.

The Iron Creek Trail (640) meanders southwest for the first 1.25 miles to the wilderness line. Next, it passes Alpine Way branching east, signed to Marshall Lake. (Alpine Way also accesses the following hike to Goat Lake.) The route west curves gently to a second junction in a boggy flat then angles up an open slope above Iron Creek Valley. Splash across Iron Creek and climb to an overlook of lovely Alpine Lake in 4 miles. A spur drops to the north shore and Alpine Peak stands out to the south above the treetops.

The main trail snakes above Alpine Lake. The ridgetop has views of peaks to the north and south and overlooks the Iron Creek Valley stretching east toward Stanley. A little more scenic climbing brings you past a small tarn in an alpine valley to the outlet and northern end of the largest lake in the Sawtooths at 5 miles, 8,430 feet.

Starkly beautiful Sawtooth Lake stretches a full mile from head to toe and a half mile across. A deep basin of granite slabs outlines the oval shape, and a few twisted trees cling for survival to the steep walls. The jagged contours of Mount Regan shoot 1,760 feet skyward from the surface at the far end.

Looking down the length of mile-long Sawtooth Lake, craggy Mount Regan dominates the southern horizon.

There's a junction by the outlet. Before going on to McGown Lakes, take the left fork to a granite knoll with a full view across the lake. The scenic path hugs the shore for an easygoing mile to a flower-lined pond directly beneath Mount Regan before dropping through a glacier-cut gap to reach Baron Creek Trail in 6 lightly traveled miles.

The main trail branches west to climb 360 feet in a 0.5-mile traverse across the north wall. This spectacular stretch offers an eagle's perspective across the full length of the lake to Mount Regan and the gap carved in the far wall. The path crests at 8,800 feet, the high point on the hike, then quickly drops into a rocky valley to reach the largest McGown Lake just south of the trail at 6 miles.

The McGown Lakes lie in shallow rock basins below low peaks. They haven't much to offer other than a couple of campsites, a few stunted trees, and the magnificent route connecting them with Sawtooth Lake a mile away.

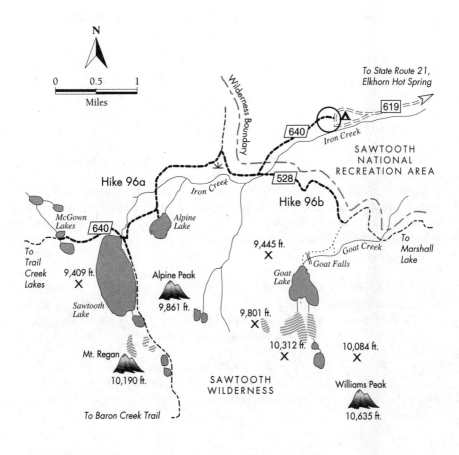

N

0   0.5   1
Miles

To State Route 21,
Elkhorn Hot Spring

619

640

Iron Creek

SAWTOOTH
NATIONAL
RECREATION AREA

Wilderness Boundary

Hike 96a

Iron Creek

528

Hike 96b

McGown
Lakes   640

Alpine
Lake

9,445 ft.
X

Goat Creek

To
Marshall
Lake

To
Trail
Creek
Lakes

9,409 ft.
X

Alpine Peak

9,861 ft.

Goat Falls

Goat
Lake

Sawtooth
Lake

9,801 ft.
X

Mt. Regan

10,312 ft.
X

10,084 ft.
X

10,190 ft.

SAWTOOTH
WILDERNESS

Williams Peak

To Baron Creek Trail

10,635 ft.

HIKE 96b *Goat Lake*

General description:	A day hike or overnighter for experienced hikers only to a rock-walled lake in the Sawtooths, near Elkhorn Hot Spring.
Difficulty:	Strenuous.
Distance:	7 miles round trip.
General location:	5.5 miles west of Stanley.
Elevation gain:	+1,750 feet, -240 feet.
High point:	Goat Lake, 8,220 feet.
Maps:	Same as above.
Restrictions:	Recreational user pass required.
Contact:	Sawtooth NRA.

Finding the trailhead: Follow the road access above.

The hike: A second trek from the Iron Creek Trailhead offers a challenging route to a lake hemmed in by sheer granite cliffs. Hanging snowfields on the far wall cast chunks of ice into the water. A misty waterfall threads down from two higher lakes, and another borders the hike into the lake. The trip isn't recommended for inexperienced hikers, as much of the route is a steep scramble on loose rock. Good hiking boots are a must. *Note:* Campfires are prohibited within 200 yards of Goat Lake.

Follow Iron Creek Trail (640) 1.25 miles southwest through a lodgepole pine forest, past the wilderness boundary, to a trail junction in a grassy valley. The right fork continues up Iron Creek Valley to Alpine, Sawtooth, and McGown lakes (see above); the left fork is signed to Marshall Lake and traces the wilderness line southeast.

Turn east onto Alpine Way (528) and cross Iron Creek. Pass through a boggy forest, then wade a small stream laced with wildflowers where the trail contours around a wooded ridge. It swings slowly southward and then veers sharply northeast a second time at 2.75 miles.

Leave the main trail by turning right on a primitive path that climbs below a cliff. A spur branches downhill in 0.25 mile to the base of Goat Creek Falls. The track to the lake becomes increasingly eroded and slippery. Look south at the first switchback to another ribbon of falls across the basin; farther south, Williams and Thompson Peaks slice into the horizon. The path shoots up the north wall to the top of the falls, gaining 800 feet in the 0.75-mile climb from Alpine Way.

Cross the creek above the falls, then hike the last hundred yards to reach the north shore of Goat Lake at 3.5 miles. Cliffs on three sides rise 1,500 feet above the surface, and jagged towers lean out as if ready to leap. Experts can boulder-hop around the east shore to compare views, but the traverse is steep and tricky.

The Leaning Latrine. *The first time I was there, Iron Creek Campground had an unusual feature, an outhouse tipped forward on a slant. I was unaware of this as I approached one night without a flashlight. The door seemed hard to open, and then it slammed shut behind me! In total darkness, I found myself staggering to stand upright and reach the seat. I couldn't understand what was wrong—I'd only had one beer after the hike. The following morning it all became clear when I saw that it was the outhouse, and not me, that was tipsy.*

HIKE 96c *Cramer Lakes*

General description:	A backpack up a glacial canyon to high lakes, wildflowers, and breathtaking views in the Sawtooths, near Elkhorn Hot Spring.
Difficulty:	Moderate.
Distance:	14.5 miles round trip.
General location:	6.5 miles south of Stanley.
Elevation gain:	1,840 feet.
High point:	Upper Cramer Lake, 8,400 feet.
Hiking quads:	Mount Cramer and Warbonnet Peak USGS.
Road map:	Sawtooth National Forest.
Restrictions:	Recreational user pass required.
Contact:	Sawtooth NRA.

Finding the trailhead: Drive 4.5 miles south of Stanley on State Route 75 and turn right on Redfish Lake Road. Drive 2 miles to a sign on the right marking the backpacker's parking lot. This is the only spot you can leave your car for overnight trips.

The hike: A boot-beaten path up a deep canyon bordered by the best known and most climbed peaks in the Sawtooths branches south to the Cramer Lakes in a popular hike from Redfish Lake. Inviting campsites at Middle Cramer face a waterfall across the blue green water. Upper Cramer, the largest of the three, sits directly beneath the towering face of a 10,500-foot peak. Mount Cramer peeks from behind the canyon leading south to Cramer Divide.

With the help of the Redfish Lake ferry, you can save 5.5 miles of walking to the far end. The scenic 20-minute ride offers close views of Mount Heyburn's sheer cliffs and the sharp pinnacles of The Grand Mogul guarding the head of the lake. The ferry drops hikers at Inlet Transfer Camp. Trail mileage and elevation gain are given from this point.

Redfish Lake Creek Trail (101) starts above the inlet campground in heavy timber and climbs alongside the rushing creek into the wide, U-shaped canyon. Pop out of the woods at the base of Mount Heyburn and zigzag past a junction with the lakeside trail. Continue with a moderate climb past a stretch where house-sized boulders almost block the path. Climbers enjoy this area for its solid rock and easy access.

The path continues alongside the plunging creek and passes occasional waterfalls, then climbs through a forest of lodgepole pines, spruce, and fir. There are frequent glimpses of the spires and domes rimming the canyon walls. You'll pass the orange-hued Saddleback at 2 miles, nicknamed by climbers "Elephant's Perch." Continue past Goat and Eagle Perches to reach Flatrock Junction at 3.5 miles, 7,400 feet.

Cramer Lakes

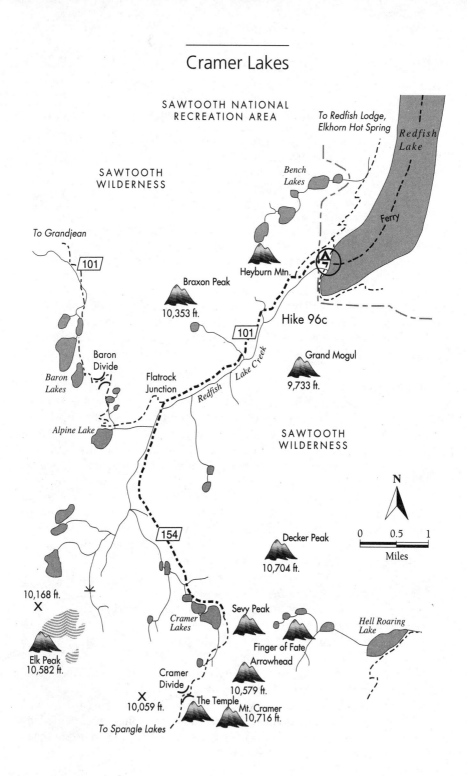

SAWTOOTH NATIONAL
RECREATION AREA

To Redfish Lodge,
Elkhorn Hot Spring

*Redfish
Lake*

SAWTOOTH
WILDERNESS

*Bench
Lakes*

To Grandjean

101

Ferry

Braxon Peak

Heyburn Mtn.

Hike 96c

10,353 ft.

101

Baron
Divide

Grand Mogul

9,733 ft.

Flatrock
Junction

Lake Creek

*Baron
Lakes*

Redfish

Alpine Lake

SAWTOOTH
WILDERNESS

N

154

Decker Peak

0   0.5   1

10,704 ft.

Miles

10,168 ft.
X

*Cramer
Lakes*

Sevy Peak

*Hell Roaring
Lake*

Finger of Fate
Arrowhead

Elk Peak
10,582 ft.

Cramer
Divide

10,579 ft.

X
10,059 ft.

The Temple

To Spangle Lakes

Mt. Cramer
10,716 ft.

At Flatrock Junction, named for the granite slabs filling the canyon floor, the trail splits. The right fork branches off to cross Baron Divide, drop to Baron Lakes, and finally exit at Grandjean in a total of 18.5 miles. The left fork climbs past the Cramer Lakes over 9,480-foot Cramer Divide, and offers access to many classic lakes and peaks farther south.

Turn south onto Cramer Lakes Trail (154). Cross Redfish Lake Creek and stroll 0.5 mile upstream through forest, then follow switchbacks up the wall to a hanging valley where the route swings southeast. Enjoy views across to craggy Reward and Elk Peaks. A last gentle stretch brings you to Lower Cramer Lake at 6.8 miles. Settle down here for a bit of solitude, or walk another 0.5 mile to the upper lakes for less privacy but wall-to-wall views.

The graceful 20-foot waterfall at Middle Cramer Lake makes an idyllic setting for the large campsite facing it at the outlet, while tiny tentsites along the narrow shelf between the upper two lakes combine a vertical view down the broad falls with a panorama of jagged peaks rimming Upper Cramer Lake. It's a delightfully difficult choice to make!

97 Mormon Bend Hot Spring

General description:	A hot dip on the far side of the Salmon River, near the eastern Sawtooth trailheads. Swimwear advised when standing up.
Elevation:	6,100 feet.
General location:	2 miles east of Stanley.
Map:	Sawtooth National Forest.
Restrictions:	Recreational user pass required.
Contact:	Sawtooth NRA.

Finding the hot spring: From Lower Stanley, go 2 miles east to the first bend in the river past Elkhorn Hot Spring and just west of Milepost 193. Dig out your wading shoes and aim for the far bank, but only when the river is low. The hot spring is not shown on the forest map and is misplaced 3 miles east on the state geothermal.

The hot spring: A channel of 100-degree water flows across a meadow into a small rock-lined soaking pool. The pool, 350 yards downstream from the boat box at Elkhorn, is barely visible on the far bank. It requires a major river ford, which by late summer shouldn't be too tricky, but offers the finder a high chance of a quiet soak unobserved by passing cars. An inner tube might ease the crossing.

98 Basin Creek Campground Hot Spring

General description:	Soaking pool(s) hiding in a campground, near the eastern Sawtooth trailheads. Daytime skinnydipping not recommended.
Elevation:	6,100 feet.
General location:	7 miles east of Stanley.
Map:	Sawtooth National Forest.
Restrictions:	Recreational user pass required.
Contact:	Sawtooth NRA.

Finding the hot spring: Drive 7 miles east of Stanley on State Route 75 to Basin Creek Campground. Pull into campsite 4 and wander casually into the bushes. You'll have to wade the creek to reach the pools. The spring isn't marked on the forest map.

The hot spring: What some folks stopping here never discover is that there happens to be a hot spring on the far bank of the creek flowing past the campsites; the bushy border screens a pleasant soaking pool or two from view. Control the temperature by adjusting the creekside rocks. A semi-private spot in a public campground!

99 Basin Creek (Kem) Hot Spring

General description:	Hot dips sandwiched between the highway and the Salmon River, near the eastern Sawtooth trailheads. Swimwear advised.
Elevation:	6,100 feet.
General location:	7 miles east of Stanley.
Map:	Sawtooth National Forest.
Restrictions:	Recreational user pass required.
Contact:	Sawtooth NRA.

Finding the hot spring: Drive 7 miles east of Stanley on State Route 75. Just beyond Basin Creek Campground (see above), there's a pullout on the right with a "Day Use Only" sign, where a short path now drops to the hot spring. As of the summer of 1997, there is no more driving or camping down by the pools. The spring isn't shown on the forest map.

The hot spring: This site offers a bit more seclusion than the other roadside dips east of Stanley. It's at the base of a bank below the busy

A good time to visit Basin Creek Hot Spring is just after the spring runoff.

highway; motorists aren't likely to notice a few bathers unless they know just where to look.

Two family-sized soaking pools, often filled to capacity, border the river. You can move the rocks to either divert the 133-degree inflow or admit river water. The pools swamp during high water and the rocks wash away; they take on a new look every summer depending on the talents of the volunteers who rebuild them.

100 Sunbeam Hot Springs

General description:	Highly visible pools squeezed between the highway and the Salmon River. No nudes, just "prudes and prunes."
Elevation:	6,100 feet.
General location:	11 miles east of Stanley.
Map:	Sawtooth National Forest.
Restrictions:	Recreational user pass required.
Contact:	Sawtooth NRA.

Despite high visibility, summer visitors flock to the shallow soaking pools at Sunbeam Hot Springs.

Finding the hot springs: Drive 11 miles east of Stanley on State Route 75 (4 miles past Basin Creek Hot Spring or a mile west of Sunbeam Resort). Look for an old stone bathhouse and interpretive signs at a large turnout. A short path leads down the bank to the pools. The springs are named on the forest map.

The hot springs: One last cluster of highway hot soaks lines the Salmon River Scenic Biway from Stanley to Challis. Boiling water at 169 degrees is piped beneath the highway from the springs and flows across a gravel beach into several popular pools at the river's edge. Bathers can adjust the rocks to create a variety of soaking temperatures. Succeeding pools, each cooler than the one above, emerge as the river recedes through the summer.

The historical bathhouse has recently been repaired and restored, and a stone outhouse in the same style has been built nearby. This work was done in conjunction with the Idaho Centennial Historical Site near Sunbeam Dam.

101 Upper Loon and Owen Cabin Hot Springs

HIKE 101 *To Both Hot Springs*

General description:	A day hike or overnighter to a chain of pearls lost in the River of No Return Wilderness. A skinnydipper's delight.
Difficulty:	Easy.
Distance:	11.5 miles round trip.
General location:	45 miles northeast of Stanley.
Elevation gain:	+240 feet, -640 feet.
High point:	Trailhead, 5,400 feet.
Hiking quad:	River of No Return Wilderness, South half.
Road map:	Same or Challis National Forest.
Contact:	Middle Fork Ranger District, Salmon and Challis National Forest.

Finding the trailhead: Drive 12 miles east of Stanley on State Route 75 (a mile past Sunbeam Hot Springs) to Sunbeam Resort. Turn left on the Yankee Fork Road (13) and drive 8 easy miles north to Bonanza, home of the historic Yankee Fork Dredge that sits marooned in a small pond walled in by the rocks it dredged out of the creek.

Bear left beyond the barge onto rocky Loon Creek Road (172), which follows Jordan Creek north past other historic sites to Loon Creek summit. The seasonal road, open from July 1 to November 1, snakes over the 8,700-foot crest that forms the wilderness boundary and down the far side to eventually reach the road-end trailhead 33 dusty miles from the highway. Tin Cup Campground, a mile from the end, provides a welcome rest. The springs are marked on the map.

The hike: A series of wilderness hot springs lie at close intervals on Upper Loon Creek in the Salmon River Mountains north of Sunbeam. All are located on the east side, which is also the trail side, of the broad creek, and all branch into steamy channels that either trickle or tumble down the rocky banks. They vary in appearance from unimpressive to spectacular. Some are for display purposes only, while some are outstanding soaks.

Loon Creek Trail (101), a pleasant stroll, is far less tiring than the access road. The canyon walls are coated with grass and sagebrush on the south-facing slopes while the hills facing north are lightly wooded with Douglas-fir. The upper canyon consists of talus slopes and rock outcrops patched

Upper Loon and Owen Cabin Hot Springs

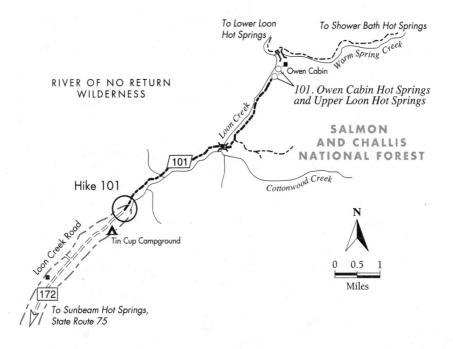

To Lower Loon
Hot Springs

To Shower Bath Hot Springs

Warm Spring Creek

Owen Cabin

RIVER OF NO RETURN
WILDERNESS

*101. Owen Cabin Hot Springs
and Upper Loon Hot Springs*

Loon Creek

**SALMON
AND CHALLIS
NATIONAL FOREST**

101

Hike 101

Cottonwood Creek

N

0   0.5   1

Miles

Loon Creek Road

▲
Tin Cup Campground

172

To Sunbeam Hot Springs,
State Route 75

with lime-yellow and orange lichen. Beyond an 800-foot rock face, the path fords small streams fringed by grassy flats. The route closely follows the lively creek. In August and September you can sometimes see salmon struggling up the rapids to reach their spawning grounds.

The trail bridges Loon Creek at 3 miles, passes a few campsites, and soon reaches a stretch of midsummer berry picking interspersed with more easy stream hopping. At 5 miles are the remains of a log cabin hidden in a tangle of greenery down by the creek. The first hot spring branches into a broad flow over the rocky flat, and a few shallow pools edge the creek. There's a shaded campsite in the grass beside the cabin.

The hot springs: Just around the next bend, hot waterfalls from the two largest springs, both at 145 degrees, plunge over 20-foot cliffs into Loon Creek. One or more seasonal soaking pools are usually dug out against the cliff directly below the falls. Green moss and ferns hug the bank beneath the misty spray. The temperature may be a smidge too hot, but the rocks can be rearranged to admit a cold mix from the creek. The outflow swirls with a marbling of hot and cold currents into a protected alcove.

Owen Cabin Hot Springs emerge at 133 degrees in a meadow a scant 0.5 mile farther on. Two channels flow gently through the grass into pools of rust-colored algae, then continue down the bank to fill shallow, rock-lined soaking pools by the creek. The crumbling ruins of the historic Owen cabin, engulfed in vegetation, lie just beyond the wide meadow.

With time to spare: From this point, there's a choice of extensions to this trip. You could take Warm Spring Creek Trail 8.5 miles upstream as an alternate way to Shower Bath (see Hike 106). The primitive route involves fording the creek six times, but it passes another wild gem, a privately owned but rarely visited shower shack and hot tub at Foster Ranch. You could also continue down Loon Creek Trail all the way to Lower Loon and Whitey Cox Hot Springs (see Hike 107), which might be an easier access than the one described.

102 Slate Creek (Hoodoo) Hot Spring

General description:	A hot bath in an up-again/down-again bath house on a dirt road in the White Clouds. Keep swimwear handy.
Elevation:	7,040 feet.
General location:	30 miles east of Stanley.
Map:	Sawtooth National Forest.
Restrictions:	Recreational user pass required.
Contact:	Sawtooth NRA.

Finding the hot spring: Drive 23 miles east of Stanley on State Route 75. Turn right on Slate Creek Road (666) just beyond a bridge over the Salmon River. Drive south 7 bumpy miles or so to a narrow pullout by the bathhouse, a few hundred yards past a formerly closed gate. The spring is named on the forest map.

The hot spring: This spring has had its ups and downs. The original funky but functional bathhouse, which, as reported in the last edition of this guide, was torn down a few years back, was standing once again in the summer of 1997. The walls are a mixture of loose planks and warped plywood. The roof is more open to the elements than ever, and a hole for a window lets the bather enjoy the view uphill.

The shack straddles a hot spring on the wooded bank above a lively creek. An incoming pipe feeds 122-degree water into an aging, recessed box big enough to hold two cozy couples. A second crucial pipe admits cold water, but the present plumbing badly needs replacing. A removable slat in the wall lets the water drain out. With or without the bathhouse it's still a scenic soak, but if all else fails there's a shower at the culvert down the road.

Slate Creek Hot Spring and Crater Lake

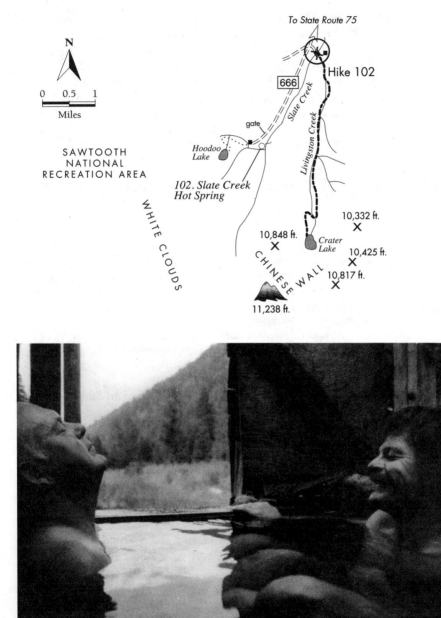

N

0   0.5   1
Miles

SAWTOOTH
NATIONAL
RECREATION AREA

To State Route 75

666

Slate Creek

Livingston Creek

Hike 102

gate

Hoodoo
Lake

102. Slate Creek
Hot Spring

WHITE CLOUDS

CHINESE WALL

10,332 ft.
X

10,848 ft.
X

Crater
Lake

10,425 ft.
X

10,817 ft.
X

11,238 ft.

The shack at Slate Creek Hot Spring still has a way of eliciting smiles of contentment from those who venture within its patchwork walls.

HIKE 102 *Crater Lake*

General description:	A day hike or overnighter to a quiet lake in the White Clouds, near Slate Creek Hot Spring.
Difficulty:	Moderate.
Distance:	8 miles round-trip.
General location:	29 miles east of Stanley.
Elevation gain:	2,480 feet.
High point:	Crater Lake, 8,920 feet.
Hiking quad:	Livingston Creek USGS.
Road map:	Sawtooth National Forest.
Restrictions:	Recreational user pass required.
Contact:	Sawtooth NRA.

Finding the trailhead: Follow the directions above to Slate Creek Road and drive upcanyon 5.6 miles. Turn left at the second ranch to the road-end parking area at Slate Creek. The trail is shown on the forest map but not on the USGS quad.

The hike: A pleasant walk up a lively creek reaches blue-grey Crater Lake tucked between twisted ridges in a lightly used part of the Sawtooth NRA. The route has many stream fords but is easy to follow.

Cross the creek on a footbridge and walk up an abandoned mining road. At most of the stream crossings, you'll find rocks or logs. The route for the first mile or so is a fairly gentle climb through deep woods, then it begins to steepen. At 3 miles, there's an open traverse with increasingly broad views as the track heads up the rocky canyon wall. Make one giant switchback at the head of the canyon to reach the outlet of Crater Lake at 4 miles.

Wander around the lake on either side and enjoy views of the contorted Chinese Wall, a striated ridge that buckles in the center as if someone had tried to lift it off the ground from both ends. Across from the Chinese Wall is the rounded end of Railroad Ridge. A sawtoothed crest fills the gap in between. The unusual basin gives a touch of class to an otherwise modest lake.

Pain remedy: *I was halfway through a peanut butter and carrot sandwich as I sat on a warm rock gazing up at the Chinese Wall. The sky suddenly turned darker than Slate Creek below. I'd just gulped down the last bite when the drops started to fall, and the drizzle turned to a spitting downpour before I was halfway down the trail. The harder it poured, the faster I ran!*

I'd no sooner leaped into the car when the sky turned a sickly shade of yellow and let loose a wild volley of hailstones. The ground, covered with dancing snow peas, turned white in an instant. I slithered the last mile up the road with a smile on my face because the perfect antidote to nasty weather was close at hand. Ten minutes later, I slid into a cocoon of steamy water and leaned back against a handy plank.

Sleet and hail pelted the crude shelter at Slate Creek Hot Spring while I waited out the storm in total comfort.

103 West Pass Hot Spring

General description:	A remote trio of bathtubs below a dirt road in the White Clouds. Wear what you normally bathe in.
Elevation:	6,800 feet.
General location:	65 miles southeast of Stanley.
Map:	Sawtooth National Forest.
Restrictions:	Recreational user pass required.
Contact:	Sawtooth NRA.

Finding the hot spring: From Stanley, take State Route 75 east, 36 miles (4 miles past Clayton) and turn south, across from a highway campground onto the East Fork Salmon River Road (120). Pavement turns to gravel in 15 to 16 miles, and Big Boulder Creek Road (see following hike) goes straight where the main road veers left at 18 miles.

The seasonal road, open from May 1 through December 1, soon passes a winter gate and 10 miles later a camping area. Next come two gates a mile apart, which you must leave as you find them. Between the gates, the road bridges West Pass Creek by a cabin. Bear left just past the second gate on a track that climbs above the creek to a grassy flat. Park here and take a short path past an abandoned mine down to the tubs. The spring, a total of 29 miles from the highway, is marked on the forest map.

The hot spring: Hoses running from the old mine shaft supply 112-degree water to three bathtubs perched side by side above West Pass Creek. The two old tubs with gaping holes have finally been replaced, with a third thrown in for good measure. Lower the soaking temperature by diverting the hoses. A lime-green cast to the water makes you feel like you're afloat in a margarita.

104 Bowery Hot Spring

General description:	A high-tech spa on the East Fork Salmon River, in the White Clouds. Highly skinnydippable.
Elevation:	6,800 feet.
General location:	66 miles southeast of Stanley.
Map:	Sawtooth National Forest.
Restrictions:	Recreational user pass required.
Contact:	Sawtooth NRA.

New arrivals prepare for a hot bath with a view at West Pass Hot Spring.

Finding the hot spring: Follow the road access above past the turnoff to West Pass Hot Spring and continue 0.6 mile to a locked gate. Park here and walk the road toward Bowery Guard Station, turning left just before the bridge on a path to the tub, a scant half mile altogether. The spring, 30 miles from the highway, isn't marked on the forest map but the guard station is.

The hot spring: The latest news at Bowery is a barn red fiberglass spa with all the bells and whistles still attached. This one looks like it's here to stay, as it's been recessed, along with a matching tongue-and-groove skirting, into a custom-fit plywood deck. It features a sturdy railing at one end for clothes and towels, and a pair of young aspen trees have holes for their trunks in the floor.

Steamy water is gravity-fed from the 125-degree spring. Lower the temperature by diverting the hose and adding a few dozen buckets of river water. The spa can be refilling while you sun bathe on the deck. Two buckets and a broom are currently on hand.

Warning: Visitors to West Pass and Bowery should contact the Forest Service for an update on access. The road crosses private land, and the gates are sometimes locked.

The 6-foot diameter spa at Bowery Hot Spring takes a good hour to fill and many trips back and forth with the bucket.

HIKE 104 *Island and Goat Lakes*

General description:	A long day hike or overnighter to alpine lakes in the White Clouds, en route to West Pass and Bowery Hot Springs.
Difficulty:	Strenuous.
Distance:	13 miles round trip.
General location:	59 miles southeast of Stanley.
Elevation gain:	+2,220 feet, -240 feet.
High point:	Island Lake, 9,240 feet.
Hiking quads:	Boulder Chain Lakes and Livingston Creek USGS.
Road map:	Sawtooth National Forest.
Restrictions:	Recreational user pass required.
Contact:	Sawtooth NRA.

Finding the trailhead: Follow the road access above to Big Boulder Creek Road (667) and drive 4 miles to a trail sign near the dilapidated Livingston Mill. Turn left to the trailhead parking area.

The hike: This popular trail, which also accesses Walker Lake and the Big Boulder Lakes, is the shortest route into the White Cloud Mountains. The Boulder Chain Lakes to the south see fewer visitors but also require twice the hiking distance to reach. Bordered by granite slabs and lofty peaks, these lakes

Island and Goat Lakes

offer stiff competition to the well-known Sawtooth Range farther west.

Big Boulder Creek Trail (680) crosses sagebrush flats backed by redrock towers. At 2 miles a side path branches south to Frog Lake and Boulder Chain Lakes. The main trail works up through a forest of lodgepole and aspen, dips across Quicksand Meadows, crosses side creeks on logs, then climbs past the rushing outlet of Goat Lake to the Walker Lake junction in just over 5 miles.

Climbing to Island Lake, the path weaves back and forth across the stream. In a marsh 0.4 mile up, a half-mile path forks left across a rocky saddle to Goat Lake. You'll reach a campsite at Island Lake less than a mile from the Walker Lake junction. Talus slopes and trees border Goat Lake beneath a wall of colorfully banded rock which striates Granite Peak beneath a skyline of pinnacles. Narrow Island Lake, dotted with two islands, is rimmed by granite benches, a cliff on one side, and a small meadow at the upper end.

With time to spare, this trip combines well with Walker Lake just a mile above the junction. The half-mile-long lake, misnamed Walter on the USGS quad, is backed by cliffs and a double-tipped peak. A cross-country route from here climbs 2 miles to the Big Boulder Lakes—Cove, Sapphire, and Cirque—nestled in the White Clouds at a high point of 10,000 feet.

J. OUT OF CHALLIS

AN OVERVIEW

Hot springs and hikes: This frisbee-shaped area will send you flying all the way from Barney Warm Springs (105) on BLM land in the remote Pahsimeroi Valley 65 miles southeast of Challis, to a hair-raising but spectacular drive northwest of town that climbs a convoluted crest deep into the River of No Return Wilderness. At 30 miles, a path plunges to geothermal delights at Shower Bath (106). At the road's end, a long descent to the Middle Fork Salmon River reaches hot soaks at Lower Loon and Whitey Cox (107).

Season: Barney, a cool soak at a high elevation, is best on a hot summer day. Prime time for the wilderness hot spring treks is midsummer through early fall. Off-season use is hampered by seasonal road closures, high-elevation trailheads, and spring runoff on all but Barney. Hikers should prepare for nippy or foul weather at the start of the season that shifts to hot and dry toward the end.

Challis Area Map

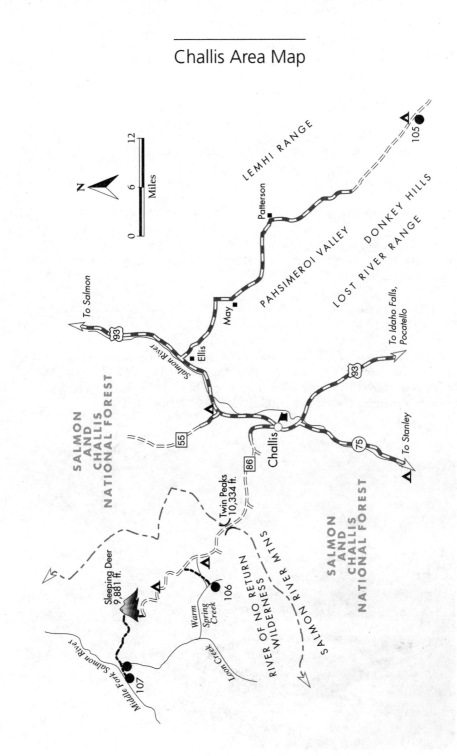

105 Barney Warm Springs

General description:	A roadside warm pond in a remote desert valley. Skinnydippable with discretion.
Elevation:	6,400 feet.
General location:	65 miles southeast of Challis.
Map:	Challis National Forest.
Contact:	Salmon Field Office, BLM.

Finding the warm springs: Go north from Challis 18 miles on U.S. Highway 93 to Ellis. Take the Pahsimeroi Road 34 miles southeast on pavement then another 13 on gravel to Summit Creek BLM Campground. At the south end of camp, a short spur goes west to the pond. Barney is named on the forest map but misleadingly called *hot*.

The warm springs: Barney flows to the surface of a waist-deep pond within an enclosure of logs. The temperature may be marginally warmer deep in the pool, but it generally hovers around 83 degrees. One oldtimer says the logs were once a corral, back before the pond was filled by damming the springs. Another story has it that the logs are the remains of an old house that once sat over the pond. The group that spins this tale can all remember swimming underneath the house as kids back in the '40s.

Folks with any sense visit Barney Warm Springs at midday, but one brave soul opted for a night soak under a full moon. Marty "Splash" Nelson photo

In any case, the pond makes a refreshing stop on a hot summer day. On one side of the sagebrush valley are the Donkey Hills backed by the Lost River Range. On the other side is the Lemhi Range capped by 11,612-foot Bell Mountain.

Note: Barney supports a healthy population of tiny tropical fish that someone planted years back.

106 Shower Bath Hot Springs

HIKE 106 *To Shower Bath Hot Springs*

General description:	A grueling day hike or overnighter to a geothermal fairyland in the River of No Return Wilderness. Swimwear superfluous baggage.
Difficulty:	Strenuous.
Distance:	12 miles round trip.
General location:	29 miles northwest of Challis.
Elevation gain:	+100 feet, -2,340 feet.
High point:	Trailhead, 8,040 feet.
Hiking quad:	River of No Return Wilderness, South half.
Road map:	Same or Challis National Forest.
Contact:	Middle Fork Ranger District, Salmon and Challis National Forest.

The vision and the challenge: Imagine stumbling knee-deep in a torrent of icy water through a deep chasm that sees maybe an hour of sun a day, rounding the last bend numb and exhausted, and finding paradise spread out before you. Steamy water flows over the sides of a wide alcove and splashes into rocky bowls below. Clouds of spray billow out over a soft green carpet beyond the pools.

Like the legendary Shangri-la, Shower Bath lies at the end of an exhausting and difficult trek. Some 29 teeth-jarring miles on a knife-edged road are followed by a trail diving downhill into a stream that you must navigate through a narrow gorge. The last 300-yard stretch can be waist deep through late July; when flooded, Warm Spring Creek can't be waded with any degree of safety. Be sure to check with the Forest Service in Challis before attempting the trip.

Finding the trailhead: The odyssey begins by taking U.S. Highway 93 or State Route 75 to Challis. Go west into town and turn right on Challis Creek

Shower Bath Hot Springs

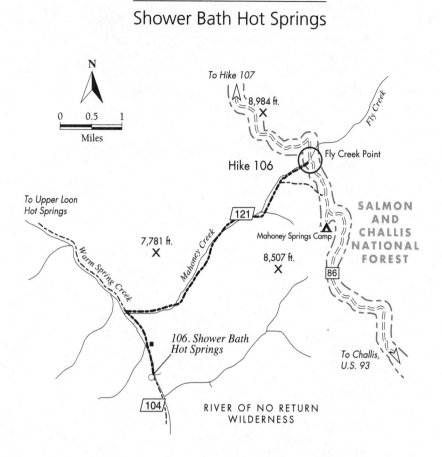

To Hike 107

8,984 ft.
X

Fly Creek

Hike 106

Fly Creek Point

To Upper Loon Hot Springs

121

7,781 ft.
X

Warm Spring Creek

Mahoney Creek

Mahoney Springs Camp

8,507 ft.
X

SALMON
AND
CHALLIS
NATIONAL
FOREST

86

N

0   0.5   1
Miles

106. Shower Bath Hot Springs

To Challis, U.S. 93

104

RIVER OF NO RETURN
WILDERNESS

Road. Drive 9 paved miles into Salmon and Challis National Forest, where pavement ends and Sleeping Deer Road (86) begins. Bear right at 10.5 miles and right again at a confusing junction at 15 miles. Climb a rocky surface to crest at 10,334 feet on Twin Peaks (the wilderness boundary). The seasonal road, open from August 1 to October 1, irons out somewhat beyond the top but becomes very narrow; sheer dropoffs are offset by wall-to-wall views.

Shortly past a turnoff to Mahoney Springs Camp at 28 miles, you'll see the first of two signs a mile apart that both read "to Warm Spring Creek Trail;" the second, located opposite the Fly Creek trailhead, is the shorter route. See the following hike for another adventure at the end of the road and Hike 101 for an alternate route to Shower Bath by way of Upper Loon Hot Springs. Shower Bath is named on the map.

The hike: Drop over the edge on a path that plunges 760 feet in the first mile to reach a spring, two old log huts, and a junction where the two trails join together to follow Mahoney Creek downhill. The route dives another mile through heavy timber to a side stream, after which the grade becomes more

Hikers will find one or more rocky soaking pools at Shower Bath Hot Springs hidden behind a curtain of steam and fine spray.

moderate. The sinuous track weaves across Mahoney Creek wherever the canyon walls get too snug on one side. When you're not fording the creek, you'll be jumping the many side streams that feed it. Continue down through a blend of pine, fir, and aspen to finally bottom out on a sagebrush flat at Warm Spring Creek with a total loss of 2,340 feet in 5 miles.

Take a breather and stroll upstream on Warm Spring Creek Trail past the old Warm Spring Ranger Cabin, built in 1910, and on to the mouth of the narrows. Prepare for a cold plunge as rock walls 200 feet high funnel the path into the swift moving creek. Work your way upstream taking care to avoid the deeper holes. The path emerges briefly along the west bank, then drops back into the stream. Tiny hot springs trickle down the sheer walls, but these aren't the ones you came this far to see. Round the final bend and haul out on dry land on the west bank at 6 miles (5,800 feet).

The hot springs: A broad wall of water trickles and tumbles in a 40-foot drop over the rim, and rainbows shimmer as sunlight pours through the mist. Gushing from the ground above at 120 degrees, the flow cools to a perfect soak in the tiny pools directly below.

Lichen speckles the rock-ribbed walls, and thick grasses carpet the floor with inviting campsites. A warm stream meanders through the meadow to another soaking pool spread out by the creek. Enjoy your stay, but please treat the fragile ecosystem around the springs with the respect it deserves.

107 Lower Loon & Whitey Cox Hot Springs

HIKE 107 *To Both Hot Springs*

General description:	A rugged backpack featuring wilderness hot dips in the depths of the Middle Fork Salmon River Canyon. Public nudity prohibited within the river corridor.
Difficulty:	Extremely strenuous. See Appendix C for alternate route.
Distance:	35 miles round trip.
General location:	43 miles northwest of Challis.
Elevation gain:	+ 120 feet, -5,420 feet.
High point:	Trailhead, 9,340 feet.
Hiking quad:	River of No Return Wilderness, South half.
Road map:	Same or Challis National Forest.
Contact:	Middle Fork Ranger District, Salmon and Challis National Forest.

Lower Loon and Whitey Cox Hot Springs

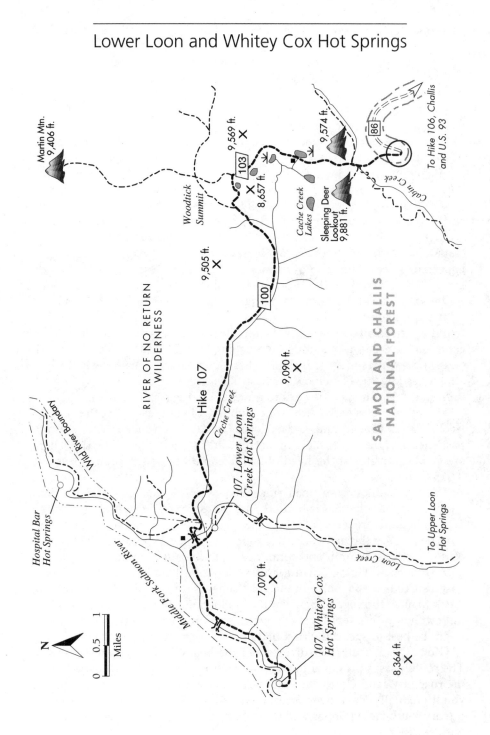

Finding the trailhead: Follow the spine-tingling access road described above. Continue along the narrow crest to reach the road-end trail sign at 43 total miles. Perch your car in the tiny pullout and dig out your dusty boots. Only Cox is marked on the map.

The hike: A long and lonesome journey offers the more adventurous hiker a chance to sample a broad cross section of the River of No Return Wilderness as well as a steamy double dip at the rainbow's end. The primitive path begins in subalpine forest on a frosty mountaintop. Two life zones, 14 miles, and well over 5,000 feet below, it comes to rest in the semi-arid canyon carved by the Middle Fork Salmon River. Sagebrush lines the way to Whitey Cox Hot Springs, and a twilight forest of ponderosa pine frames the stroll up Loon Creek to one of the finest hot pools in the wilderness.

High lakes below the trailhead draw an occasional fisherman, and the distant hot springs attract seasonal boatloads of river rats, but the rugged backcountry sees almost no visitors at all. Pristine scenery and solitude more than make up for the roundabout route.

The first mile of the Martin Mountain Trail (103) contours around a knoll studded with whitebark pine to a four-way junction on a high saddle. The left fork drops to Cabin Creek while the middle path climbs a mile to the lookout cabin on the 9,881-foot summit of Sleeping Deer Mountain. The right fork takes you down a precipitous slope, where it traverses beneath the lookout to another saddle 200 feet below the first. This stretch is usually snow covered until mid-July. The path is hard to trace across the second saddle.

The route drops between granite slabs to a long meadow at the head of Cache Creek. Five glacially carved lakes fan out at half-mile intervals. You'll pass the first lake in the marshy meadow and see a log cabin nearby. There are good campsites at the head of the lake and beside the cabin, elevation 8,685 feet.

The trail contours an open ridge that overlooks Cache Creek Canyon and the second lake that is bordered by meadows. As it swings around the headwall, there are views of other lakes and the rugged Salmon River Mountains below. You'll reach a signed junction at 4 miles. The right fork branches off to Woodtick Summit and continues on to Martin Mountain.

Turn left and zigzag down a grassy slope on the Woodtick Cutoff Trail past a small lake to reach a branch of Cache Creek 400 feet below. Ford the creek to meet the rugged trail you'll be following down to the river. This 10-mile stretch offers few level campsites and difficult access to water, so it might be best to spend the first night somewhere around the lakes.

Cache Creek Trail (100) dives down the headwall of the craggy canyon. The route passes primeval forests and lush meadows; at times you'll hear the roar of Cache Creek far below. As you continue the grueling plunge, you'll gradually leave deep forests. Grass and sagebrush begin to speckle the dry south-facing slopes, and the cooler hills facing north become wooded with stocky pines.

The soaking pool at Lower Loon Hot Springs, visited chiefly by river rafting groups, has all the key ingredients to keep a boater or backpacker happy for hours.

Near the bottom of the plunge, cross the stream at two crossings where you can count on wet feet. Shortly beyond the last ford, the trail comes to rest at a junction. Bear left on the Middle Fork Trail to Loon Creek Pack Bridge, at 4,030 feet, 14 miles and 5,300 feet below the trailhead on Sleeping Deer Mountain. Turn left across the bridge to find Lower Loon 0.25 mile upstream.

Note: There's an alternate way to these hot springs, via Loon Creek (see Hike 101), that's even more roundabout but with a far easier grade and a better trail. There's also a similar soaking box to that at Lower Loon that can be reached with half the hiking miles but with a grueling plunge of 4,300 feet (see Hike 109a below).

The hot springs: At Lower Loon you'll discover a rectangular pool lined with split logs and at least 20 feet long, 10 feet across, and 3 feet deep. Fed by several springs with temperatures up to 120 degrees, the flow cools to a blissful soak en route through a long pipe to the crystal-clear pool. One side is shaded by a canopy of evergreen boughs while a few planks on the creek side form a sun deck. The setting is a blend of seclusion and open views.

For the 7-mile round trip from here to Whitey Cox, head 0.5 mile downstream to the river and swing west up the Middle Fork Trail. The gentle route passes sagebrush slopes dotted with age-old ponderosas. You'll spot some campsites down on a sand bar dominated by one tall pine 3 miles upstream. The springs are on the second bench above it, at 4,160 feet. The lower bench holds a tadpole-laden pond and the grave of Whitey Cox, a miner who died in a rockslide while prospecting the area.

The few shallow soaking pools at Whitey Cox lie in a meadow strewn with wildflowers. By late summer the 130-degree springs have slowed in their flow, and their silty bottoms stir up easily. The pools don't have much to offer the gourmet hot springer other than countless acres of solitude, a pleasant view across the canyon, and the highly scenic stroll along a wild and grand old river.

Note: Both of these hot springs receive high use during the float season. Please treat them with TLC and practice low-impact camping techniques.

K. OUT OF SALMON

AN OVERVIEW

Hot springs and hikes: Running south of Salmon, U.S. Highway 93 accesses a hike to Goldbug's thermal cascades (108). Far west of town, a remote trail in the River of No Return Wilderness plummets to Mormon Ranch Hot Springs (109) while another climbs to the Bighorn Crags. A trip southeast of town passes Sharkey (110), while a jump north and west hits a soak at popular Panther (111). Back roads farther northwest climb to a remote bathhouse at Horse Creek (112). This dispersed batch of bubblies resides in Salmon and Challis National Forest with the exception of Sharkey, which sits on BLM land.

Salmon Area Map

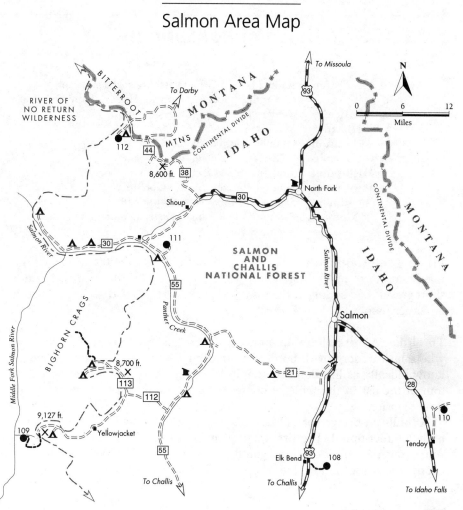

Season: Goldbug is at its best from late runoff in early summer through the fall months. The wilderness treks are limited to midsummer through early fall due to high-elevation trailheads and seasonal roads. Sharkey and Panther can be accessed most of the year, but high elevation narrows access to Horse Creek to the few months between snowfalls. Summer weather varies from hot and dry at lower elevations to cool and frequently rainy at higher elevations.

108 Goldbug (Elk Bend) Hot Springs

HIKE 108 *To Goldbug Hot Springs*

General description:	A day hike climbing to steamy soaks and hot waterfalls in a desert canyon. Highly skinnydippable.
Difficulty:	Moderate.
Distance:	4 miles round trip.
General location:	23 miles south of Salmon.
Elevation gain:	+920 feet, -120 feet.
High point:	Goldbug, 5,200 feet.
Hiking quad:	Goldbug Ridge USGS (optional).
Road map:	Salmon National Forest (optional).
Contact:	Salmon/Cobalt Ranger District, Salmon and Challis National Forest.

Finding the trailhead: Drive 23 miles south of Salmon (0.8 mile past the Elk Bend store) on U.S. Highway 93. Near Milepost 282, turn east on a short gravel road ending at the trailhead parking area. Goldbug isn't marked on either map.

The hike: A brisk climb up a craggy desert canyon ends at a green oasis where lush undergrowth borders a tumbling geothermal stream. Goldbug, known locally as Elk Bend or simply Warm Springs, may be near the bottom of the list in the table of contents but certainly ranks tops as an all-time favorite.

A trailhead bridge spans Warm Spring Creek, and switchbacks drag the path 200 feet uphill. The first quarter mile crosses private land, but as the route traverses an open slope you'll pass a gate onto BLM land. The trail drops across a second bridge where greedy cottonwoods and willows choke

Goldbug Hot Springs offers delightful hideouts to those who enjoy a bit of privacy.

Goldbug Hot Springs

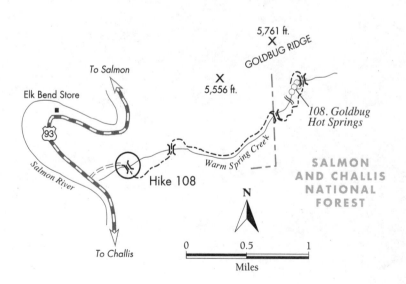

the creek in a green line winding up the valley between dry sagebrush slopes dotted with pinyon and juniper. Ahead of you, Goldbug Ridge reveals a jagged slit. The path crosses a third bridge near the canyon's mouth then zigzags up the wall. The last half mile (from the national forest boundary to the springs) is extremely steep and slippery and can be icy in the winter.

Start peering through the foliage for pools interspersed in the cascade. First comes the rollercoaster pool, which is very easy to miss. It features a bizarre waterslide that tumbles down from upper pools, then bounces up and billows out over the surface. Beyond are many others, most of them closer to the far bank. To reach these pools, climb to the fourth bridge and drop down the other side.

Camping at the springs is discouraged by the Forest Service and next to impossible because of the tight canyon, but you'll pass a grassy campsite or two near the creek between the second and third bridge. Many pools disappear during spring runoff and the creek temperature becomes somewhat cooler, so it may not be worth the trip at that time.

The hot springs: Hot and cold springs mix underground here and emerge as geothermal cascades that flow over dropoffs. A chain of bubbly pools of varying size, shape, and temperature punctuates the spaces between falls. The hottest pools are found on the trail side of the canyon, cold in the center, and warm to hot pools on the far side. The current keeps them scoured clean. Lush greenery hugs the banks and overhangs the stream to create a private world around each sparkling pool.

109 Mormon Ranch Hot Springs

The time to visit Mormon Ranch Hot Springs is NOT when the air temperature matches that in the box.

HIKE 109a *To Mormon Ranch Hot Springs*

General description:	A rugged overnighter to a remote wilderness soaking box near the Middle Fork Salmon River. Swimwear optional.
Difficulty:	Strenuous. See Appendix C for alternate route.
Distance:	14 miles round trip.
General location:	73 miles southwest of Salmon.
Elevation gain:	+120 feet, -4,760 feet.
High point:	Trailhead, 8,940 feet.
Hiking quad:	River of No Return Wilderness, both halves.
Road maps:	Both wilderness quads or Salmon National Forest.
Contact:	North Fork Ranger District, Salmon and Challis National Forest.

Mormon Ranch Hot Springs

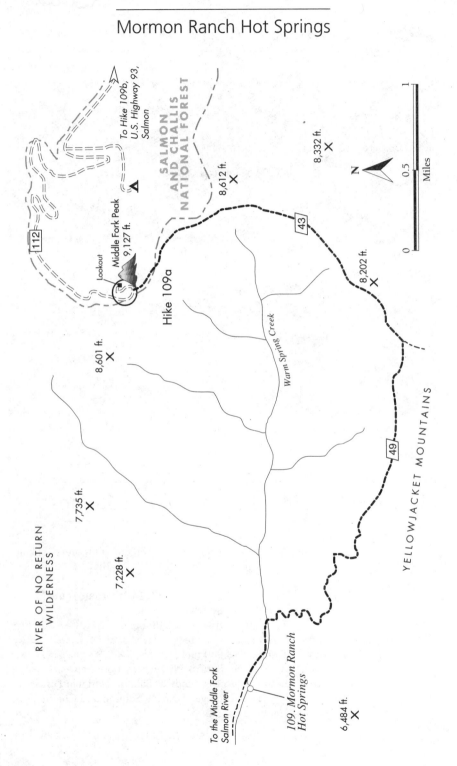

To Hike 109b,
U.S. Highway 93,
Salmon

SALMON
AND CHALLIS
NATIONAL FOREST

8,332 ft.
X

8,612 ft.
X

112

43

N

Miles

0.5

1

0

Middle Fork Peak
9,127 ft.

Lookout

8,202 ft.
X

Hike 109a

Warm Spring Creek

8,601 ft.
X

49

YELLOWJACKET MOUNTAINS

RIVER OF NO RETURN
WILDERNESS

7,735 ft.
X

7,228 ft.
X

To the Middle Fork
Salmon River

109. Mormon Ranch
Hot Springs

6,484 ft.
X

Finding the trailhead: From Salmon, drive 5 miles south on U.S. Highway 93. Bridge the river onto Williams Creek Road (21) and climb 24 dusty miles west to Panther Creek Road (55), where a right turn is a back way to Panther Hot Springs (see 111). Hang a left and go 13 miles to Porphyry Creek Road (112). Turn right and follow signs to Middle Fork Peak. After a few more miles, you'll pass the turnoff to the Bighorn Crags (see below). Next, you'll pass the rustic remains of Yellowjacket, a ghost town featuring a five-story hotel.

The seasonal road, open from July 15 to October 15, deteriorates badly in the final 14 miles, but those with high clearance should survive. Continue a few miles past the tiny campground to Middle Fork Peak Lookout (9,127 feet) at the end, a total of 68 long and dusty miles from the highway. The springs are faintly marked on the map.

The lowdown: Did you read the review of Lower Loon (Hike 107) but decide, like a true couch potato, that it wasn't worth such a hike? Here's a chance to sample a carbon copy at less than half the price. The soaking box at Mormon is identical to the one at Lower Loon but half the size. The hike here, however, plunges nearly 5,000 feet downhill. You could almost dive into the pool from the trailhead, but then there's the trip back out. What, no chairlift? I didn't claim free admission, just 50 percent off (7 trail miles versus 15). In any case, if you're a dyed-in-the-wool hot springer, Mormon is worth the experience.

The hike: Middle Fork Peak caps a sinuous ridge high in the Yellowjacket Mountains. The lonesome trail begins just south of the manned lookout and follows the ridge, dropping steadily in a giant half circle around the Warm Spring Creek drainage. As it circles the head of the broad canyon, you'll enjoy panoramic views framed by tall trees.

High-elevation forests are replaced by drier slopes dotted with sagebrush and ponderosa. When you reach a point looking back to the lookout, the path begins plummeting in earnest, weaving in and out of gullies and across open slopes in a long descent to the canyon floor. The path crosses Warm Spring Creek and hugs the north bank en route to the river. Start watching about half a mile downstream for a side path through the grass on your left. Follow it across the creek and just beyond the woods to the springs (4,300 feet).

The hot springs: A length of pipe transports spring water into a tongue-and-groove soaking box that measures 4 x 8 feet. The sturdy box can hold up to eight cozy bodies in over 2 feet of crystal clear water. The temperature runs a bit high, and there isn't any way to cool it short of diverting the pipe and waiting for the water to cool. When I was there in midsummer, the tub clocked in at 106 degrees, as did the air temperature, but in cooler weather I'm sure it would feel great.

There's a small deck adjoining the soaking box, handy for changing clothes.

The setting is a sunny meadow screened by bushes from the creekside path, and you can pitch a tent nearby. The box gets far less use by passing river rats than the one at Lower Loon since it's located 1.5 miles up the trail from the river.

HIKE 109b *Bighorn Crags*

General description:	An overnighter to the first in a chain of wilderness lakes, en route between Mormon and Panther hot springs.
Difficulty:	Strenuous.
Distance:	14 miles round trip.
General location:	61 miles west of Salmon.
Elevation gain:	+1,400 feet, -1,520 feet.
High point:	9,000 feet.
Hiking quad:	River of No Return Wilderness, North half.
Road map:	Same or Salmon National Forest.
Contact:	North Fork Ranger District, Salmon and Challis National Forest.

Finding the trailhead: Follow the directions above to Porphyry Creek Road (112) and drive 8.7 miles to a four-way intersection. Turn right on Forest Road 113 and go north over Quartzite Mountain. Pass the turnoff to Yellowjacket Lake and cross a pass at 8,700 feet, which is usually passable between July 15 and October 15, to Crags Campground, 10.7 miles from Forest Road 112 or a total of about 56 dusty miles from the highway. The register box is at the north end of the loop.

The hike: The Bighorn Crags area is a backpacker's paradise of tiny alpine lakes and jagged granite towers, and the Crags Campground trailhead, at 8,460 feet, offers by far the shortest access. The hike to Welcome Lake, a fine introduction in itself, also offers a tempting array of side trips, loops, and extensions to those with time to spare.

Ship Island Lake Trail (21) climbs a wooded ridge above Golden Trout Lake to a summit at 8,720 feet, then dips and climbs another ridge north to a high point of 9,000 feet at 2 miles. Here you'll pass nine or ten rocky towers, then drop past Cathedral Rock to a junction, at 4 miles, with the scenic route over Fishfin Ridge to Harbor and Wilson Lakes.

Turn left onto the Waterfall or Welcome Lake Trail (45) and plummet down and across Wilson Creek Canyon. At 6.2 miles, at the third stream crossing, a 1-mile trail branches north to Wilson Lake. Across the creek, the route switchbacks up to Welcome Lake at 7 miles.

From Welcome Lake, the sharp spires and triangular peaks of Fishfin Ridge stand out to the northeast across Wilson Creek Canyon. A dark wall

Bighorn Crags

Ship Island Lake

Airplane Lake

RIVER OF NO RETURN
WILDERNESS

CRAGS

Wilson Lake

FISHFIN RIDGE

Cathedral Rock
9,400 ft.

Terrace Lakes

Harbor Lake

45

Heart Lake

BIGHORN

Welcome Lake

9,000 ft.
X

Wilson Creek

21

Golden Trout Lake

Hike 109b

Reflection Lake

N

113

SALMON AND CHALLIS
NATIONAL FOREST

To Mormon Ranch Hot Springs
or U.S. 93, Salmon

0   1   2
Miles

of cliffs towers above granite slabs and scattered trees at the upper end of the narrow lake, and meadows of tiny wildflowers carpet the convoluted shoreline.

Options: The Waterfall Trail continues to Heart Lake and over the divide to the four tiny Terrace Lakes set below a needle-tipped cliff. This 3.6-mile section has a gain of 670 feet and a loss of 680 feet. South of Welcome Lake, a trail to Puddin Mountain Lakes crosses the divide and drops to Reflection Lake whose surface mirrors a granite wall. The 5-mile route gains 850 feet and loses 1,080 feet. Beyond are Buck, Doe, Fawn, Echo, Twin Cove, and Turquoise lakes.

Harbor and Wilson lakes are found north of Welcome Lake at the base of Fishfin Ridge. From the junction at 4 miles (see above) it's a 3-mile trip with a gain of 820 feet and a loss of 360 feet. It is possible to do a loop that includes all three lakes in a total of 16.5 scenic miles. Farther north are even more lakes to visit.

110 Sharkey Hot Spring

General description:	A hot spring with a colorful past, on a dirt road above the Lemhi Valley. Keep swimwear handy.
Elevation:	5,400 feet.
General location:	25 miles southeast of Salmon.
Map:	Salmon National Forest.
Contact:	Salmon Field Office, BLM.

Finding the hot spring: From Salmon, take State Route 28, 20 miles southeast. Turn left at the Tendoy store, then left again on gravel for 3 miles to Warm Springs Road (185). Turn right and go 2 miles uphill, then right on a short spur that ends at the tub. The road is usable most of the year. Sharkey is named on the forest map but sits on BLM land.

The hot spring: What I found here was a tiny recessed box, water piped in at 112 degrees and no means of cooling it. What someone else finds may be something else entirely. A different tub or no tub. The site periodically gets destroyed by the powers that be, only to be reborn. The setting is a sagebrush slope with not a shade tree in sight.

Sharkey had its heydey in the mid-1920s. A local with a lease on the land and a claim to the water rights built a swimming pool with changing rooms and cabins. He piped cold water from a quarter mile away and built the road up the hill. A swim cost two bits, and you could rent a swimsuit for the same price. All went well for many years, and Sharkey enjoyed great popularity as the community plunge. In the meantime the BLM came into being, took a glance at the aging structures, and decided that Sharkey wasn't

Sharkey Hot Spring

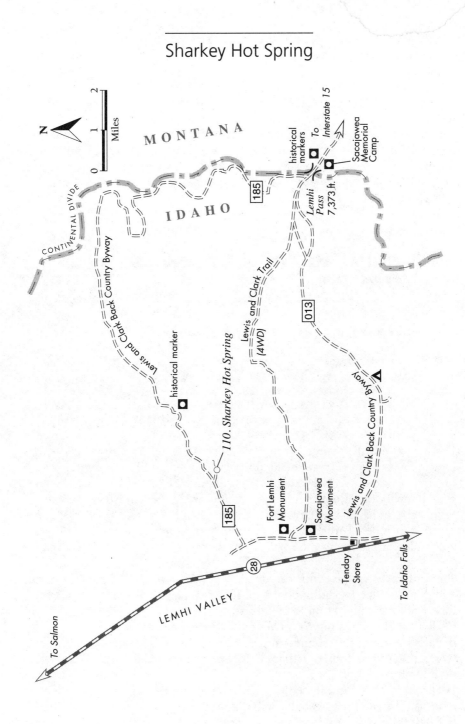

N

0 1 2
Miles

MONTANA

IDAHO

CONTINENTAL DIVIDE

Lewis and Clark Back Country Byway

historical markers

To Interstate 15

Sacajawea Memorial Camp

Lemhi Pass 7,373 ft.

185

Lewis and Clark Trail (4WD)

013

historical marker

110. Sharkey Hot Spring

185

Fort Lemhi Monument

Sacajawea Monument

Lewis and Clark Back Country Byway

28

Tenday Store

To Idaho Falls

LEMHI VALLEY

To Salmon

up to code. The whole works came down in the 1970s, and the site returned to the natural state you see it in today.

Historical note: The BLM marks the access road as a Lewis and Clark Back Country Byway. Sharkey is the first unofficial stop on this 39-mile scenic drive that loops over Lemhi Pass. Lewis and Clark crossed the Continental Divide here in 1805, and also met the legendary Sacajawea here. Her memorial is found at the summit where the Lewis and Clark Trail bisects the loop, and down the far side you'll find a campground on Agency Creek Road 4 miles east of Tendoy. **Note:** The narrow dirt roads can be impassable when wet.

111 Panther (Big Creek) Hot Springs

General description:	A Texas-style soaker on a grassy hillside near a dirt road. Skinnydippable with discretion.
Elevation:	4,400 feet.
General location:	55 miles northwest of Salmon.
Map:	Salmon National Forest.
Contact:	Salmon/Cobalt Ranger District, Salmon and Challis National Forest.

Finding the hot springs: From Salmon, take U.S. Highway 93, 21 miles north to North Fork. Here the Salmon River Road (30) heads west, past the turnoff to Horse Creek (see below) and Shoup. At 26 miles comes the Outpost, home of the "Booker Burger," named for chief cook and bottle washer John Booker. At this venerable landmark, Panther Creek Road (55) turns south. At 4 miles, Forest Road 60 climbs 4 miles uphill to a pullout where a 0.25-mile path drops to the springs. Panther is marked on the forest map.

The hot springs: On a hillside edged by ponderosas, users have carved out a huge waist-deep soaking pool and dug trenches to regulate the temperature. Scalding water at up to 199 degrees channels toward the pool but can be diverted by adjusting rocks. A small cold water source, sometimes gone by late summer, also funnels in, and the balance is critical. The system works fine unless someone there before you starts tinkering and messes up the plumbing.

Panther's at its best in cooler weather and shines on through the winter months. The final road gets icy about halfway up, but locals often walk the last half for a steamy winter soak. For those into steam heat, there's even a sauna hut built from rocks. The nearest campground is down on Panther Creek.

At Panther Hot Springs, it pays to test the water before you take the plunge.

Historical note: Panther Creek itself was originally called Big Creek. The name changed in the 1920s when someone reportedly went shooting every panther in sight until the creek was littered with them. It's been Panther Creek ever since, but you'll still see Big Creek Hot Springs labeled on the older maps.

112 Horse Creek Hot Springs

General description:	A roadside bathhouse near a remote campground in the Bitterroots. A haven for skinnydippers or chunkydunkers.
Elevation:	6,200 feet.
General location:	65 miles northwest of Salmon.
Map:	Salmon National Forest.
Contact:	North Fork Ranger District, Salmon National Forest.

Finding the hot springs: From Salmon, zip 21 miles north on U.S. Highway 93 to North Fork and take the Salmon River Road (30) west. At 17 miles, where the pavement peters out, turn right on Forest Road 38 and climb switchbacks to the Bitterroot Divide on the Idaho-Montana border. The sinuous road follows the crest and state line over a high point of 8,600 feet and becomes FR 44, eventually passing a turnoff to Darby, MT, at Horse Creek Pass (see below). A few more miles brings you to FR 65 on the left and the shortest route to Darby on the right. The final lap plummets 3.6 miles to the bathhouse. Horse Creek is named on the forest map.

Note to hikers: Those who enjoy fishing might consider a side trip to Reynolds Lake. The trailhead, signed to Reynolds Creek and Divide trails, is found at the end of FR 44, 8 miles past the turnoff to Horse Creek. The 1.5-mile path is a moderate climb, and the marshy lake sits in a basin of granite benches.

The hot springs: Bubbles stream up through the slab rock and sand bottom of a soaking pool big enough to float a small family. Over the 100-degree pool sits a crude 8- x 10-foot bathhouse, roofless except for a covered area on the side for hanging clothes. A window looks out across a tree-lined meadow. A footbridge from the picnic area to the shack spans the outflow, which flows through an outdoor dip into Horse Creek. The nearby campground makes a peaceful spot to hang your hat.

The name game: *While contentedly afloat, I began to notice the many names inscribed on the walls around the pool. Out of the chaos, a pattern began to emerge: "Abe 'n Deb," "Bear 'n Deb," "Jo & Jack & Deb," "Deb + Jim," "Pete 'n Deb," "Zeek 'n Deb." In the far corner was the exception—"Rob '90, w/o Deb." And in case any reader is interested, at the bottom of one wall you'll even find "Deb alone" plus a telephone number.*

TWO FOR THE ROAD

Those who scan backcountry maps with a fine-toothed comb for stray goodies may have noticed one labeled **Owl Creek Hot Springs** on the Salmon Forest map or the River of No Return Wilderness quad, North half. It's just off the Salmon River Road a few miles west of the Panther Creek junction, and the landmark is an Owl Creek Trail sign on your right.

Two miles up the Forest Service path sits a cabin with a hot tub near the creek. Promising, but obviously private property. So you ford the creek and bushwhack upstream through poison ivy in search of a second spring which, since it's reported to be located on the far bank, must be back on public land, right? Wrong. This parcel happens to cross the creek. So, both halves of Owl Creek Hot Springs are, unfortunately, off limits. But read on. . .

The last little teaser, **Overwhich Hot Spring**, hides just over the Montana border, on public land, but tougher to access. It's faintly labeled "hot spring" on the Bitterroot Forest Map. To find it, drop over the Divide at Horse Creek

Pass on FR 91 signed to Darby. Go roughly 18 miles north, and just before Painted Rocks Lake hang a right on Overwhich Creek Road (5703). It's gated at 5 miles, but a motorscooter could probably take you as far as a major stream ford in 4 miles. By late summer this should be safe enough, and your boots could take you the final 4 miles up the creek.

I have no idea how rough the route is or what's up there worth finding. I was hot in pursuit with a friend who possesses both a Honda 90 and an internal divining rod for "witching" (hot) water. We got nearly to Overwhich Road but were forced to give up the chase due to some very nasty weather. But tune in to the next edition of Hiking Hot Springs and hopefully you'll find a full description on the final page.

Appendix A

HOT TIPS

Help! I'm up to my neck in hot water with a current total of 118 hot springs to keep track of. It's not easy staying abreast of all the changes they undergo. You can help to keep the book afloat with accurate up-to-date information by reporting any significant improvements, changes, or problems you've encountered at any spring or with any access road or hiking trail. Recent photos are also gratefully accepted, and small size color prints are fine. Label the back with your name, hot spring, and date. Your name will be credited under any photo used. Please send me your contributions c/o Falcon Publishing, Box 1718, Helena, MT 59624. Many thanks and happy soaks!

Appendix B

Who To Contact

Contact the following agencies for updates on weather and road conditions, hiking trails and stream crossings, hot springs, and other miscellaneous information. If the receptionist can't answer your questions, ask for someone in recreation. Maps may be purchased here, and many districts offer free trail printouts.

Oregon

Bureau of Land Management

Burns District
HC 74-12533
Highway 20 West
Hines, OR 97738
541-573-4400

Vale District
100 Oregon St.
Vale, OR 97918
541-473-3144
or
Rome Launch Site Ranger Station

Bureau of Reclamation

Central Snake Project
214 Broadway Ave.
Boise, ID 83702

Deschutes National Forest

Bend/Fort Rock Ranger District
1230 NE Third, A-262
Bend, OR 97701
541-388-5664

Mount Hood National Forest

Clackamas River Ranger District
595 NW Industrial Way
Estacada, OR 97023
503-630-6861

Willamette National Forest

Blue River Ranger District
51668 Blue River Drive
Blue River, OR 97413
541-822-3317

McKenzie Ranger District
57600 McKenzie Highway
McKenzie Bridge, OR 97413
541-822-3381

Oakridge Ranger District
49098 Salmon Creek Rd.
P.O. Box 1410
Oakridge, OR 97463
541-782-2283

Umpqua National Forest

Diamond Lake Ranger District
2020 Toketee Ranger Station Rd.
Idleyld Park, OR 97447
541-498-2531
or
Toketee Lake Ranger Station

Washington

Gifford Pinchot National Forest

Wind River Ranger District
1262 Hemlock Rd.
Carson, WA 98610
509-427-3200

Mount Hood National Forest

Columbia Gorge Ranger District
70220 East Highway 26
Zigzag, OR 97049
503-622-3191

Mount Baker-Snoqualmie National Forest

Darrington Ranger District
1405 Emmens St.
Darrington, WA 98241
360-436-1155

Mount Baker Ranger District
2105 Highway 20
Sedro Woolley, WA 98284
206-856-5700

Skykomish Ranger District
74920 NE Stevens Pass Hwy
P.O. Box 305
Skykomish, WA 98288
360-677-2414

Olympic National Park

600 East Park Ave.
Port Angeles, WA 98362
206-452-4501
or
Elwa Ranger Station
Olympic Hot Springs Rd.

British Columbia

BC Forests

Arrow Forest District
845 Columbia Ave.
Castlegar, BC V1N 1H3
250-365-8600

Chilliwack Forest District
9880 S McGrath Rd.
P.O. Box 159
Rosedale, BC V0X 1X0
604-794-2100

Cranbrook Forest District
1902 Theatre Rd.
Cranbrook, BC V1C 4H4
250-426-3391

Invermere Forest District
625 - 4th St.
P.O. Box 189
Invermere, BC V0A 1K0
250-342-4200

Squamish Forest District
42000 Loggers Lane
Squamish, BC V0N 3G0
604-898-2100

BC Parks

East Kootenay District
(Wasa Lake Park)
Box 118
Wasa, BC V0B 2K0
250-422-4200

Garibaldi/Sunshine Coast District
(Alice Lake Park)
Box 220
Brackendale, BC V0N 1H0
604-898-3678

Strathcoma District
(Rathtrevor Beach Park)
Box 1479
Parksville, BC V9P 2H4
250-954-4600

Idaho

Boise National Forest

Cascade Ranger District
540 N Main
P.O. Box 696
Cascade, ID 83611
208-382-4271

Emmett Ranger District
1805 Highway 16 #5
Emmett, ID 83617
208-365-7000
or
Garden Valley Ranger Station
208-462-3241

Lowman Ranger District
Highway 21
HC-77, Box 3020
Lowman, ID 83637
208-259-3361

Mountain Home Ranger District
2180 American Legion
Mountain Home, ID 83647
208-587-7961
or
Atlanta Ranger Station

Bureau of Land Management

Salmon Field Office
Highway 93 South
Route 2, Box 610
Salmon, ID 83467
208-756-5400

Shoshone District
400 W First
Shosone, ID 83352
208-886-2206

Canyon Cats

215 N Main
P.O. Box 11
Riggins, ID 83549
888-628-3772

Clearwater National Forest

Lochsa Ranger District
Route 1, Box 398
Kooskia, ID 83539
208-926-4274

Powell Ranger District
Lolo, MT 59847
208-942-3113

Payette National Forest

Council Ranger District
500 East Whitley
P.O. Box 567
Council, ID 83612
208-253-0100

Krassel Ranger District
500 S Mission St.
P.O. Box 1026
McCall, ID 83638
208-634-0600

McCall Ranger District
202 W Lake St.
P.O. Box 1026
McCall, ID 83638
208-634-0400

New Meadows Ranger District
700 Virginia St.
P.O. Box J
New Meadows, ID 83654
208-347-2141

Salmon and Challis National Forest

Middle Fork Ranger District
Highway 93 North
P.O. Box 750
Challis, ID 83226
208-879-4101

North Fork Ranger District
P.O. Box 180
North Fork, ID 83466
208-865-2700

Salmon/Cobalt Ranger District
Route 2, Box 600
Salmon, ID 83467
208-756-5100

Sawtooth National Forest

Fairfield Ranger District
P.O. Box 189
Fairfield, ID 83327
208-764-3203

Ketchum Ranger District
Sun Valley Road
P.O. Box 2356
Ketchum, ID 83340
208-622-5371

Sawtooth NRA
Headquarters Office
Star Route (Hwy 75)
Ketchum, ID 83340
208-727-5000
or
Stanley Ranger Station
208-774-3681

Appendix C

Hot water rafting

Any couch potatoes out there interested in sampling the toughest-to-hike-to springs? How about getting together for whitewater raft trips down hot spring–infested rivers? We're talking multi-day wilderness expeditions guided by professional outfitters: major rapids, pristine scenery, and hot springs you might otherwise never see. Two wild and woolly rivers fit the bill.

The winner, hands down, for hot springs is the renowned Middle Fork Salmon River in Idaho. It boasts several that are virtually unreachable by foot, and the rafts stop at as many as time and the river allow. Prime time for a hot spring trip is the second half of July, but these trips usually book up by the end of the previous season. It's a six day, five night package that covers 100 miles of first-class whitewater paddling.

A second choice is the lesser known, but equally wild and scenic Owyhee River in eastern Oregon. You can count on a stop at two of the area's most remote hot springs. Peak rafting season here is late April through May. The Owyhee is a deep canyon chiseled out of the desert, with 65 miles of fun paddling. Trips go for 5 to 7 days and are easier to book and less expensive than those on the Middle Fork.

Interested? Know any other hot spring buffs to inspire? Many outfitters offer a discount to groups of ten or more. Write to me at 6301 Squaw Valley Road #2582, Pahrump, NV 89048. I'll be choosing an outfitter and the best available date for each river. The company will send you all the specs and you can respond to them directly c/o Evie Litton's trip. Let's make it happen!

About the Author

Evie Litton broke loose from a fifteen-year career as a technical illustrator for the University of California in Berkeley to hit the road in 1983. She happily traded her civilized life for a camperized van she now calls home and has been busy exploring the backcountry to find out what secrets lie around the next bend. She prefers the adventure of personal discovery and avoids developed recreation areas and advertised tourist attractions. Her nomadic odyssey stretches from the saguaro deserts, canyon country "slots," and hot watering holes of the southwest to the mountain country and wild hot springs of Idaho.

Author Evie Litton can usually be found somewhere in her natural habitat, in this case, Pine Flats Hot Spring in Idaho. Bob Westerberg photo

Index

FALCON GUIDES® Leading the Way™

FALCON GUIDES® are available for where-to-go hiking, mountain biking, rock climbing, walking, scenic driving, fishing, rockhounding, paddling, birding, wildlife viewing, and camping. We also have FalconGuides on essential outdoor skills and subjects and field identification. The following titles are currently available, but this list grows every year. For a free catalog with a complete list of titles, call FALCON toll-free at 1-800-582-2665.

HIKING GUIDES

Hiking Alaska
Hiking Arizona
Hiking Arizona's Cactus Country
Hiking the Beartooths
Hiking Big Bend National Park
Hiking the Bob Marshall Country
Hiking California
Hiking California's Desert Parks
Hiking Carlsbad Caverns
    and Guadalupe Mtns. National Parks
Hiking Colorado
Hiking Colorado, Vol. II
Hiking Colorado's Summits
Hiking Colorado's Weminuche Wilderness
Hiking the Columbia River Gorge
Hiking Florida
Hiking Georgia
Hiking Glacier & Waterton Lakes National Parks
Hiking Grand Canyon National Park
Hiking Grand Staircase-Escalante/Glen Canyon
Hiking Grand Teton National Park
Hiking Great Basin National Park
Hiking Hot Springs in the Pacific Northwest
Hiking Idaho
Hiking Maine
Hiking Michigan
Hiking Minnesota
Hiking Montana
Hiking Mount Rainier National Park
Hiking Mount St. Helens
Hiking Nevada
Hiking New Hampshire

Hiking New Mexico
Hiking New York
Hiking North Carolina
Hiking the North Cascades
Hiking Northern Arizona
Hiking Olympic National Park
Hiking Oregon
Hiking Oregon's Eagle Cap Wilderness
Hiking Oregon's Mount Hood/Badger Creek
Hiking Oregon's Three Sisters Country
Hiking Pennsylvania
Hiking Shenandoah National Park
Hiking the Sierra Nevada
Hiking South Carolina
Hiking South Dakota's Black Hills Country
Hiking Southern New England
Hiking Tennessee
Hiking Texas
Hiking Utah
Hiking Utah's Summits
Hiking Vermont
Hiking Virginia
Hiking Washington
Hiking Wyoming
Hiking Wyoming's Cloud Peak Wilderness
Hiking Wyoming's Wind River Range
Hiking Yellowstone National Park
Hiking Zion & Bryce Canyon National Parks
The Trail Guide to Bob Marshall Country
Wild Country Companion
Wild Montana
Wild Utah

■ *To order any of these books, check with your local bookseller
or call FALCON ® at **1-800-582-2665**.
Visit us on the world wide web at:*
www.FalconOutdoors.com

FALCON®

FALCONGUIDES ® Leading the Way™

WILDLIFE VIEWING GUIDES
Alaska Wildlife Viewing Guide
Arizona Wildlife Viewing Guide
California Wildlife Viewing Guide
Colorado Wildlife Viewing Guide
Florida Wildlife Viewing Guide
Indiana Wildlife Vewing Guide
Iowa Wildlife Viewing Guide
Kentucky Wildlife Viewing Guide
Massachusetts Wildlife Viewing Guide
Montana Wildlife Viewing Guide
Nebraska Wildlife Viewing Guide
Nevada Wildlife Viewing Guide
New Hampshire Wildlife Viewing Guide
New Jersey Wildlife Viewing Guide
New Mexico Wildlife Viewing Guide
New York Wildlife Viewing Guide
North Carolina Wildlife Viewing Guide
North Dakota Wildlife Viewing Guide
Ohio Wildlife Viewing Guide
Oregon Wildlife Viewing Guide
Puerto Rico and the Virgin Islands WVG
Tennessee Wildlife Viewing Guide
Texas Wildlife Viewing Guide
Utah Wildlife Viewing Guide
Vermont Wildlife Viewing Guide
Virginia Wildlife Viewing Guide
Washington Wildlife Viewing Guide
West Virginia Wildlife Viewing Guide
Wisconsin Wildlife Viewing Guide

HISTORIC TRAIL GUIDES
Traveling California's Gold Rush Country
Traveling the Lewis & Clark Trail
Traveling the Oregon Trail
Traveler's Guide to the Pony Express Trail

SCENIC DRIVING GUIDES
Scenic Driving Alaska and the Yukon
Scenic Driving Arizona
Scenic Driving the Beartooth Highway
Scenic Driving California
Scenic Driving Colorado
Scenic Driving Florida
Scenic Driving Georgia
Scenic Driving Hawaii
Scenic Driving Idaho
Scenic Driving Michigan
Scenic Driving Minnesota
Scenic Driving Montana
Scenic Driving New England
Scenic Driving New Mexico
Scenic Driving North Carolina
Scenic Driving Oregon
Scenic Driving the Ozarks including the
    Ouchita Mountains
Scenic Driving Pennsylvania
Scenic Driving Texas
Scenic Driving Utah
Scenic Driving Washington
Scenic Driving Wisconsin
Scenic Driving Wyoming
Scenic Driving Yellowstone & Grand Teton
    National Parks
Back Country Byways
Scenic Byways East
Scenic Byways Farwest
Scenic Byways Rocky Mountains

■ *To order any of these books, check with your local bookseller*
*or call FALCON ® at **1-800-582-2665**.*
Visit us on the world wide web at:
www.FalconOutdoors.com

FALCON®

FALCONGUIDES® Leading the Way™

Mountain Biking Guides

Mountain Biking Arizona
Mountain Biking Colorado
Mountain Biking Georgia
Mountain Biking New Mexico
Mountain Biking New York
Mountain Biking Northern New England
Mountain Biking Oregon
Mountain Biking South Carolina
Mountain Biking Southern California
Mountain Biking Southern New England
Mountain Biking Utah
Mountain Biking Wisconsin
Mountain Biking Wyoming

Local Cycling Series

Fat Trax Bozeman
Mountain Biking Bend
Mountain Biking Boise
Mountain Biking Chequamegon
Mountain Biking Chico
Mountain Biking Colorado Springs
Mountain Biking Denver/Boulder
Mountain Biking Durango
Mountain Biking Flagstaff and Sedona
Mountain Biking Helena
Mountain Biking Moab
Mountain Biking Utah's
   St. George/Cedar City Area
Mountain Biking the White
   Mountains (West)

■ *To order any of these books, check with your local bookseller
or call FALCON ® at **1-800-582-2665**.
Visit us on the world wide web at:
www.FalconOutdoors.com*

FALCON®

FALCON GUIDES® Leading the way™

FalconGuides® are available for where-to-go hiking, mountain biking, rock climbing, walking, scenic driving, fishing, rockhounding, paddling, birding, wildlife viewing, and camping. We also have FalconGuides on essential outdoor skills and subjects and field identification. The following titles are currently available, but this list grows every year. For a free catalog with a complete list of titles, call FALCON toll-free at 1-800-582-2665.

BIRDING GUIDES
Birding Minnesota
Birding Montana
Birding Northern California
Birding Texas
Birding Utah

ROCKHOUNDING GUIDES
Rockhounding Arizona
Rockhounding California
Rockhounding Colorado
Rockhounding Montana
Rockhounding Nevada
Rockhound's Guide to
    New Mexico
Rockhounding Texas
Rockhounding Utah
Rockhounding Wyoming

WALKING
Walking Colorado Springs
Walking Denver
Walking Portland
Walking St. Louis
Walking Virginia Beach

CAMPING GUIDES
Camping California's
    National Forests
Camping Colorado
Camping Southern California
Camping Washington

ALL FIELD GUIDES
Bitterroot: Montana State Flower
Canyon Country Wildflowers
Central Rocky Mountain
    Wildflowers
Great Lakes Berry Book
New England Berry Book
Ozark Wildflowers
Pacific Northwest Berry Book
Plants of Arizona
Rare Plants of Colorado
Rocky Mountain Berry Book
Scats & Tracks of the Pacific
    Coast States
Scats & Tracks of the Rocky Mtns.
Southern Rocky Mountain
    Wildflowers
Tallgrass Prairie Wildflowers
Western Trees
Wildflowers of Southwestern Utah
Willow Bark and Rosehips

PADDLING GUIDES
Floater's Guide to Colorado
Paddling Minnesota
Paddling Montana
Paddling Okefenokee
Paddling Oregon
Paddling Yellowstone & Grand
    Teton National Parks

HOW-TO GUIDES
Avalanche Aware
Backpacking Tips
Bear Aware
Desert Hiking Tips
Hiking with Dogs
Leave No Trace
Mountain Lion Alert
Reading Weather
Route Finding
Using GPS
Wilderness First Aid
Wilderness Survival

MORE GUIDEBOOKS
Backcountry Horseman's
    Guide to Washington
Camping California's
    National Forests
Exploring Canyonlands & Arches
    National Parks
Exploring Hawaii's Parklands
Exploring Mount Helena
Recreation Guide to WA
    National Forests
Touring California & Nevada
    Hot Springs
Trail Riding Western
    Montana
Wild Country Companion
Wilderness Directory
Wild Montana
Wild Utah

■ *To order any of these books, check with your local bookseller*
or call FALCON ® at 1-800-582-2665.
Visit us on the world wide web at:
www.FalconOutdoors.com

FALCON®

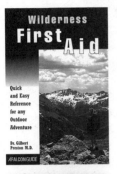

WILDERNESS FIRST AID

By Dr. Gilbert Preston M.D.

Enjoy the outdoors and face the inherent risks with confidence. By reading this easy-to-follow first-aid text, all outdoor enthusiasts can pack a little extra peace of mind on their next adventure. *Wilderness First Aid* offers expert medical advice for dealing with outdoor emergencies beyond the reach of 911. It easily fits in most backcountry first-aid kits.

LEAVE NO TRACE

By Will Harmon

The concept of "leave no trace" seems simple, but it actually gets fairly complicated. This handy quick-reference guidebook includes all the newest information on this growing and all-important subject. This book is written to help the outdoor enthusiast make the hundreds of decisions necessary to protect the natural landscape and still have an enjoyable wilderness experience. Part of the proceeds from the sale of this book go to continue leave-no-trace education efforts. The Official Manual of American Hiking Society.

BEAR AWARE

By Bill Schneider

Hiking in bear country can be very safe if hikers follow the guidelines summarized in this small, "packable" book. Extensively reviewed by bear experts, the book contains the latest information on the intriguing science of bear-human interactions. *Bear Aware* can not only make your hike safer, but it can help you avoid the fear of bears that can take the edge off your trip.

MOUNTAIN LION ALERT

By Steve Torres

Recent mountain lion attacks have received national attention. Although infrequent, lion attacks raise concern for public safety. *Mountain Lion Alert* contains helpful advice for mountain bikers, trail runners, horse riders, pet owners, and suburban landowners on how to reduce the chances of mountain lion-human conflicts.

Also Available

***Wilderness Survival • Reading Weather • Backpacking Tips • Climbing Safely •
Avalanche Aware • Desert Hiking Tips • Hiking with Dogs • Using GPS •
Route Finding • Wild Country Companion***

To order check with your local bookseller or
call FALCON® at **1-800-582-2665.**
www.FalconOutdoors.com